토익, 생각의 순서를 잡아주는

유수연 토익 RC PART 7 강의노트

유수연 토익 RC PART 7 강의노트

지은이 유수연
초판 1쇄 발행 2017년 7월 31일
초판 4쇄 발행 2020년 8월 20일

발행인 박효상 **편집장** 김현 **기획·편집** 김준하, 김설아 **디자인책임** 이연진
디자인 싱타디자인 고희선
마케팅 이태호, 이전희 **관리** 김태옥

종이 월드페이퍼 **인쇄·제본** 현문자현

출판등록 제10-1835호 **발행처** 사람in **주소** 121-839 서울시 마포구 양화로 11길 14-10 (서교동) 3F
전화 02) 338-3555(代) **팩스** 02) 338-3545 **E-mail** saramin@netsgo.com
Website www.saramin.com

책값은 뒤표지에 있습니다.
파본은 바꾸어 드립니다.

ⓒ 유수연 2017

ISBN
978-89-6049-637-8 14740
978-89-6049-634-7 (세트)

우아한 지적만보, 기민한 실사구시 사람in

토익, 생각의 순서를 잡아주는

유수연 토익 RC PART 7 강의노트

유수연 지음

사람in

ALL ABOUT TOEIC

TOEIC (Test of English for International Communication)
토익은 업무상 커뮤니케이션을 위한 듣기와 문서 등에 대한 이해를 원활하게 할 수 있는지를 묻는 TEST이다. 현재 한국과 일본을 비롯하여 전 세계 약 150여개 국가의 기업과 기관에서 인력채용 및 평가, 승진, 영어 학습 프로그램 등에 활용되고 있다.

출제 의도를 알아야 토익은 단기간에 끝낼 수 있다.
토익은 각 파트별 구성과 묻고자 하는 출제자의 의도를 정확하게 파악해야 단기간에 원하는 점수를 얻을 수 있다.
PART 5는 주로 기본적인 품사의 배치와 문법을 알고 있는지를 묻고 PART 6에서는 문서의 문맥과 내용을 파악할 수 있는지를 묻는다. 더 나아가서 PART 7에서는 문서에 나온 정보의 진위여부와 다수 문서(지문)의 연관된 정보를 통해서 사실 여부를 확인할 수 있는 정보 검색 능력을 묻는다.

TOEIC 시험 구성

구성	PART	유형		문항 수	시간	점수
Listening	PART 1	사진 묘사		6	45분	495점
	PART 2	질의응답		25		
	PART 3	짧은 대화		39		
	PART 4	설명문		30		
Reading	PART 5	단문 공란 메우기		30	75분	495점
	PART 6	장문 공란 메우기		16		
	PART 7	독해	단일 지문 (10)	29		
			이중 지문 (2)	10		
			삼중 지문 (3)	15		
	총 7개 PART			200문항	120분	990점

출제 범위 및 기준
출제 기관인 ETS에 따르면, TOEIC의 출제 기준은
영어를 모국어로 사용하는 특정 국가에서만 쓰이는 표현이나 문법, 관용어들은 피한다.
또 특정 문화나 직업 분야에만 해당되거나 생소한 상황은 나오지 않는다.
L/C의 경우 여러 나라 사람들의 이름, 다양한 영어 발음과 악센트(미국, 영국, 캐나다, 호주, 뉴질랜드)가 출제된다.

출제 분야	세부 분야
General Business (일반 업무)	계약, 협상, 마케팅, 세일즈, 비즈니스 계획, 회의
Manufacturing (제조)	공장 관리, 조립 라인, 품질 관리
Finance, Budgeting (금융, 예산)	은행, 투자, 세금, 회계, 청구
Corporate Development (개발)	연구, 제품 개발
Office Work (사무실 업무)	임원회의, 위원회의, 편지, 메모, 전화, 팩스, E-mail, 사무 장비와 가구
Personnel (인사)	구인, 채용, 퇴직, 급여, 승진, 취업 지원과 자기소개
Housing, Corporate Property (주택, 기업 부동산)	건축, 설계서, 구입과 임대, 전기와 가스 서비스
Travel (여행)	기차, 비행기, 택시, 버스, 배, 유람선, 티켓, 일정, 역과 공항 안내, 자동차 렌트, 호텔, 예약, 연기와 취소

유수연 토익 RC PART 7
강의노트

정답의 위치를 찾아 키워드를 검색하는 능력이 중요하다.
답은 포괄적인 단어로 Paraphrasing 된다는 것을 알아 두자.

1. 토익 독해는 수능 독해가 아니다. 빠르게 정보를 검색하는 능력이 필요하다.

수능 독해에 익숙해져 있는 학습자들은 토익의 기본적인 배경을 충분히 이해할 필요가 있다. 토익은 비즈니스 업무 상황에서 커뮤니케이션을 위해 개발된 시험이다. 그러므로 단순히 해석만으로 문제를 푸는 것이 아니라 정보를 검색, 분류, 비교, 판단하는 능력을 훈련하는 것이 중요하다.

2. 꼭 필요한 정보만 찾을 수 있는 Skimming과 Scanning 스킬

정답의 위치와 키워드 정보를 검색하는 훈련을 해야 한다. 이때 필요한 것이 skimming과 scanning이다. skimming은 빠른 속도로 훑어 읽어 내려가는 것으로 글의 주제를 파악할 때 꼭 필요한 스킬이다. scanning은 필요한 정보를 찾는 데 집중하면서 지문을 읽어 내려가는 것이다.

3. 질문의 유형별 전략을 학습하라.

일상적인 업무 상황에서 자주 등장하는 문서들은 일반적으로 그 형식이 정형화되어 있다. 예를 들어 목적을 묻는 문제는 지문의 처음 2줄에 90%가 답이 있다. 주제나 목적은 지문의 초반부에 요구나 요청사항들은 후반부에 나오기 때문이다. 그러므로 질문의 유형별 전략을 학습하는 것은 답의 위치를 쉽게 파악할 수 있기 때문에 매우 중요하다.

4. not question이나 사실·확인을 요하는 indicate/suggest 유형의 문제는 소거법을 사용한다.

이 같은 질문 유형은 문서상 정형화된 위치에서 답을 찾을 수 없다. Part 7에서 가장 어려운 문제 중에 하나이다. 주로 사람의 이름이나 행사 등의 키워드를 중심으로 출제되기 때문에 각각의 보기 내용들이 어디에 위치해 있는지를 파악하고 하나씩 소거하면서 풀어야 한다.

5. 다중 지문의 연계 문제 유형은 지문을 연결하고 있는 키워드를 찾아야 한다.

이중 지문이 2개, 삼중 지문이 3개가 출제된다. 지문과 지문을 연결하는 공통적인 키워드를 찾아야 한다. 키워드와 함께 정답이 있는 해당 위치를 검색하면 답이 없고 다른 키워드를 남긴다. 다른 키워드는 다른 지문에 중복되어 있기 때문에 연결되는 키워드를 찾아내는 것이 중요하다.

이렇게 활용하세요!

유수연의 토익 노하우가 고스란히 담긴 핵심 강의노트
스스로 문제 풀면서 전수 받는다!

CHAPTER 1
SINGLE PASSAGE

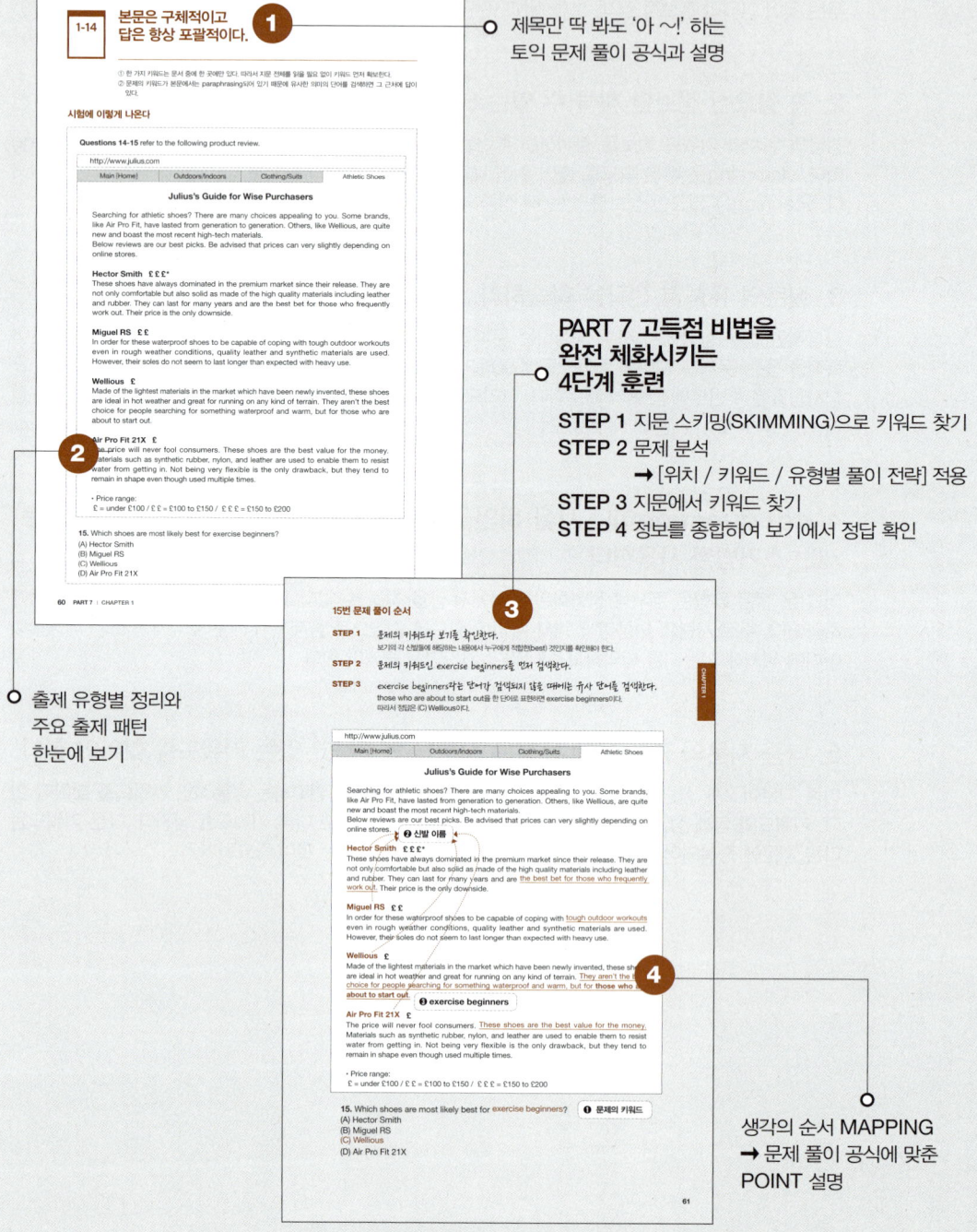

○ 제목만 딱 봐도 '아 ~!' 하는 토익 문제 풀이 공식과 설명

○ 출제 유형별 정리와 주요 출제 패턴 한눈에 보기

PART 7 고득점 비법을 완전 체화시키는 4단계 훈련

STEP 1 지문 스키밍(SKIMMING)으로 키워드 찾기
STEP 2 문제 분석
→ [위치 / 키워드 / 유형별 풀이 전략] 적용
STEP 3 지문에서 키워드 찾기
STEP 4 정보를 종합하여 보기에서 정답 확인

○ 생각의 순서 MAPPING
→ 문제 풀이 공식에 맞춘 POINT 설명

CHAPTER 2
DOUBLE PASSAGE

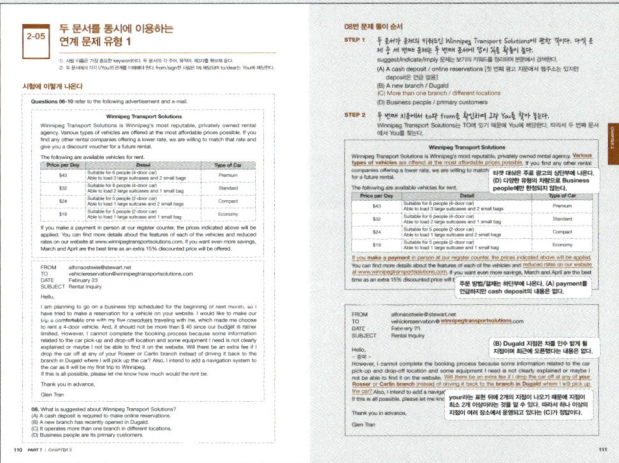

CHAPTER 3
TRIPLE PASSAGE

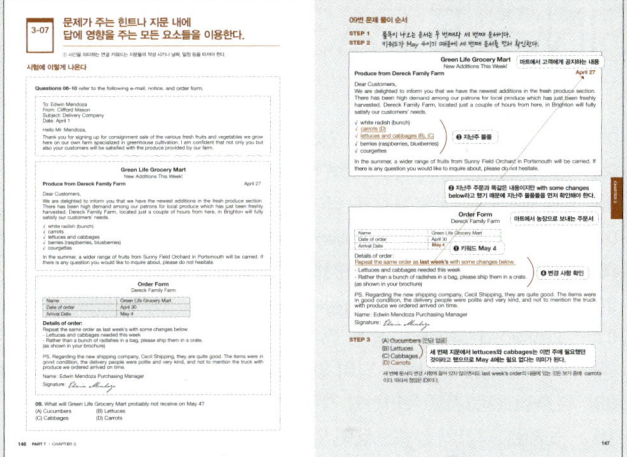

FINAL TEST

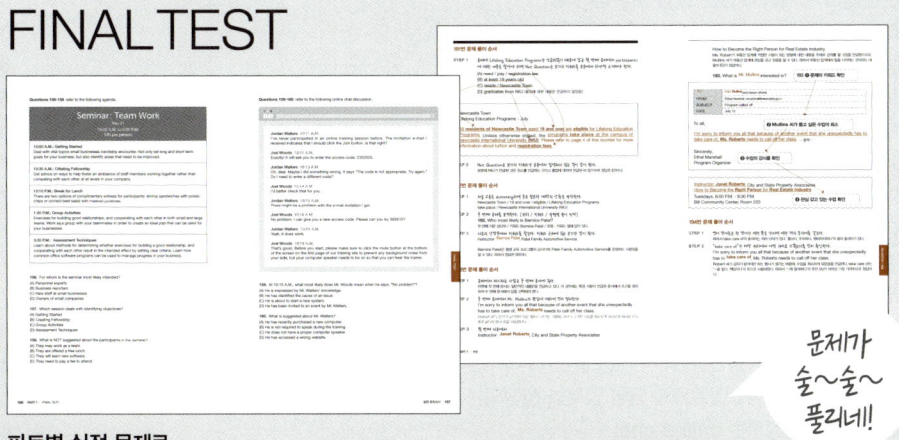

파트별 실전 문제로
확실한 마무리

문제가
술~술~
풀리네!

차례

ALL ABOUT TOEIC … 4
유수연 토익 RC PART 7 강의노트 … 5
이렇게 활용하세요! … 6

PART 7

토익의 독해는 수능 독해가 아니다

0-01	PART 7 한눈에 보기	12
0-02	PART 7 고득점을 위해 꼭 필요한 5가지	13
0-03	PART 7 문제 풀이 기본 원칙	14

질문 유형별 전략을 학습하라

CHAPTER 1
SINGLE PASSAGE

	ACTUAL TEST	20
1-01	답은 항상 keyword 옆에 있다.	34
1-02	요구 사항은 답이 지문의 하단부에 있다.	36
1-03	목적은 처음 두 줄에 90% 답이 있다.	38
1-04	기간, 요일, 숫자 등은 keyword 옆에 있는 것이 답이다.	40
1-05	업종을 묻는 문제는 표의 구체적인 명목들이 답을 보여 준다.	42
1-06	답은 항상 paraphrasing된다.	44
1-07	keyword 옆에 답이 없는 경우는 또 다른 keyword를 남긴다.	46
1-08	목적은 처음 2~3줄에 답이 있을 확률이 90%이며 하단부 요구 사항에 답이 있을 확률은 10%이다.	48
1-09	I/You/제3자를 확인하고 각각의 직업을 파악하라.	50
1-10	문제점, 과거의 정보는 답이 앞에 있다.	52
1-11	'사실'인 것을 찾는 문제는 보기의 keyword를 먼저 정리한 후 본문을 검색한다.	54
1-12	추후 연락처/연락 방법/지원 방법 등은 지문의 하단부에 답이 있다.	56
1-13	but, however, unfortunately 등 역접 뒤에 답이 있다.	58
1-14	본문은 구체적이고 답은 항상 포괄적이다.	60
1-15	Not Question은 소거법을 이용한다.	62
1-16	동의어 찾기 문제는 진짜 동의어를 찾는 것이 아니다.	64
1-17	보기 문장 중에 한 단어 오류를 찾아라.	66
1-18	답은 순서대로 배치된다.	68
1-19	사람 이름은 항상 중요한 keyword이다.	70
1-20	'문맥' 추가 문제는 위치와 연결어가 관건이다.	72
1-21	동의어는 문맥상 대체할 수 있는 단어를 찾는 것이다.	74
1-22	'문맥' 추가 문제는 지시형용사, 지시대명사, 부사들이 답을 연결한다.	76
1-23	문맥 추가 문제는 위아래 문맥을 연결해 주는 논리의 근거를 확보해야 한다.	78
1-24	온라인 채팅 '의도' 문제는 위아래 연결어가 있거나 전체적인 상황을 포괄적으로 묘사하는 것이 답이다.	80
1-25	online chat은 등장인물들의 관계도를 먼저 이해한다.	82
1-26	online chat은 등장인물들의 담당 업무와 진행되는 일의 상황을 파악해야 한다.	84
1-27	3인 이상이 등장하는 online chat	86
1-28	미래의 계획은 상대방 대사에서 권유/제안으로 답이 제시되기도 한다.	88

CHAPTER 2
DOUBLE PASSAGE

	ACTUAL TEST	94
2-01	본문 중에 구체적인 단서들을 모아서 포괄적인 답을 찾는다.	102
2-02	4가지 항목이 있는 문서는 공통 정보를 찾는 문제가 출제된다.	104
2-03	5문제 중 반드시 한 문제 이상은 두 문서를 동시에 이용해야 답이 나온다.	106
2-04	표나 시각 자료 등에는 직접적인 답이 많지 않다.	108
2-05	두 문서를 동시에 이용하는 연계 문제 유형 1	110
2-06	두 문서를 동시에 이용하는 연계 문제 유형 2	112
2-07	수동태형 문제는 상대방이 작성한 문서에 답이 있다.	114
2-08	키워드를 이용하는 문제	116
2-09	두 문서를 동시에 이용하는 연계 문제 유형 3	118
2-10	두 문서를 동시에 이용하는 연계 문제 유형 4	120
2-11	요구와 제안은 하단부에 답이 있다.	122

CHAPTER 3
TRIPLE PASSAGE

	ACTUAL TEST	128
3-01	표나 그래프 등 시각 자료는 다른 문서와 연결하여 답을 찾는 문제가 주로 출제된다.	134
3-02	가격/비용/날짜 등을 묻는 문제는 본문에서 모든 정보를 찾아서 순서대로 배열한 후에 최종 답을 찾는다.	136
3-03	마지막 문제의 답은 주로 세 번째 문서에 등장한다.	138
3-04	목적이 앞부분에 없을 때는 하단부에 나오는 요구 사항에 답이 있다.	140
3-05	보기가 모두 장소이거나 시간, 사람 이름 등이면 모두 본문에서 검색해 두어야 한다.	142
3-06	Paraphrasing된 표현을 주의하라.	144
3-07	문제가 주는 힌트나 지문 내에 답에 영향을 주는 모든 요소들을 이용한다.	146
3-08	한 단어로만 답을 찾으려 하지 말고 구체적인 정보들을 모아서 포괄적인 답을 찾는다.	148
3-09	문제 중에 키워드가 있으면 해당 지문에서 검색된 키워드 위주로 정보를 연결한다.	150
3-10	특정 명사가 지칭하는 대상을 확인하라.	152
3-11	차액/변경 사항들은 original과 new로 정보를 구분해 두어야 한다.	154
3-12	할인의 조건/자격은 빈출 연계 문제이다. 문제의 키워드 옆에 답이 없다면 또 다른 키워드를 남긴다.	156
3-13	특정인과 관련한 사실 확인 문제는 해당 지문과 연계 지문을 동시에 봐야 한다.	158

FINAL TEST 실전 모의고사   162

해설
본문 해석/정답	184
FINAL TEST 실전 모의고사 해설	216

토익의 독해는
수능 독해가 아니다

PART 7
한눈에 보기

0-01

1. **문제 유형**: 독해 지문과 관련된 질문의 답을 고르는 문제로, 단일 지문(Single Passage)과 복수 지문(Double Passage + Triple Passage)으로 구성된다.

2. **문제 개수**: 총 54문제가 출제된다.

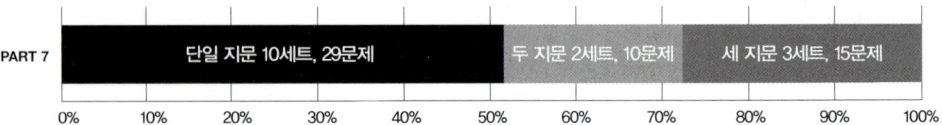

3. **풀이 시간**: 54분(문제당 1분 이내에 풀어야 함)

4. **Part 7은 실제 업무 문서상의 정보를 정확하게 이해할 수 있는지를 묻는 파트이다.**

우리가 그동안 공부했던 지문들은 거의 대부분 학문적인(academic) 영어였으며 주로 번역을 통해 지문의 내용을 이해하는 것이 그 목적이었다. 따라서 수능 독해에서는 영어로 지식을 습득하는 것을 목적으로, 전체 지문을 이해하고 번역하는 능력을 키웠다.

그러나 토익은 영어로 업무를 처리하는 능력을 테스트하는 시험이다. 따라서 토익에서는 전체 지문을 이해하거나 번역하는 것보다는 업무에 필요한 정보를 빠르고 효율적으로 파악해 처리하는 능력을 키우는 것이 그 목적이다. 토익의 독해는 정보를 비즈니스 문서상에서 검색하고 분류하고 비교하고 판단하는 능력을 키우는 것이 학습의 목적이다. 문제에서 주어진 키워드와 보기의 키워드를 최대한 이용하여 빠른 시간 내에 본문 중에 필요한 정보를 찾고 문제를 해결하는 능력이 관건이다.

5. **토익 독해 공부**

비즈니스 문서들은 양식이 있기 때문에 모든 문제의 답의 위치는 이미 정해져 있다. 따라서 출제되는 문제 유형을 분석하고 유형별로 연습하고 문제의 키워드와 보기의 키워드를 최대한 이용하여 문제는 푼다.
전체 지문을 한 번에 읽고 이해하는 것이 아니라 문단별로 나누어 해당 문제와 함께 끊어서 읽어야 한다.

6. **전략적 문제 풀이 접근법**

   Step 1 지문의 앞부분을 스키밍(skimming)하여 기본 정보를 정리한다.
   Step 2 질문을 분석하여 키워드와 답의 위치를 찾는다.
   Step 3 질문의 키워드와 보기 (A)~(D)의 키워드를 정리한다.
   Step 4 지문에서 보기의 키워드들을 스키밍(skimming)으로 검색한다.
   Step 5 지문에서 검색한 내용과 보기 (A)~(D)를 대조하여 정답을 찾는다.

★ 최근 토익의 추세는 언뜻 보아서는 (A)~(D) 모두 답이 되는 것 같지만, 한 단어 때문에 오답이 되는 경우가 많으므로 신속하면서도 꼼꼼하게 확인하면서 풀어야 한다.

PART 7 고득점을 위해 꼭 필요한 5가지

0-02

토익의 독해는 정보를 검색하고 분류하는 능력을 묻는다.

1 지문 속에서 질문의 키워드 위치를 파악하는 능력
업무에서 사용되는 기본적인 문서의 유형에 따라 정해진 작성 순서와 방법이 있다. 유형별 문서의 작성 순서를 이해하고 있으면 질문과 보기의 키워드가 지문의 어디에 있는지 쉽게 찾을 수 있다.

2 키워드를 빠르게 검색하는 Skimming & Scanning
질문과 보기의 키워드 내용을 스키밍(skimming)과 스캐닝(scanning)을 이용해서 빠르게 검색하는 스킬이다. 이때 앞서 언급한 첫 번째 스킬을 기반으로 스키밍과 스캐닝을 하게 되면 좀 더 빠르게 키워드를 찾아낼 수 있다. '스키밍(skimming)'이란 전체 지문을 모두 읽고 이해하는 것이 아니라 한 지문을 20~30초 정도에 훑어 내리는 것으로 평균 한 줄에 하나의 키워드를 빠르게 체크하여 주요 정보들을 미리 확보해 두는 것이다.

3 보기의 오답을 소거하는 능력
최근 토익 경향은 단순히 유형별 문서의 작성 순서에 대한 이해와 키워드 내용만으로는 풀 수 없는 문제들이 많이 등장한다. 따라서 오답을 소거하는 능력은 보기와 전체 지문을 파악해야 풀 수 있는 추론 문제뿐만 아니라 일반적인 문제들에서도 답을 고를 때 필요한 스킬이다. 여기서 주의해야 할 것은 보기 중에 키워드가 등장하긴 하지만 동시에 오답을 결정하는 단어도 함께 숨어 있어서 보기의 내용을 꼼꼼하게 지문에서 확인해야 실수를 피할 수 있다. 이런 유형의 문제는 단순한 위치 파악이나 키워드로 해결되는 문제보다 시간이 많이 걸리기 때문에 스키밍(skimming)과 스캐닝(scanning)을 이용한 연습이 많이 필요하다.

4 Paraphrasing 능력
보기의 내용은 구체적이고 답은 포괄적으로 제시된다.

5 토익 독해의 문제들은 반드시 정해진 유형과 패턴들만이 출제된다.
무조건 지문을 읽고 답을 찾으려 하지 말고 먼저 시험에 나오는 문제 유형별로 풀이 전략을 학습하는 것이 효율적이다. 토익이라는 시험은 문제 은행식이기 때문에 새로운 문제가 출제되지는 않는다. 따라서 시험에 출제되는 문제 유형별 스킬과 정확한 풀이 훈련이 중요하다.

독해 4대 원칙
① 답은 순서대로 배치된다.
② 문제를 먼저 분석한 후에 지문의 해당 위치를 검색한다.
③ 본문은 구체적이고 답은 포괄적이다.
④ 보기의 오답들은 한 단어의 오류를 숨기고 있다.

PART 7
0-03 문제 풀이 기본 원칙

Questions 147-148 refer to the following announcement.

> We are happy to tell you all that Evelyn Nguyen has agreed to take on a position as an associate attorney here at the Salvatore Law Firm. Ms. Nguyen studied the law at Harold National University and specialized in the field of patent and copyright law. She has constantly improved her career in the field even during her school years at the university. Last year, she did an internship at the Eduardo Law Association which focuses on clients such as inventors, technicians, and machinists in the engineering industry. Indubitably, Ms. Nguyen is highly qualified the position and will be a valuable addition to our team. Please attend a welcoming reception for her this Friday in the main conference hall.

147. Where does the announcement most likely appear?
(A) In a printing office
(B) In an employment agency
(C) In a law firm
(D) In an engineering team

148. What are staff members invited to do on Friday?
(A) Attend a law seminar
(B) Meet a new employee
(C) Visit a local university
(D) Join an engineering conference

STEP 1
지문의 앞부분을 skimming하여 기본 정보를 정리한다.

> We are happy to tell you all that <u>Evelyn Nguyen</u> has agreed to <u>take on</u> a position as an <u>associate attorney</u> here at the Salvatore Law Firm. Ms. Nguyen studied the law at Harold National University and specialized in the field of patent and copyright law. She has constantly improved her career in the field even during her school years at the university. Last year, she did an internship at the Eduardo Law Association which focuses on clients such as inventors, technicians, and machinists in the engineering industry. Indubitably, Ms. Nguyen is highly qualified the position and will be a valuable addition to our team. Please attend a welcoming reception for her this Friday in the main conference hall.

- 공부에도 리더십이 있다. 지문 내용에 끌려 다니지 말고 상황을 빠르게 장악해야 한다.
- 처음 2~3줄을 가볍게 읽으며 중요 단어들을 빠르게 skimming하여 전체 상황을 한 줄로 정리한다.
- [Evelyn Nguyen이라는 사람이 소속 변호사로 법률 회사에 합류했다는 공지]

STEP 2
질문을 분석하여 키워드와 답의 위치를 찾는다.

- 전체 지문을 한 번에 읽지 않는다.
- 한 문단씩 끊어서 문제를 읽고 교차하여 지문을 분석한다.
- 처음 2~3줄을 읽고 내용을 파악하면 첫 번째 문제를 먼저 분석한다.

STEP 3

문제의 키워드와 보기 (A) – (D)의 키워드를 정리한다.

문제는 항상 3가지를 알려 준다. 문제를 최대한 이용하라.
1) 답의 위치 – 답은 순서대로 배치된다.
2) 문제의 키워드와 보기마다의 키워드를 확인한다.
3) 모든 문제는 풀이 전략이 있다.

147. **Where** does the **announcement** most likely appear?
(A) In a **printing** office
(B) In an **employment agency**
(C) In a **law firm** ▶ 정답
(D) In an **engineering** team

---

147 We are happy to tell you all that **Evelyn Nguyen** has agreed to **take on** a position as an **associate attorney here at** the **Salvatore Law Firm.** Ms. Nguyen studied the law at Harold National University and specialized in the field of patent and copyright law. She has constantly improved her career in the field even during her school years at the university. Last year, she did an internship at the Eduardo Law Association which focuses on clients such as inventors, technicians, and machinists in the engineering industry. Indubitably, Ms. Nguyen is highly qualified the position and will be a valuable addition to our team. **148** Please attend a welcoming **reception** for her this **Friday** in the main conference hall.

> 147번 장소나 목적을 묻는 문제는 지문의 상단부에 위치한다.

> 148번 보기의 키워드 Friday와 답의 위치(하단부) 분석

148. What **are staff members invited to do on Friday**?
(A) Attend a **law seminar**
(B) Meet a **new employee** ▶ 정답
(C) Visit a local **university**
(D) Join an engineering **conference**

> ❶ 마지막 문제의 답은 주로 하단부에 있다.
> ❷ 요구 사항은 대부분 하단부에 답이 있다.
> ❸ 키워드는 Friday이다.

STEP 4

문제별 유형에 따른 풀이 훈련을 한다.

147. 장소나 목적을 묻는 문제는 지문의 상단부에 답이 나온다.
148. 요구 사항은 답이 하단부에 있으며 주로 Please, You should, We ask 등으로 시작한다.

STEP 5

답은 항상 포괄적인 단어로 paraphrasing된다.

오답은 본문 중에 있다. 따라서 본문 중에 conference나 engineer 등이 보인다고 해도 Please 뒷부분을 포괄적으로 설명한 것이 답이 된다. 키워드인 Friday 근처에서 답을 찾는다.

Please attend a welcoming reception for her this Friday in the main conference hall.
금요일에 그녀를 환영하는 리셉션에 오라는 것은 '새로 오는 직원을 만나라'는 뜻이다.
정답은 (B)이다.

질문 유형별 전략을
학습하라

CHAPTER 1
SINGLE PASSAGE

CHAPTER 1

ACTUAL TEST

Questions 01-02 refer to the following receipt.

> Receipt No. 7484920
> (Please keep this receipt number for reference. You may need it when you contact the customer service.)
>
> **Tickets for Gerald Murray in Jazz concert Saturday, June 12, 8:00 P.M.**
>
> [Charged to credit card ending in 7758-XXXX]
> Paid by Justin Morris: $43 to Darrell Theater
>
> **Note:** Be advised that tickets ordered in advance are nonrefundable. In order to check your name on the pre-order list, please arrive at the ticket office before the event. Any other form of receipt will not be accepted, so make sure to print this receipt and bring it with you to the arena.

01. What is Mr. Morris supposed to do on June 12?
(A) Request a refund
(B) Call the ticket office
(C) Go to a musical event
(D) Make a card payment

02. What must Mr. Morris bring with him?
(A) Pre-order lists
(B) A copy of receipt
(C) Reference numbers
(D) A printed ticket

Questions 03-04 refer to the following letter.

Dear Mr. Colin,

We are writing to you to provide you with information regarding your order. Your confirmation number is DM-4382. Please do not lose this number. You will be asked to provide it in order to discuss your order.

The book titles you requested are in stock and will be shipped to you within a week. However, the audio tape you requested is on back order at the moment. We cannot guarantee an arrival date, but we estimate that you will receive the tape within seven to eight weeks. If you still have not received all of the materials after ten weeks, please contact us so that we can take care of the matter quickly.

To make this process more clear, our company has established an online tracking map that allows customers to see the current location of their orders. You can log on to view your order using your confirmation number at www.Fantasy4you.com.

To contact us directly you can call our toll-free number at 800-452-7245 to speak with a customer service representative from Monday to Friday, 9 A.M. - 6 P.M. Eastern Standard time.

03. What is the purpose of this letter?
(A) To confirm the order for books and the audio tape
(B) To inform the client that the book is out of stock
(C) To provide information regarding a customer order
(D) To request confirmation of the order

04. When will the audio tape be shipped to the customer?
(A) Within a week
(B) In 9 weeks
(C) In 7-8 weeks
(D) After 10 weeks

Questions 05-07 refer to the following invoice.

From: Eunice Loyal Services, Co.
Levi Road, Rex Park, Wales 45T-3CH

Invoice:
Delivered to (on July 12) & Billed to
Terry Nunez and Ortiz Oak Restaurant
345 Ronnie, Westwood

Item No.	Description	Quantity
345Q	Various Vegetables Crate	10
*96H	Mixed Seafood Bag	20
42YN	Utensil Set	3
68UT	Sanitary Cap Box	10

* Item No. 96H will be shipped at a later date since it is out of stock at the moment.

05. What most likely is Eunice Loyal Services?
(A) A catering company
(B) A restaurant supplier
(C) A shipping firm
(D) A restaurant chain

06. What will most likely happen on July 12?
(A) An item will run out of stock.
(B) A payment will be made.
(C) A shipment will arrive.
(D) An invoice will be corrected.

07. What is suggested about the seafood bag?
(A) It is not currently available.
(B) It will be on sale soon.
(C) It is cheaper than usual.
(D) It will be produced soon.

Questions 08-09 refer to the following e-mail.

To: Johnny Perry <jperry@carlexpert.co.au>
From: Holly Pierce <hpierce@carlexpert.co.au>
Date: January 21
Subject: Singapore

Hello, Perry.

It seems to take much longer than estimated for the team I am supervising to complete the report on the progress of the highway construction. I need to prolong our stay here in Singapore, so please cancel my Thursday meetings in New York, which will allow me to be well prepared for the meeting with a client, Ms. Ramsey, next week.

Also, I need you to copy and forward the current contract details to me as soon as possible. You may be able to find it in my cabinet or on my desk with the TCY documents. I have a copy at the moment, but it is an outdated version.

You can reach me by phone or e-mail for the next few days, so if there are calls regarding the schedule change from any of my clients, please do not hesitate to transfer the calls to my cell phone.

Thank you in advance for your help.

Holly
Holly Pierce, Vice President, Carl Expert Inc.

---

08. Why most likely was the e-mail written?
(A) To set up a job interview
(B) To ask for help to change a schedule
(C) To approve a construction plan
(D) To report the status of a project

09. Who most likely is Mr. Perry?
(A) A construction worker
(B) An architect
(C) A personal assistant
(D) A telephone operator

Questions 10-11 refer to the following text message.

From: Arturo Powell, Wednesday, 11 September, 1:25 P.M.

Myron, I'm setting up our new meeting room sound system at the Sammy Conference Center. Andy is busy doing his job at the Patel Hotel, so it is too much work for me to do it on my own. It's more time consuming than expected. They want me to install two separate systems in case the room is divided into different spaces for more than one event at the same time. Would you mind getting hold of Herman and asking whether he has any extra time to help me? His number should be in the company directory on our website.

10. What challenge is Mr. Powell facing?
(A) He is scheduled to do some other work.
(B) He is having difficulty completing a job.
(C) He is not able to divide some rooms.
(D) He will be late for a meeting.

11. Why did Mr. Powell leave the text message to Myron?
(A) To tell him to contact a colleague
(B) To reschedule a client meeting
(C) To ask him to reserve a conference room
(D) To cancel a work schedule

Questions 12-13 refer to the following notice.

Attention Business owners in Canberra City

The directory of businesses in Canberra City has increased so rapidly that publishing them in the local newsletter takes up too much space. Therefore, a printed directory will not be available anymore. Instead, it will be offered online.

The directory has not been posted yet, but it will be listed at www.canberracitygo.com soon. We recommend you go over your listing and check if it is accurate once it is available. If you notice that any information is wrong or any link is not connected properly, please inform us so that we can correct the errors.

Thanks,

Lothian Payne
Canberra City Council
334-2241

---

12. What is suggested about the business directory?
(A) Businesses in more than one area will be covered.
(B) The distribution date is going to be changed.
(C) Only an online version is scheduled to be available.
(D) The listing in it will be shortened.

13. Why might someone contact Mr. Payne?
(A) To renew an access code
(B) To request a deadline extension
(C) To correct some information
(D) To contribute to a newsletter

Questions 14-15 refer to the following product review.

http://www.julius.com

| Main [Home] | Outdoors/Indoors | Clothing/Suits | Athletic Shoes |

Julius's Guide for Wise Purchasers

Searching for athletic shoes? There are many choices appealing to you. Some brands, like Air Pro Fit, have lasted from generation to generation. Others, like Wellious, are quite new and boast the most recent high-tech materials.

Below reviews are our best picks. Be advised that prices can very slightly depending on online stores.

Hector Smith   £ £ £*
These shoes have always dominated in the premium market since their release. They are not only comfortable but also solid as made of the high quality materials including leather and rubber. They can last for many years and are the best bet for those who frequently work out. Their price is the only downside.

Miguel RS   £ £
In order for these waterproof shoes to be capable of coping with tough outdoor workouts even in rough weather conditions, quality leather and synthetic materials are used. However, their soles do not seem to last longer than expected with heavy use.

Wellious   £
Made of the lightest materials in the market which have been newly invented, these shoes are ideal in hot weather and great for running on any kind of terrain. They aren't the best choice for people searching for something waterproof and warm, but for those who are about to start out.

Air Pro Fit 21X   £
The price will never fool consumers. These shoes are the best value for the money. Materials such as synthetic rubber, nylon, and leather are used to enable them to resist water from getting in. Not being very flexible is the only drawback, but they tend to remain in shape even though used multiple times.

* Price range:
£ = under £100 / £ £ = £100 to £150 / £ £ £ = £150 to £200

14. What is mentioned as a problem with Miguel RS shoes?
(A) They are not very flexible.
(B) They are not light enough.
(C) They are not as durable as they should be.
(D) They are more expensive than any other shoes.

15. Which shoes are most likely best for exercise beginners?
(A) Hector Smith
(B) Miguel RS
(C) Wellious
(D) Air Pro Fit 21X

Questions 16-19 refer to the following article.

Books loved for good

March 18 – In West Randwick town, Jennie Walsh, who has been teaching European literature at Birchgrove City College for fifteen years, is perhaps better known as the owner of the region's oldest bookstore, The Lance Reading Place. The store is also famous for its unusual features such as its selection of rare books and only opens for business on Sundays. Obviously, orders placed by online or telephone from private collectors, museums, and universities are the bookstore's main source of revenue while walk in sales account only for a small part of Ms. Walsh's business.

On Saturday, Lance Reading Place is going to celebrate its fiftieth anniversary. "When my father, Horace, started this business many years ago on South Clovery Avenue, several blocks from here, he may never have expected that it would still be in business five decades later." Ms. Walsh said. Its original sign is still displayed over the entrance.

The exterior keeps the front porch atmosphere like a normal house with a swing, a rocking chair and benches. A corner of the store is full of books about chess, an everlasting passion of the Walsh family. On Friday afternoons, the store becomes a place for a casual social club. Apparently, the members are fascinated in literature, rare books, and chess.

Next month, Ms. Walsh will reach another milestone; she intends to retire as a professor. However, even though she is retiring, The Lance Reading Place is not going to extend its hours and still will be open only once a week. "My retirement from one job is not to allow more time for another." Ms. Walsh added. "Instead, I will be able to spend more time with my children and friends because I don't need to do any time consuming preparation for classes or tests.

16. What is the main purpose of the article?
(A) To bring in more people to a book club
(B) To announce the relocation of well-known business
(C) To celebrate the achievements of a local entrepreneur
(D) To report some benefits of selling rare items

17. What is NOT indicated about Ms. Walsh?
(A) She plans to end her career as a teacher.
(B) She enjoys talking about chess with others.
(C) She has resided in Birchgrove City over fifteen years.
(D) She has read many books written by European writers.

18. The word "keeps" in paragraph 3, line 1 is closest in meaning to
(A) prevents
(B) maintains
(C) protects
(D) connects with

19. What is mentioned about The Lance Reading Place?
(A) Its sales may have increased significantly.
(B) It opens every weekday.
(C) Its children's book section will be expanded.
(D) Its current business hours will be unchanged.

Questions 20-23 refer to the following article.

Tuesday, May 11

Sylvester Cinema on Devin Road will be closed to the public at the beginning of next month, yet this beautiful structure won't be unavailable for very long. The structure has been sold to Shawn Theater Group (STG), owned by John Cooper.

According to STG Vice President Loretta Spencer, the group has a plan to renovate the structure before it starts its operation. She claimed that all of the equipment such as screens, sound systems, and seats in the cinema will be replaced. — [1] — "Still," Ms. Spencer added, "One of the Sylvester Cinema's old projectors will be kept so as to continue to show classic pieces in their original format to the public."

Formerly, the Sylvester Cinema focused on showing artistic, noncommercial, and international movies. — [2] —. The previous owner, Mr. J.Terry, who retired recently, wanted to make the Sylvester Cinema the best place for artistic movies. For over a decade, it seemed successful, but the number of customers has dropped significantly in the past few years and the owner made the decision to sell the cinema. — [3] —.

"It wasn't easy for me to make a such decision," said Mr. J.Terry, "I already miss not only the cinema, but also everyone working with me. However, it's great that STG will revitalize the old cinema."

Under its new management, the cinema is planning to continue to show artistic films occasionally, as well as mainstream ones in order to bring more people to the cinema.

The cinema is scheduled to reopen to the public on August 5. Besides, the annual film festival focusing on classical pieces will be continuously hosted by the cinema starting September 11 for two weeks. Nothing about the event will be changed except one thing. It will not be called Sylvester Film Festival, but the Shawn Theater Group Movie Festival. — [4] —.

20. What is indicated about the Sylvester Cinema?
(A) It will reopen next month.
(B) Its customers will miss Mr. J.Terry's performance.
(C) Its equipment will be replaced soon.
(D) It will show only artistic movies.

21. According to the article, what was hard for Mr. J.Terry?
(A) Locating the most suitable equipment
(B) Selecting artistic films for his cinema
(C) Determining to put the cinema on sale
(D) Finding a place for his retirement party

22. Who is Ms. Spencer?
(A) A constructor
(B) A business owner
(C) An executive
(D) An engineer

23. In which of the positions marked [1], [2], [3], and [4] does the following sentence best belong to?
"The lobby on the ground floor is going to be removed."
(A) [1]
(B) [2]
(C) [3]
(D) [4]

Questions 24-26 refer to the following article.

The Stuart Park to be Refurbished
By Forrest Paul

Camden (August 21) - A resolution to refurbish the ten-year-old Stuart Park has been unanimously approved by Camden Town Council. This initiative has been considered since originally proposed four years ago. However, it was not approved until Rick Shalib was officially appointed as mayor. "I promised the town that my first priority in office would be to put the project into action, and I intend to keep my word." he said in an interview. — [1] —.

When the park was completed, its four kilometer trail-lined with trees along a stream seemed to serve as a place for Camden residents' walk. But it did not last long because people found that the place is not the best choice for their kids. — [2] —.

"We often come to the path to take a walk, but our children would feel like playing with a ball," said one of the town residents, Alvin Rice. "There is not enough space for our kids to run and play freely. And since it doesn't have enough tables or benches, the park is not appropriate for a picnic lunch." — [3] —.

A series of tasks will be required to make a spacious green spot available for various outdoor activities. Picnic tables, benches, and a playground with an outdoor football field and a basketball court would be great additions. — [4] —. These were requested by one of the town's sport groups for those wishing to exercise at any time of the day.
The overall refurbishment process will be done during the winter season, and the park will be set for the public in the coming spring.

24. What is suggested about the park's refurbishment?
(A) It is scheduled to start the coming spring.
(B) None of the council members disagreed to it.
(C) It needs more than a year to be done.
(D) Mayor Shalib proposed it a long time ago.

25. The word "initiative" in paragraph 1, line 4, is closest in meaning to
(A) start
(B) advantage
(C) action
(D) plan

26. In which of the positions marked [1], [2], [3], and [4] does the following sentence best belong?
    "And lampposts are planned to be installed along the park's path for evening visitors."
(A) [1]
(B) [2]
(C) [3]
(D) [4]

Questions 27-29 refer to the following article.

Briefing on High Street Business

Keith's Bookstore has closed a deal to acquire the retail premises by its current space at 223 Bond Street in Victoria East. The well-known high street fixture will utilize the new premises for its needed expansion. — [1] —. "Since our store opened four years ago, our business has always been hitting the ground running." says Todd Sanders, cofounder and owner. "People said to us that small businesses like our bookstore are not as successful as they once were anymore." — [2] —. Sanders added, "The renovated Keith's Bookstore will be more spacious than the original one."

"The reopening ceremony will be held on June 25." said Sanders. — [3] —. "The extra space makes our customers as well as us very excited. — [4] —. It will allow us to hold more interesting events such as publication parties, book signings, and meetings with authors."

27. What is the article mainly about?
(A) A book signing event
(B) The launch of a publication
(C) Some changes to a local business
(D) A brief profile of a famous author

28. Who most likely is Mr. Sanders?
(A) A building inspector
(B) A famous writer
(C) An entrepreneur
(D) A news reporter

29. In which of the positions marked [1], [2], [3], and [4] does the following sentence best belong?
    "We have proved that the opposite case exists."
(A) [1]
(B) [2]
(C) [3]
(D) [4]

Questions 30-31 refer to the following text message chain.

Lettie Arron   **[12:14 A.M.]**
Mr. Wolfe, I sent you the updated contract by e-mail.
Did you get it?

Neal Wolfe   **[12:16 A.M.]**
Yeah, I'm just looking at it now. Thank you for making those revisions.

Lettie Arron   **[12:17 A.M.]**
No problem. Thanks for notifying me of the issue.
The contract now clearly indicates that $150 will be paid for an accepted article instead of $100.

Neal Wolfe   **[12:18 A.M.]**
Excellent. I'm going to go over the details once again and sign it to mail it to you as soon as possible.

Lettie Arron   **[12:20 A.M.]**
Thanks and please let me know if you need anything else. As you know we have a range of rental spaces and properties.

---

30. At 12:17 A.M., what does Ms. Arron mean when she writes, "No problem"?

(A) She has willingly fulfilled a request.
(B) She is still considering signing a contract.
(C) She is clear about the contract details.
(D) She was aware that an e-mail had already been sent.

31. Where most likely does Ms. Arron work?

(A) A consulting firm
(B) A legal firm
(C) A bank
(D) A real estate agency

Questions 32-33 refer to the following text message chain.

Julia Ross [10:36 A.M.]
Is it okay to begin the presentation before you arrive? The client is already here.

Jesus Ruiz [10:38 A.M.]
Yes, please go ahead. I think I won't be able to make it in time.

Julia Ross [10:40 A.M.]
All right then, I'll start with the overview and move onto the discussion on the new features of our product. You should arrive here no later than 11:00, right?

Jesus Ruiz [10:41 A.M.]
Sure, and you will do a great job.

Julia Ross [10:42 A.M.]
Yeah, but I think you had better present the expense savings. It isn't really my field.

Jesus Ruiz [10:44 A.M.]
No problem. I'll be there as soon as I can.

32. At 10:38 A.M., what most likely does Mr. Ruiz mean when he writes, "Yes, please go ahead"?
(A) He wants some figures to be forwarded to him.
(B) He wants Ms. Ross to stick to schedule.
(C) He thinks a short break should be added.
(D) He is unhappy with a scheduling conflict.

33. According to Ms. Ross, what is Mr. Ruiz most familiar with?
(A) Sales
(B) Design
(C) Finance
(D) Shipping

Questions 34-37 refer to the following online chat discussion.

Deanna Schultz [2:32 P.M.] In order to prepare for next week's branch managers' meeting, I have to arrange transportation from the airport. So, everyone needs to provide me your flight information. It is the first time we hold a meeting like this, and everything should be organized properly.

Lynn Santos [2:33 P.M.] It's unbelievable. If I use a car, will the travel costs be reimbursed to me? I tried to book a flight from New York, but all the seats have been sold out already.

Celia Sharp [2:34 P.M.] I have booked a seat on Leroy Airlines, flight 31, arriving in Washington, DC from San Francisco at 7:10 A.M.

Deanna Schultz [2:35 P.M.] Oh my! That's bad news. I'd better check that for you.

Seth Stanley [2:35 P.M.] All the flights from Detroit were fully booked as well. So I'm going to catch a bus to New Jersey to take a plane from there, getting in at 7:05 A.M. I barely managed to make a reservation for the last seat to Washington, DC.

Deanna Schultz [2:37 P.M.] I just checked the policy that driving to any event over 60 miles away does not qualify for reimbursement. And there is no available flight from any airport in the cities nearby at the moment. Why don't you consider catching a train? You'd better make a reservation as soon as possible and notify me of the travel arrangements.

Lynn Santos [2:38 P.M.] That might be possible. I will do that.

Deanna Schultz [2:40 P.M.] Mr. Sharp and Ms. Stanley, grateful for the information. Taxis will be arranged to wait for your arrivals.

34. At 2:33 P.M., what most likely does Ms. Santos mean when she writes, "It's unbelievable"?
(A) She thought the meeting had been put off to next week.
(B) She was not able to book her flight ticket.
(C) She did not expect that Ms. Schultz would ask about her travel destination.
(D) She had not been informed of free transportation from the airport.

35. At 2:35 P.M., what will Ms. Schultz check?
(A) Available transportation options from the airport
(B) Information on Mr. Sharp's travel arrangement
(C) The company policy for reimbursement
(D) A discounted flight ticket from New York

36. What is suggested about the branch managers?
(A) They will arrive from the same city.
(B) They will arrange their own taxi from the airport.
(C) They need to make a presentation at the meeting this year.
(D) They are having a meeting in Washington, DC.

37. How most likely will Ms. Santos get to the branch managers' meeting?
(A) She will ride a bus.
(B) She will catch a train.
(C) She will use an airline.
(D) She will take her own car.

답은 항상 keyword 옆에 있다.

① 질문의 키워드를 파악하고 어디서 나올 만한 내용인지 확인하라.
② 본문의 단어는 구체적이고 답은 항상 포괄적으로 paraphrasing이 된다.

시험에 이렇게 나온다

Questions 01-02 refer to the following receipt.

> Receipt No. 7484920
> (Please keep this receipt number for reference. You may need it when you contact the customer service.)
>
> **Tickets for Gerald Murray in Jazz concert Saturday, June 12, 8:00 P.M.**
>
> [Charged to credit card ending in 7758-XXXX]
> Paid by Justin Morris: $43 to Darrell Theater
>
> **Note:** Be advised that tickets ordered in advance are nonrefundable. In order to check your name on the pre-order list, please arrive at the ticket office before the event. Any other form of receipt will not be accepted, so make sure to print this receipt and bring it with you to the arena.

01. What is Mr. Morris supposed to do on June 12?
(A) Request a refund
(B) Call the ticket office
(C) Go to a musical event
(D) Make a card payment

01번 문제 풀이 전략

STEP 1 처음 2줄을 skimming하여 주요 정보와 대략의 상황을 파악한다.
receipt number / Tickets / Jazz concert

STEP 2 첫 번째 문제를 분석한다. [위치 / 키워드 / 유형별 풀이 전략]
147. What is Mr. Morris supposed to do on June 12?
첫 번째 문제 - 지문 상단부 / 키워드 12일 / 유형 - 키워드 옆에 답이 있다.

STEP 3 지문의 상단부에서 키워드를 찾는다.
키워드 근처에 있는 보기가 답이 된다.
in Jazz concert Saturday, June 12, 8:00 P.M.

STEP 4 본문은 구체적 Jazz concert이지만
답은 포괄적 musical event가 답이 된다.
Morris 씨가 7월 12일에 하기로 예정된 일이 무엇인지 묻는 문제이다. 지문의 Tickets for Gerald Murray in Jazz concert Saturday, June 12, 8:00 P.M.에서 Morris 씨가 6월 12일에 열리는 Gerald Murray 콘서트의 티켓을 구매했음을 알 수 있다. 따라서 (C)가 정답이다.

최신 함정 유형

refund/card 등 보기에 있는 모든 단어들은 본문에서 검색된다. 토익에서 오답의 특징은 본문 중에서 뽑아낸 정보로 만든다는 것이다. 따라서 본문을 처음부터 끝까지 다 읽고 나면 모든 보기가 답인 것처럼 느껴진다. 무조건 본문을 먼저 읽기보다는 문제를 먼저 분석한 후에 답의 위치를 확보해야 한다. 모든 답은 유형별로 정해진 위치에서 찾아야 오히려 혼동을 줄일 수 있다.

생각의 순서 MAPPING

Receipt No. 7484920
(Please keep this receipt number for reference. You may need it when you contact the customer service.)

Tickets for Gerald Murray in **Jazz concert** Saturday, **June 12, 8:00 P.M.**

[Charged to credit card ending in 7758-XXXX]
Paid by Justin Morris: $43 to Darrell Theater

Note: Be advised that tickets ordered in advance are nonrefundable. In order to check your name on the pre-order list, please arrive at the ticket office before the event. Any other form of receipt will not be accepted, so make sure to print this receipt and bring it with you to the arena.

❶ skimming
❸ 키워드
❷ 문제 분석
❹ 포괄적인 답

01. What is Mr. Morris supposed to do on June 12?
(A) Request a refund
(B) Call the ticket office
(C) Go to a musical event
(D) Make a card payment

요구 사항은 답이 지문의 하단부에 있다.

① 결론이나 미래에 대한 전망, 계획 또는 제안이나 요구, 요청 사항은 본문의 후반부에 주로 등장한다.
② 요구 사항은 주로 〈require/ask/invite/encourage + 목적어 + to do〉의 형태나 must/should/have to/need 등으로 질문한다.
③ 지문의 후반부에서 아래의 표현들을 잡아야 답이 나온다.

Please	Why don't you/Let's	If you want
You should/need/have to	We want you/We ask you	명령문

시험에 이렇게 나온다

Questions 01-02 refer to the following receipt.

Receipt No. 7484920
(Please keep this receipt number for reference. You may need it when you contact the customer service.)

Tickets for Gerald Murray in concert Saturday, June 12, 8:00 P.M.

[Charged to credit card ending in 7758-XXXX]
Paid by Justin Morris: $43 to Darrell Theater

Note: Be advised that tickets ordered in advance are nonrefundable. In order to check your name on the pre-order list, please arrive at the ticket office before the event. Any other form of receipt will not be accepted, so make sure to print this receipt and bring it with you to the arena.

02. What must Mr. Morris bring with him?
(A) Pre-order lists
(B) A copy of receipt
(C) Reference numbers
(D) A printed ticket

02번 문제 풀이 순서

STEP 1 이번을 해결한 후에는 중반부 이후의 나머지 지문을 읽지 않고, 바로 02번 문제 분석을 먼저 한 후에 나머지 지문을 읽어야 한다.

STEP 2 문제를 분석한다. [위치 / 키워드 / 유형별 풀이 전략]
What must Mr. Morris bring with him? 마지막 문제 - 지문 하단부 / must 요구

SETP 3 지문의 하단부에서 be advised/please/make sure/명령문을 찾는다.
그 중에 bring이라는 keyword와 유사 어휘가 있는 부분이 답이다.

STEP 4 문제에서 bring이라는 키워드를 확인하고 답을 찾는다.
Morris 씨가 가지고 와야만 하는 것이 무엇인지 묻는 문제이다. 지문의 so make sure to print this receipt and bring it with you to the arena.에서 Morris 씨에게 공연장으로 인쇄된 영수증을 가지고 올 것을 언급하고 있다. 따라서 영수증 사본임을 알 수 있으므로 정답은 (B)이다.

최신 함정 유형

본문의 요구 사항은 현재 총 4가지이다. 1. 주문을 미리 해라 2. 일찍 도착해라 3. 프린트해라 4. 프린트한 것을 가지고 와라. 따라서 이때 또 다른 키워드인 bring을 놓치게 되면 답을 찾을 수 없다. 그러니 문제를 분석할 때는 항상 [위치 + 키워드+ 유형별 풀이 전략]을 항상 동시에 염두에 두어야 한다.

생각의 순서 MAPPING

Receipt No. 7484920
(Please keep this receipt number for reference. You may need it when you contact the customer service.)

Tickets for Gerald Murray in Jazz concert Saturday, June 12, 8:00 P.M.

[Charged to credit card ending in 7758-XXXX]
Paid by Justin Morris: $43 to Darrell Theater

Note: Be advised that tickets ordered in advance are nonrefundable. In order to check your name on the pre-order list, please arrive at the ticket office before the event. Any other form of receipt will not be accepted, so **make sure** to print this **receipt** and **bring** it with you to the arena.

❶ skimming

❸ 키워드 (make sure + bring)

❷ 문제 분석
요구 사항(must/bring) 하단부

02. What must Mr. Morris bring with him?
(A) Pre-order lists
(B) A copy of receipt
(C) Reference numbers
(D) A printed ticket

목적은 처음 두 줄에 90% 답이 있다.

① 목적은 본문의 상단부를 확인하라.
② 보기의 키워드를 먼저 확인한 후에 본문에서 보기를 꼼꼼하게 확인하면서 오답을 소거한다.

시험에 이렇게 나온다

Questions 03-04 refer to the following letter.

Dear Mr. Colin,

We are writing to you to provide you with information regarding your order. Your confirmation number is DM-4382. Please do not lose this number. You will be asked to provide it in order to discuss your order.

The book titles you requested are in stock and will be shipped to you within a week. However, the audio tape you requested is on backorder at the moment. We cannot guarantee an arrival date, but we estimate that you will receive the tape within seven to eight weeks. If you still have not received all of the materials after ten weeks, please contact us so that we can take care of the matter quickly.

To make this process more clear, our company has established an online tracking map that allows customers to see the current location of their orders. You can log on to view your order using your confirmation number at www.Fantasy4you.com.

To contact us directly you can call our toll-free number at 800-452-7245 to speak with a customer service representative from Monday to Friday, 9 A.M. - 6 P.M. Eastern Standard time.

03. What is the purpose of this letter?
(A) To confirm the order for books and the audio tape
(B) To inform the client that the book is out of stock
(C) To provide information regarding a customer order
(D) To request confirmation of the order

03번 문제 풀이 순서

STEP 1 문서의 기본적인 정보인 편지의 목적을 묻는 문제이다.
목적은 본문의 상단부에서 언급된다. 본문의 첫 문장에서 We are writing to you to ~로 보아 이 편지의 주제나 목적을 말하고 있음을 알 수 있다.

STEP 2 본문에서 사용된 단어를 이용한 오류를 제거하라.
(A)는 book과 audio tape의 주문(order)에 대한 편지는 맞지만 주문(order)을 확인(confirm)하고자 하는 것이 아니므로 오답이다.
(B)는 어떤 정보를 알려주는 것은 맞지만 책(book)의 품절(out of stock)이 아니라 audio tape이 품절(on backorder)되었음을 알려주는 것이므로 오답이다.
(C)는 첫 번째 줄에서 주문에 대한 정보를 제공하고자 한다는 내용으로 보아 정답이 된다.
(D)는 confirmation number를 알려주고 있는 것이지 요청(request)하는 것이 아니므로 오답이 된다.

토익은 전체 내용에 대한 이해보다는 정확한 정보를 정확한 위치에서 검색하고 오류를 제거하는 데이터(data) 관리 능력을 중요시 여긴다. 따라서 보기의 한 단어 오류를 먼저 제거하는 습관이 중요하다.
오류를 모두 제거하고 남은 것을 답으로 선택한다.

생각의 순서 MAPPING

Dear Mr. Colin,

We are writing to you to provide you with information regarding your order. Your confirmation number is DM-4382. Please do not lose this number. You will be asked to provide it in order to discuss your order.

The book titles you requested are in stock and will be shipped to you within a week. However, the audio tape you requested is on backorder at the moment. We cannot guarantee an arrival date, but we estimate that you will receive the tape within seven to eight weeks. If you still have not received all of the materials after ten weeks, please contact us so that we can take care of the matter quickly.

To make this process more clear, our company has established an online tracking map that allows customers to see the current location of their orders. You can log on to view your order using your confirmation number at www.Fantasy4you.com.

To contact us directly you can call our toll-free number at 800-452-7245 to speak with a customer service representative from Monday to Friday, 9 A.M. - 6 P.M. Eastern Standard time.

❶ 편지의 목적은 상단부에 등장한다.

03. What is the purpose of this letter?
(A) To confirm the order for books and the audio tape
(B) To inform the client that the book is out of stock
(C) To provide information regarding a customer order
(D) To request confirmation of the order

기간, 요일, 숫자 등은 keyword 옆에 있는 것이 답이다.

① 숫자, 기간, 요일 등은 보기의 정보가 본문에 모두 언급되면서 난이도가 올라간다.
② 본문에 있는 정보들 중에 문제에서 제시하는 keyword 옆에 있는 정확한 정보를 찾아내는 것이 관건이다.

시험에 이렇게 나온다

Questions 03-04 refer to the following letter.

Dear Mr. Colin,

We are writing to you to provide you with information regarding your order. Your confirmation number is DM-4382. Please do not lose this number. You will be asked to provide it in order to discuss your order.

The book titles you requested are in stock and will be shipped to you within a week. However, the audio tape you requested is on backorder at the moment. We cannot guarantee an arrival date, but we estimate that you will receive the tape within seven to eight weeks. If you still have not received all of the materials after ten weeks, please contact us so that we can take care of the matter quickly.

To make this process more clear, our company has established an online tracking map that allows customers to see the current location of their orders. You can log on to view your order using your confirmation number at www.Fantasy4you.com.

To contact us directly you can call our toll-free number at 800-452-7245 to speak with a customer service representative from Monday to Friday, 9 A.M. - 6 P.M. Eastern Standard time.

04. When will the audio tape be shipped to the customer?
(A) Within a week
(B) In 9 weeks
(C) In 7-8 weeks
(D) After 10 weeks

04번 문제 풀이 순서

STEP 1 구체적인 내용을 묻는 문제이다.
When, audio tape, shipped를 키워드로 잡고 본문에서 스키밍(skimming)과 스캐닝(scanning)을 하여 찾아낸다.

STEP 2 두 번째 단락에서 However 이후에 audio tape을 찾았고 앞뒤 문맥에서 배송(ship)되는 날짜를 확인해야 한다.
다음 문장에서 you will receive the tape within seven to eight weeks를 통해 배송은 7-8주 후임을 알수 있다. (A) Within a week이라는 표현은 두 번째 단락, 첫 번째 줄에 나왔지만 이것은 책이 도착하는 시기이므로 정답이 될 수 없다.

보기의 숫자가 모두 본문에 있지만 어떤 키워드와 관련이 되어 있는지를 꼼꼼히 확인해야 답이 나오는 패턴을 파악할 수 있다. 배송되는 것이 book titles인지 audio tape인지를 반드시 확인해야 한다.
But이나 However 뒤에 답이 있다는 것을 항상 명심하자.

생각의 순서 MAPPING

Dear Mr. Colin,

We are writing to you to provide you with information regarding your order. Your confirmation number is DM-4382. Please do not lose this number. You will be asked to provide it in order...

❶ 키워드 audio tape

The book titles you requested are in stock and will be shipped to you within a week. **However, the audio tape** you requested is on backorder at the moment. We cannot guarantee an arrival date, **but** we estimate that you will receive **the tape within seven to eight weeks**. If ...materials after ten weeks, please contact us so that...

❷ 키워드인 audio tape을 중심으로 앞뒤 문장에서 정답을 확인할 수 있다.

To make this process more clear, our company has established an online tracking map that allows customers to see the current location of their orders. You can log on to view your order using your confirmation number at www.Fantasy4you.com.

To contact us directly you can call our toll-free number at 800-452-7245 to speak with a customer service representative from Monday to Friday, 9 A.M. - 6 P.M. Eastern Standard time.

04. When will the audio tape be shipped to the customer?
(A) ~~Within a week~~ → book titles의 배송 일정
(B) ~~In 9 weeks~~
(C) In 7-8 weeks
(D) ~~After 10 weeks~~

1-05 업종을 묻는 문제는 표의 구체적인 명목들이 답을 보여 준다.

① 업종을 묻는 문제는 단순하게 회사 이름에서 답이 나올 수 있는 것이 아니다. 누가 누구에게 즉, 두 회사의 관계를 이해하고 I에 해당하는 편지를 보내는 회사와 you에 해당하는 받는 회사를 분명히 밝혀야 한다.
② 편지의 최상단 letterhead에 명시되는 회사는 항상 편지를 보내는 I에 해당하는 회사이다.
③ 표에 있는 구체적인 품목들은 회사에 대한 정보를 보여 준다.

시험에 이렇게 나온다

Questions 05-07 refer to the following invoice.

From: Eunice Loyal Services, Co.
Levi Road, Rex Park, Wales 45T-3CH

Invoice:
Delivered to (on July 12) & Billed to
Terry Nunez and Ortiz Oak Restaurant
345 Ronnie, Westwood

Item No.	Description	Quantity
345Q	Various Vegetables Crate	10
*96H	Mixed Seafood Bag	20
42YN	Utensil Set	3
68UT	Sanitary Cap Box	10

* Item No. 96H will be shipped at a later date since it is out of stock at the moment.

05. What most likely is Eunice Loyal Services?
(A) A catering company
(B) A restaurant supplier
(C) A shipping firm
(D) A restaurant chain

05번 문제 풀이 순서

STEP 1 먼저 보내는 회사와 받는 회사를 찾아야 한다.
보내는 회사는 지문 최상단의 Eunice Loyal Services, Co.이고 받는 회사는 Terry Nunez and Ortiz Oak Restaurant이다.

STEP 2 명세서의 표를 보면 주문한 물품 내역이 레스토랑에 사용되는 물품들임을 보여 준다.

STEP 3 From(보낸 회사)에 해당하는 회사는 물건을 보낸 회사이다. 또한 하단부에 재고가 없다는 의미는 배송만을 하는 회사는 아니라는 것이다.

STEP 4 to(받는 회사)에 해당하는 회사가 Restaurant이다.

 보기의 모든 회사들이 지문에 나오기 때문에 등장 회사들의 관계를 잘 이해해야 한다.
from에 해당하는 회사와 to에 해당하는 회사를 찾는 것이 관건이다.

생각의 순서 MAPPING

From: Eunice Loyal Services, Co.
Levi Road, Rex Park, Wales 45T-3CH   ❶ 보내는 회사

Invoice:
Delivered to (on July 12) & Billed to   ❶ 받는 회사 (Restaurant)
Terry Nunez and Ortiz Oak Restaurant
345 Ronnie, Westwood

Item No.	Description	Quantity
345Q	Various Vegetables Crate	10
*96H	Mixed Seafood Bag	20
42YN	Utensil Set	3
68UT	Sanitary Cap Box	10

❷ 보내는 물품들이 식자재나 식기류이다.

* Item No. 96H will be shipped at a later date since it is out of stock at the moment.

❸ 재고가 없다는 것은 이 회사가 배송 회사가 아니라는 것을 의미한다.

05. What most likely is Eunice Loyal Services?
(A) A catering company [행사 등에 음식과 직원을 파견하는 회사]
(B) A restaurant supplier
(C) A shipping firm [배달만을 전문으로 하는 회사, from이 아니라 through/by 등으로 명시해야 한다.]
(D) A restaurant chain [Terry Nunez and Ortiz Oak restaurant이다.]

답은 항상 paraphrasing된다.

① 영어는 중복을 싫어하며 본문에 있는 단어를 그대로 다시 보기에서 답으로 제시하는 단순한 문제는 출제하지 않는다.
② 본문의 답에 해당하는 단어와 정답은 항상 유사 어휘로 전환하여 제시된다.
③ paraphrasing될 때 동의어나 포괄적인 단어로 바뀐다.

시험에 이렇게 나온다

Questions 05-07 refer to the following invoice.

From: Eunice Loyal Services, Co.
Levi Road, Rex Park, Wales 45T-3CH

Invoice:
Delivered to (on July 12) & Billed to
Terry Nunez and Ortiz Oak Restaurant
345 Ronnie, Westwood

Item No.	Description	Quantity
345Q	Various Vegetables Crate	10
*96H	Mixed Seafood Bag	20
42YN	Utensil Set	3
68UT	Sanitary Cap Box	10

* Item No. 96H will be shipped at a later date since it is out of stock at the moment.

06. What will most likely happen on July 12?
(A) An item will run out of stock.
(B) A payment will be made.
(C) A shipment will arrive.
(D) An invoice will be corrected.

06번 문제 풀이 순서

STEP 1 7월 12일에 무슨 일이 발생할지 묻는 문제이다. 지문에서 키워드인 12를 찾는다.

STEP 2 Delivered to (on July 12) & Billed to에서 7월 12일에 배달 물품이 도착할 것임을 알 수 있다.

STEP 3 deliver = ship이기 때문에 정답은 (C)이다.

비즈니스 문서는 반드시 해당 위치에서 답을 찾아야만 한다. 전체 지문을 모두 읽으면서 보기를 보면 오히려 모든 보기가 답인 것 같은 혼란이 생긴다.

생각의 순서 MAPPING

From: Eunice Loyal Services, Co.
Levi Road, Rex Park, Wales 45T-3CH

Invoice:
Delivered to (on July 12) **& Billed to**   ❶ 키워드 July 12
Terry Nunez and Ortiz Oak Restaurant
345 Ronnie, Westwood

Item No.	Description	Quantity
345Q	Various Vegetables Crate	10
*96H	Mixed Seafood Bag	20
42YN	Utensil Set	3
68UT	Sanitary Cap Box	10

* Item No. 96H will be shipped at a later date since it is out of stock at the moment.

---

06. What will most likely happen on July 12?
(A) An item will run out of stock.
(B) A payment will be made.
(C) A shipment will arrive.   ❷ shipment = delivery
(D) An invoice will be corrected.

keyword 옆에 답이 없는 경우는 또 다른 keyword를 남긴다.

① 문제 중에서 제시된 키워드를 본문에서 찾으면 그 근처에 답이 있다.
② 키워드 근처에 있는 내용이 보기 중에 답에 해당하는 것이 없다면 또 다른 키워드를 남기게 된다.
③ 또 다른 키워드를 연결하여 답을 찾는다.

시험에 이렇게 나온다

Questions 05-07 refer to the following invoice.

From: Eunice Loyal Services, Co.
Levi Road, Rex Park, Wales 45T-3CH

Invoice:
Delivered to (on July 12) & Billed to
Terry Nunez and Ortiz Oak Restaurant
345 Ronnie, Westwood

Item No.	Description	Quantity
345Q	Various Vegetables Crate	10
*96H	Mixed Seafood Bag	20
42YN	Utensil Set	3
68UT	Sanitary Cap Box	10

* Item No. 96H will be shipped at a later date since it is out of stock at the moment.

07. What is suggested about the seafood bag?
(A) It is not currently available.
(B) It will be on sale soon.
(C) It is cheaper than usual.
(D) It will be produced soon.

07번 문제 풀이 순서

STEP 1   질문의 키워드인 seafood bag과 관련된 내용을 지문에서 찾아 보기와 대조하는 문제이다.

STEP 2   seafood 근처에는 보기 중에 해당하는 내용이 없다.

STEP 3   seafood 근처에 또 다른 키워드는 96H와 수량 20개이다.

STEP 4   또 다른 키워드인 96H를 찾아보면 지문 하단부의 Item No. 96H will be shipped at a later date since it is out of stock at the moment.에서 물품 번호 96H인 해산물 보관 자루가 현재 일시 품절 상태임을 언급하고 있다.

 한 번에 답이 나오지 않고 키워드를 두 번에 걸쳐 비틀어 제시하는 유형으로, 정보를 복잡한 경로로 추적하게 만드는 문제는 최근에 단일 지문과 복수 지문에서 모두 등장하는 유형이다.

생각의 순서 MAPPING

From: Eunice Loyal Services, Co.
Levi Road, Rex Park, Wales 45T-3CH

Invoice:
Delivered to **(on July 12) & Billed to**
Terry Nunez and Ortiz Oak Restaurant
345 Ronnie, Westwood

Item No.	Description	Quantity
345Q	Various Vegetables Crate	10
*96H	Mixed Seafood Bag	20
42YN	Utensil Set	3
68UT		10

❶ 키워드 seafood bag
❷ 또 다른 키워드 96H

* Item No. **96H** will be shipped at a later date since it is <u>out of stock at the moment.</u>

❸ 96H 관련 설명이 답이 된다.
❹ not available

07. What is suggested about the seafood bag?

(A) It is not currently available.
(B) It will be on sale soon.
(C) It is cheaper than usual.
(D) It will be produced soon.

목적은 처음 2~3줄에 답이 있을 확률이 90%이며 하단부 요구 사항에 답이 있을 확률은 10%이다.

① 비즈니스 문서의 목적은 항상 상단부에 답이 있어야 한다.
② 상황 설명이 길거나 처음 보내는 편지의 경우에는 종종 지문의 하단부에 본론이 나온다. 따라서 목적이 하단부에 요구 사항이나 부탁, 제안 등의 표현으로 제시된다.

시험에 이렇게 나온다

Questions 08-09 refer to the following e-mail.

To: Johnny Perry <jperry@carlexpert.co.au>
From: Holly Pierce <hpierce@carlexpert.co.au>
Date: January 21
Subject: Singapore

Hello, Perry.

It seems to take much longer than estimated for the team I am supervising to complete the report on the progress of the highway construction. I need to prolong our stay here in Singapore, so please cancel my Thursday meetings in New York, which will allow me to be well prepared for the meeting with a client, Ms. Ramsey, next week.

Also, I need you to copy and forward the current contract details to me as soon as possible. You may be able to find it in my cabinet or on my desk with the TCY documents. I have a copy at the moment, but it is an outdated version.

You can reach me by phone or e-mail for the next few days, so if there are calls regarding the schedule change from any of my clients, please do not hesitate to transfer the calls to my cell phone.

Thank you in advance for your help.

Holly
Holly Pierce, Vice President, Carl Expert Inc.

08. Why most likely was the e-mail written?
(A) To set up a job interview
(B) To ask for help to change a schedule
(C) To approve a construction plan
(D) To report the status of a project

08번 문제 풀이 순서

STEP 1 편지를 쓴 목적은 앞부분을 먼저 skimming한다.
지문의 앞부분에 상황 설명이 길어 목적이 나타나지 않는다. 이런 경우에는 뒷부분에서 요구나 부탁의 표현을 찾는다.

STEP 2 요구나 부탁의 표현은 주로 Please, I need you to, If you ~ 등의 표현을 찾는다.

STEP 3 보기의 키워드를 정리하여 본문의 내용과 대조한다.
본문에 없는 내용을 포함하는 보기는 오답이다. 항상 정답은 본문의 내용보다 포괄적으로 묘사된다.
요구 사항은 3가지이다. ① 미팅 취소 / ② 계약서 사본 보내 줄 것 / ③ 일정 변동에 대해 전화할 것
이 중에서 보기에 해당하는 내용을 찾으면 (B)가 정답이다.

To: Johnny Perry <jperry@carlexpert.co.au>
From: Holly Pierce <hpierce@carlexpert.co.au>
Date: January 21
Subject: Singapore

Hello, Perry.

It seems to take much longer than estimated for the team I am supervising to complete the report on the progress of the highway construction. I need to prolong our stay here in Singapore, [상황 설명]

Hello, Perry.

It seems to take much longer than estimated for the team I am supervis... the report on the progress of the highway construction. I need to prolon... in Singapore, so ① **please cancel** my Thursday **meetings** in New York, ... me to be well prepared for the meeting with a client, Ms. Ramsey, next week.

Also, ② **I need you to copy** and **forward the current contract** details to me as soon as possible. You may be able to find it in my cabinet or on ... documents. I have a copy at the moment, but it is an outdated v...

You can reach me by phone or e-mail for the next few days, so ③ **if there are calls regarding the schedule change** from any of my clients, please do not hesitate to transfer the calls to my cell phone.

Thank you in advance for your help.

Holly
Holly Pierce, Vice President, Carl Expert Inc.

❶ 목적은 상단부에 등장한다.

❷ Please / I need / If ~

❸ cancel meetings regarding the schedule change = 목적

---

08. Why most likely was the e-mail written?
(A) To set up a job ~~interview~~
(B) To ask for help to change a schedule
(C) To approve a ~~construction~~ plan
(D) To report the ~~status of a project~~

1-09 I/You/제3자를 확인하고 각각의 직업을 파악하라.

① 편지/이메일을 보내거나 받는 사람과 관련된 문제의 경우 I와 You 그리고 본문 중에 언급되는 제3자를 찾아서 직업과 관련 정보를 정리해야 한다. 주로 사람이나 회사 이름을 키워드로 하여 직위, 회사의 업종, 부서, 직업 등을 묻는다.

② from/sign에 해당하는 사람은 본문에서 I/We에 해당하는 정보를 찾는다.
   to/dear/hello에 해당하는 사람은 본문에서 You가 언급된 부분을 찾는다.

Who is this notice from?	I에 대한 질문
To whom/For whom is the letter intended? Who will read this notice?	You에 대한 질문
Who is Ms. Brady's employer?	제3자에 대한 질문

시험에 이렇게 나온다

Questions 08-09 refer to the following e-mail.

To: Johnny Perry <jperry@carlexpert.co.au>
From: Holly Pierce <hpierce@carlexpert.co.au>
Date: January 21
Subject: Singapore

Hello, Perry.

It seems to take much longer than estimated for the team I am supervising to complete the report on the progress of the highway construction. I need to prolong our stay here in Singapore, so please cancel my Thursday meetings in New York, which will allow me to be well prepared for the meeting with a client, Ms. Ramsey, next week.

Also, I need you to copy and forward the current contract details to me as soon as possible. You may be able to find it in my cabinet or on my desk with the TCY documents. I have a copy at the moment, but it is an outdated version.

You can reach me by phone or e-mail for the next few days, so if there are calls regarding the schedule change from any of my clients, please do not hesitate to transfer the calls to my cell phone.

Thank you in advance for your help.

Holly
Holly Pierce, Vice President, Carl Expert Inc.

09. Who most likely is Mr. Perry?
(A) A construction worker
(B) An architect
(C) A personal assistant
(D) A telephone operator

09번 문제 풀이 순서

STEP 1 해당하는 사람이 I/You/제3자인지를 확인한다.
· 09. Who most likely is Mr. Perry?에서 Perry는 hello ~/to ~에 해당하는 You이다.
· 본문 중에 you가 언급된 부분을 찾는다.

STEP 2 보기에 등장하는 사람들의 역할을 파악해야 한다.
I인 Holly가 부탁한 일들을 보면 일정 변경, 서류 복사, 전화 연결 등을 부탁한다. 따라서 You는 (D) 전화 연결원은 아니다. 이런 일을 처리하는 직업은 personal assistant이다. 또한 Holly는 Carl Expert Inc.에서 일한다. 그러므로 I를 위해서 일하는 You도 Carl Expert Inc.에서 일한다는 것을 알 수 있다. 따라서 (A) A construction worker와 (B) An architect는 답이 아니다.

To: Johnny Perry <jperry@carlexpert.co.au>
From: Holly Pierce <hpierce@carlexpert.co.au>
Date: January 21
Subject: Singapore

Hello, Perry.   ❶ 받는 사람 You

It seems to take much longer than estimated for the team I am supervising to complete the report on the progress of the highway construction. I need to prolong our stay here in Singapore, so please cancel my Thursday meetings in New York, which will allow me to be well prepared for the meeting with a client, Ms. Ramsey, next week.

Also, I need you to copy and forward the current contract details to me as soon as possible. You may be able to find it in my cabinet or on my desk with the TCY documents. I have a copy at the moment, but it is an outdated version.

You can reach me by phone or e-mail for the next few days, so if there are calls regarding the schedule change from any of my clients, please do not hesitate to transfer the calls to my cell phone.
Thank you in advance for your help.

❸ You가 언급된 부분
→ Perry (You)의 역할

Holly   ❷ 보내는 사람 I
Holly Pierce, Vice President, Carl Expert Inc.

---

09. Who most likely is Mr. Perry?
(A) A construction worker
(B) An architect
(C) A personal assistant
(D) A telephone operator

1-10 문제점, 과거의 정보는 답이 앞에 있다.

① problem, concern, worry, challenge 등 어려움, 문제점, 과거의 상황은 본문의 앞부분에서 설명이 되어야 한다.
② Why did ~ not과 같은 질문의 답은 부정적인(negative) 내용을 답으로 찾는다.

시험에 이렇게 나온다

Questions 10-11 refer to the following text message.

From: Arturo Powell, Wednesday, 11 September, 1:25 P.M.

Myron, I'm setting up our new meeting room sound system at the Sammy Conference Center. Andy is busy doing his job at the Patel Hotel, so it is too much work for me to do it on my own. It's more time consuming than expected. They want me to install two separate systems in case the room is divided into different spaces for more than one event at the same time. Would you mind getting hold of Herman and asking whether he has any extra time to help me? His number should be in the company directory on our website.

10. What challenge is Mr. Powell facing?
(A) He is scheduled to do some other work.
(B) He is having difficulty completing a job.
(C) He is not able to divide some rooms.
(D) He will be late for a meeting.

11. Why did Mr. Powell leave the text message to Myron?
(A) To tell him to contact a colleague
(B) To reschedule a client meeting
(C) To ask him to reserve a conference room
(D) To cancel a work schedule

10번 문제 풀이 순서

STEP 1 첫 번째 문제의 답은 본문의 앞부분에 있다.

STEP 2 challenge는 '도전'이라는 뜻보다는 '문제점, 어려움' 등으로 해석해야 한다.

STEP 3 편지나 메모 등은 반드시 I (from)/You (to)를 구별해야 한다.
위에서 메모/메시지를 작성한 사람이 Mr. Powell이기 때문에 I의 문제점이나 이유를 찾아야 한다.

STEP 4 본문의 앞부분을 보면
Andy is busy doing his job at the Patel Hotel, so it is too much work for me to do it on my own.에서 Andy가 바빠서 올 수 없으면 혼자 하기에는 너무 많은 일이라고 언급한다. 따라서 답은 difficulty completing a job의 (B)이다.

STEP 5 보기에서 오류인 한 단어들을 제거한다.
(C) He is ~~not able to divide~~ rooms.
room은 언급되지만 나눌 수 없다는 의미는 아니다.

(D) He will be ~~late~~ for a meeting.
meeting은 언급이 되지만 늦었다는 의미는 아니다.

11번 문제 풀이 순서

STEP 1 일반적인 Why-Question 문제의 힌트는 상단부에 등장하지만 마지막 문제로 출제될 경우 답은 하단부에 나온다.

STEP 2 하단부에서 '요구/부탁/제안' 등의 표현을 찾는다.
요구나 부탁은 Please, Can you, Would you, You should, I want you to 등의 표현을 찾는다.
<u>Would you</u> mind getting hold of Herman and asking whether he has extra time to help me? His number should be in the company directory on our website.

STEP 3 사람 이름은 가장 중요한 키워드이다.
Arturo Powell이 Myron에게 연락한 이유는 Herman에게 전화해서 도움을 요청하는 것이다.
즉, 대신 전화를 대신해 달라고 하는 (A)가 정답이다.

---

❶ 보내는 사람 I

From: Arturo **Powell**, Wednesday, 11 September, 1:25 P.M.

Myron, ❷ 받는 사람 You new meeting room sound system at the Sammy Conference Center. Andy is busy doing his job at the Patel Hotel, so **it is too much work** for me to do it on my own. It's more time consuming than expected. They wa~~~ separate systems in case the room is divided into different spaces ~~~ event at the same time. Would you mind getting hold of **Herman** and asking whether he has any extra time to help me? **His number** should be in the company directory on our website.

> 10. challenge = too much work

> 11. 제3자 Herman = colleague

---

10. What challenge is Mr. Powell facing?
(A) He is scheduled to do some other work.
(B) He is having difficulty completing a job.
(C) He is not able to divide some rooms.
(D) He will be late for a meeting.

11. Why did Mr. Powell leave the text message to Myron?
(A) To tell him to contact a colleague
(B) To reschedule a client meeting
(C) To ask him to reserve a conference room
(D) To cancel a work schedule

1-11 '사실'인 것을 찾는 문제는 보기의 keyword를 먼저 정리한 후 본문을 검색한다.

주어진 보기는 모두 대충 맞는 내용이다. 문장 중에 한 단어 오류를 찾아라.
① suggest, indicate, imply, mention, true 등 사실인 것을 묻는 문제는 보기를 먼저 분석한 후에 보기의 키워드들을 찾아 두어야 한다.
② 보기의 키워드들을 본문에서 검색하여 보기의 내용과 본문의 내용을 비교하고 대조한다.
③ 보기의 내용은 모두 맞는 것처럼 제시되며 오답인 보기에는 한 단어씩 오류를 심어 놓는다.
④ 한 단어 오류를 먼저 제거하고 정답을 남긴다.

시험에 이렇게 나온다

Questions 12-13 refer to the following notice.

Attention Business owners in Canberra City

The directory of businesses in Canberra City has increased so rapidly that publishing them in the local newsletter takes up too much space. Therefore, a printed directory will not be available anymore. Instead, it will be offered online.

The directory has not been posted yet, but it will be listed at www.canberracitygo.com soon. We recommend you go over your listing and check if it is accurate once it is available. If you notice that any information is wrong or any link is not connected properly, please inform us so that we can correct the errors.

Thanks,

Lothian Payne
Canberra City Council
334-2241

12. What is suggested about the business directory?
(A) Businesses in more than one area will be covered.
(B) The distribution date is going to be changed.
(C) Only an online version is scheduled to be available.
(D) The listing in it will be shortened.

12번 문제 풀이 순서

STEP 1 처음 2줄을 skimming하여 주요 정보와 대략의 상황을 파악한다.
The directory / increased / too much space
a printed directory / not available / instead / online

STEP 2 첫 번째 문제를 분석한다. [위치 / 키워드 / 유형별 풀이 전략]
첫 번째 문제 - 지문 상단부 / 사실인 것을 묻는 문제는 보기를 먼저 정리한다.

12번 문제 풀이 순서

STEP 1 처음 2줄을 skimming하여 주요 정보와 대략의 상황을 파악한다.
The directory / increased / too much space
a printed directory / not available / instead / online

STEP 2 첫 번째 문제를 분석한다. [위치 / 키워드 / 유형별 풀이 전략]
첫 번째 문제 - 지문 상단부 / 사실인 것을 묻는 문제는 보기를 먼저 정리한다.

SETP 3 보기의 키워드를 본문에서 검색하여 나머지 문장에서 오류 요소를 제거한다.
질문의 키워드인 Canberra City business directory와 관련된 내용을 지문에서 찾아 보기와 대조하는 문제이다. 지문의 Therefore, a printed directory will not be available anymore. Instead, it will be offered online.에서 명부는 더 이상 서면으로 제공되지 않고, 온라인으로만 이용 가능함을 언급하고 있다. 따라서 정답은 (C)이다.

보기의 모든 내용이 본문에서 확인되기 때문에 모두 맞는 것처럼 생각하게 된다. 토익의 오답들이 본문 중에 있는 내용을 가지고 만들어지기 때문에 난이도가 높은 문제에 속한다. 비즈니스 문서를 다루는 데 있어 정확한 정보 분석 능력이 중요하기 때문에 자세한 내용까지 꼼꼼하게 확인하는 습관이 요구된다.

생각의 순서 MAPPING

Attention Business owner

❸ (A) business는 있지만 한 곳 이상의 지역을 커버한다는 내용은 없다.

The directory of businesses in Canberra City has increased so rapidly that publishing them in the local newsletter takes up too much space. Therefore, a printed directory will not be available anymore. Instead, it will be offered online.

❶ skimming

❹ (C) Only an online version is scheduled to be available.

The directory has not been posted yet, but it will be listed at www.canberracitygo.com soon. We recommend you go over your listing and check if it is accurate once it is available. If you notice that any information is wrong or any link is not connected properly, please inform us so that we can correct the errors.

Thanks,

Lothian Payne
Canberra City Council
334-2241

❺ (D) list는 있지만 줄인다는 것은 아니다.

12. What is suggested about the business directory?

❷ 문제 분석 + 보기 키워드 정리

(A) Businesses in more than ~~one area will be covered~~.
(B) The ~~distribution date~~ is going to be changed.
(C) Only an online version is scheduled to be available.
(D) The listing in it will be ~~shortened~~.

1-12 추후 연락처/연락 방법/지원 방법 등은 지문의 하단부에 답이 있다.

① 연락할 방법, 연락해야 하는 이유 등은 답이 지문의 하단부에 있다.
② 본문 중에서 If(~한다면), Pleases ~, You should ~ 등의 표현을 찾는다.
(*구인 광고의 지원 방법, 주소, 이메일, 전화번호 등은 지문의 하단부에 답이 있다.)

시험에 이렇게 나온다

Questions 12-13 refer to the following notice.

Attention Business owners in Canberra City

The directory of businesses in Canberra City has increased so rapidly that publishing them in the local newsletter takes up too much space. Therefore, a printed directory will not be available anymore. Instead, it will be offered online.

The directory has not been posted yet, but it will be listed at www.canberracitygo.com soon. We recommend you go over your listing and check if it is accurate once it is available. If you notice that any information is wrong or any link is not connected properly, please inform us so that we can correct the errors.

Thanks,

Lothian Payne
Canberra City Council
334-2241

13. Why might someone contact Mr. Payne?
(A) To renew an access code
(B) To request a deadline extension
(C) To correct some information
(D) To contribute to a newsletter

13번 문제 풀이 순서

STEP 1 두 문제 중 마지막 문제이기 때문에 마지막 문단을 확인한다.

STEP 2 문제를 분석한다. [위치 / 키워드/ 유형별 풀이 전략]
지문 하단부 / Mr. Payne = I에 해당한다. / someone(= You) contact me에 해당하는 정보를 찾는다.

SETP 3 지문의 하단부에서
If you notice that any information is wrong or any link is not connected properly, please inform us so that we can correct the errors.에서 글쓴이는 정보가 잘못된 경우 수정하기 위해 자신에게 알려줄 것을 요청하고 있다. 지문의 하단부에서 글쓴이가 Lothian Payne인 것을 알 수 있으므로 정보를 수정하기 위해 연락한다는 내용의 (C)가 정답이다.

 본문의 내용은 항상 보다 포괄적인 의미로 paraphrasing된다.

생각의 순서 MAPPING

Attention Business owners in Canberra City

The directory of businesses in Canberra City has increased so rapidly that publishing them in the local newsletter takes up too much space. Therefore, a printed directory will not be available anymore. Instead, it will be offered online.

The directory has not been posted yet, but it will be listed at www.canberracitygo.com soon. We recommend you go over your listing and check if it is accurate once it is available. If you notice that any information is **wrong** or any link is not connected properly, **please inform** us so that we can **correct the errors**.

Thanks,

Lothian **Payne**
Canberra City Council
334-2241

❶ 연락/수단 관련 내용은 하단부에 나온다.

❷ contact = please inform
wrong → correct the errors (= information)

보내는 사람 I

13. Why might someone **contact** Mr. **Payne**?
(A) To ~~renew~~ an access code
(B) To request a ~~deadline~~ extension
(C) To correct some information
(D) To ~~contribute~~ to a newsletter

❶ 문제 분석
contact / 하단부

but, however, unfortunately 등 역접 뒤에 답이 있다.

① 역접 구조의 앞부분에는 상황 설명이 있고 결론이 뒤에 온다.
② but, however, unfortunately 등의 표현 뒤에는 중요한 답의 정보가 있다.

시험에 이렇게 나온다

Questions 14-15 refer to the following product review.

http://www.julius.com

| Main [Home] | Outdoors/Indoors | Clothing/Suits | Athletic Shoes |

Julius's Guide for Wise Purchasers

Searching for athletic shoes? There are many choices appealing to you. Some brands, like Air Pro Fit, have lasted from generation to generation. Others, like Wellious, are quite new and boast the most recent high-tech materials.
Below reviews are our best picks. Be advised that prices can very slightly depending on online stores.

Hector Smith £ £ £*
These shoes have always dominated in the premium market since their release. They are not only comfortable but also solid as made of the high quality materials including leather and rubber. They can last for many years and are the best bet for those who frequently work out. Their price is the only downside.

Miguel RS £ £
In order for these waterproof shoes to be capable of coping with tough outdoor workouts even in rough weather conditions, quality leather and synthetic materials are used. However, their soles do not seem to last longer than expected with heavy use.

Wellious £
Made of the lightest materials in the market which have been newly invented, these shoes are ideal in hot weather and great for running on any kind of terrain. They aren't the best choice for people searching for something waterproof and warm, but for those who are about to start out.

Air Pro Fit 21X £
The price will never fool consumers. These shoes are the best value for the money. Materials such as synthetic rubber, nylon, and leather are used to enable them to resist water from getting in. Not being very flexible is the only drawback, but they tend to remain in shape even though used multiple times.

* Price range:
£ = under £100 / £ £ = £100 to £150 / £ £ £ = £150 to £200

14. What is mentioned as a problem with Miguel RS shoes?
(A) They are not very flexible.
(B) They are not light enough.
(C) They are not as durable as they should be.
(D) They are more expensive than any other shoes.

14번 문제 풀이 순서

STEP 1 문제의 키워드와 보기의 키워드를 찾는다.

STEP 2 키워드인 RS Shoes가 있는 곳에서 문제(problem)가 되는 내용을 찾아 답을 확인한다.

생각의 순서 MAPPING

http://www.julius.com

| Main [Home] | Outdoors/Indoors | Clothing/Suits | Athletic Shoes |

Julius's Guide for Wise Purchasers

Searching for athletic shoes? There are many choices appealing to you. Some brands, like Air Pro Fit, have lasted from generation to generation. Others, like Wellious, are quite new and boast the most recent high-tech materials.
Below reviews are our best picks. Be advised that prices can very slightly depending on online stores.

Hector Smith £ £ £*
These shoes have always dominated in the premium market since their release. They are not only comfortable but also solid as made of the high quality materials including leather and rubber. They can last for many years and are the best bet for those who frequently work out. Their price is the only downside.

Miguel RS £ £   ❸ 키워드 Miguel RS
In order for these waterproof shoes to be capable of coping with tough outdoor workouts even in rough weather conditions, quality leather and synthetic materials are used. **However**, their soles do not seem to last longer than expected with heavy use.

❹ 포괄적인 답
not last longer → not durable
however 뒤에 답이 있다.

Wellious £
Made of the lightest materials in the market, these shoes are ideal in hot weather and gre...
They aren't the best choice for people searching for something waterproof and ... who are about to start out.

❺ 오답 제거 (D)
다른 모든 것들보다
비싸지 않다.

... fool consumers. These shoes are the best value for the money. Materials such as synthetic rubber, nylon, and leather are used to enable them to resist water from getting in. Not being very flexible is the only drawback, but they tend to remain in shape even though used multiple times.

* Price range:
  £ = under £100 / £ £ = £100 to £150 / £ £ £ = £150 to £200

---

14. What is mentioned as a problem with Miguel RS shoes? ❶ 문제 분석
(A) They are not very flexible.
(B) They are not light enough.   ❷ 보기의 키워드 정리
(C) They are not as durable as they should be.
(D) They are more expensive than any other shoes.

본문은 구체적이고 답은 항상 포괄적이다.

① 한 가지 키워드는 문서 중에 한 곳에만 있다. 따라서 지문 전체를 읽을 필요 없이 키워드 먼저 확보한다.
② 문제의 키워드가 본문에서는 paraphrasing되어 있기 때문에 유사한 의미의 단어를 검색하면 그 근처에 답이 있다.

시험에 이렇게 나온다

Questions 14-15 refer to the following product review.

http://www.julius.com

| Main [Home] | Outdoors/Indoors | Clothing/Suits | Athletic Shoes |

Julius's Guide for Wise Purchasers

Searching for athletic shoes? There are many choices appealing to you. Some brands, like Air Pro Fit, have lasted from generation to generation. Others, like Wellious, are quite new and boast the most recent high-tech materials.
Below reviews are our best picks. Be advised that prices can vary slightly depending on online stores.

Hector Smith £ £ £*
These shoes have always dominated in the premium market since their release. They are not only comfortable but also solid as made of the high quality materials including leather and rubber. They can last for many years and are the best bet for those who frequently work out. Their price is the only downside.

Miguel RS £ £
In order for these waterproof shoes to be capable of coping with tough outdoor workouts even in rough weather conditions, quality leather and synthetic materials are used. However, their soles do not seem to last longer than expected with heavy use.

Wellious £
Made of the lightest materials in the market which have been newly invented, these shoes are ideal in hot weather and great for running on any kind of terrain. They aren't the best choice for people searching for something waterproof and warm, but for those who are about to start out.

Air Pro Fit 21X £
The price will never fool consumers. These shoes are the best value for the money. Materials such as synthetic rubber, nylon, and leather are used to enable them to resist water from getting in. Not being very flexible is the only drawback, but they tend to remain in shape even though used multiple times.

* Price range:
£ = under £100 / £ £ = £100 to £150 / £ £ £ = £150 to £200

15. Which shoes are most likely best for exercise beginners?
(A) Hector Smith
(B) Miguel RS
(C) Wellious
(D) Air Pro Fit 21X

15번 문제 풀이 순서

STEP 1 문제의 키워드와 보기를 확인한다.
보기의 각 신발들에 해당하는 내용에서 누구에게 적합한(best) 것인지를 확인해야 한다.

STEP 2 문제의 키워드인 exercise beginners를 먼저 검색한다.

STEP 3 exercise beginners라는 단어가 검색되지 않을 때에는 유사 단어를 검색한다.
those who are about to start out을 한 단어로 표현하면 exercise beginners이다.
따라서 정답은 (C) Wellious이다.

---

http://www.julius.com

| Main [Home] | Outdoors/Indoors | Clothing/Suits | **Athletic Shoes** |

Julius's Guide for Wise Purchasers

Searching for athletic shoes? There are many choices appealing to you. Some brands, like Air Pro Fit, have lasted from generation to generation. Others, like Wellious, are quite new and boast the most recent high-tech materials.
Below reviews are our best picks. Be advised that prices can vary slightly depending on online stores.

❷ 신발 이름

Hector Smith £ £ £*
These shoes have always dominated in the premium market since their release. They are not only comfortable but also solid as made of the high quality materials including leather and rubber. They can last for many years and are the best bet for those who frequently work out. Their price is the only downside.

Miguel RS £ £
In order for these waterproof shoes to be capable of coping with tough outdoor workouts even in rough weather conditions, quality leather and synthetic materials are used. However, their soles do not seem to last longer than expected with heavy use.

Wellious £
Made of the lightest materials in the market which have been newly invented, these shoes are ideal in hot weather and great for running on any kind of terrain. They aren't the best choice for people searching for something waterproof and warm, but for **those who are about to start out**.

❸ exercise beginners

Air Pro Fit 21X £
The price will never fool consumers. These shoes are the best value for the money. Materials such as synthetic rubber, nylon, and leather are used to enable them to resist water from getting in. Not being very flexible is the only drawback, but they tend to remain in shape even though used multiple times.

* Price range:
£ = under £100 / £ £ = £100 to £150 / £ £ £ = £150 to £200

15. Which shoes are most likely best for exercise beginners?   ❶ 문제의 키워드
(A) Hector Smith
(B) Miguel RS
(C) Wellious
(D) Air Pro Fit 21X

1-15 Not Question은 소거법을 이용한다.

① Not Question의 키워드를 확인한다.
② 보기의 키워드를 정리한다.
③ 보기의 키워드를 본문에서 검색한다.
④ 본문에서 검색한 내용과 보기의 내용을 비교하여 오류를 찾는다.

시험에 이렇게 나온다

Questions 16-19 refer to the following article.

Books loved for good

March 18 – In West Randwick town, Jennie Walsh, who has been teaching European literature at Birchgrove City College for fifteen years, is perhaps better known as the owner of the region's oldest bookstore, The Lance Reading Place. The store is also famous for its unusual features such as its selection of rare books and only opens for business on Sundays. Obviously, orders placed by online or telephone from private collectors, museums, and universities are the bookstore's main source of revenue while walk in sales account only for a small part of Ms. Walsh's business.

On Saturday, Lance Reading Place is going to celebrate its fiftieth anniversary. "When my father, Horace, started this business many years ago on South Clovery Avenue, several blocks from here, he may never have expected that it would still be in business five decades later." Ms. Walsh said. Its original sign is still displayed over the entrance.

The exterior keeps the front porch atmosphere like a normal house with a swing, a rocking chair and benches. A corner of the store is full of books about chess, an everlasting passion of the Walsh family. On Friday afternoons, the store becomes a place for a casual social club. Apparently, the members are fascinated in literature, rare books, and chess.

Next month, Ms. Walsh will reach another milestone; she intends to retire as a professor. However, even though she is retiring, The Lance Reading Place is not going to extend its hours and still will be open only once a week. "My retirement from one job is not to allow more time for another." Ms. Walsh added. "Instead, I will be able to spend more time with my children and friends because I don't need to do any time consuming preparation for classes or tests.

16. What is the main purpose of the article?
(A) To bring in more people to a book club
(B) To announce the relocation of well-known business
(C) To celebrate the achievements of a local entrepreneur
(D) To report some benefits of selling rare items

17. What is NOT indicated about Ms. Walsh?
(A) She plans to end her career as a teacher.
(B) She enjoys talking about chess with others.
(C) She has resided in Birchgrove City over fifteen years.
(D) She has read many books written by European writers.

16번 문제 풀이 순서

STEP 1 목적은 대부분 상단부에 답이 있다.

STEP 2 보기에서 키워드들을 먼저 정리한다.
(A) book club
(B) relocation
(C) celebrate / achievements / entrepreneur
(D) benefits / rare items

STEP 3 지문의 상단부에서 언급한 내용을 포괄적으로 묘사한 것이 답이다.

기사는 West Randwick 시내에서 Lance Reading Place를 운영하는 사업가인 Walsh를 소개하고 있다. 그리고 두 번째 문단 첫 번째 줄인 On Saturday, Lance Reading Place is going to celebrate its fiftieth anniversary.에서 Lance Reading Place는 15주년을 기념할 것임을 언급하고 있다. 따라서 기사의 목적은 15년 간 Lance Reading Place를 이끌어 온 Jennie Walsh의 업적을 기념하기 위한 것임을 알 수 있으므로 정답은 (C)이다.

17번 문제 풀이 순서

STEP 1 Not Question은 소거법을 이용한다.

STEP 2 문제의 키워드인 Ms. Walsh와 보기의 키워드들을 먼저 정리한 후 오류를 하나씩 소거한다.

보기의 키워드는 모두 본문 중에 있다. 본문의 키워드 부분을 보기와 대조하여 맞는 내용과 오류 내용을 꼼꼼하게 대조한다. 포괄적인 내용일 경우 복수의 구체적인 정보를 함께 고려해야 한다.

생각의 순서 MAPPING

Books loved for good

March 18 – In West Randwick town, (C) Jennie Walsh, who has been **teaching European literature** at **Birchgrove** City **College for fifteen years,** is perhaps ... of the region's ... nce Reading ... mous for its unusual features such as its selection of in rare books and only opens for business on Sundays. — 중략 —

On Saturday, Lance Reading Place is going to celebrate its fiftieth anniversary. "When my father, Horace, started this business many years ago on South Clovery Avenue, several blocks from here, he may never have expected that it would still be in business five decades later." Ms. Walsh said. Its original sign is still displayed over the entrance.

The exterior keeps the front porch atmosphere like a normal house with a swing, a rocking chair and benches. A corner of the store is full of books about **chess**, an everlasting passion of the Walsh family. On Friday afternoons, the store becomes a place for a casual social club. Apparently, the members are fascinated in literature, rare books, and **chess** (B).

Next month, Ms. Walsh will reach another milestone; (A) she intends to retire as a professor. However, even though she is retiring, The Lance Reading Place is not going to extend its hours and still will be open only once a week.

(C) 강의를 한다는 것이지 거주를 하는 것이 아니므로 정답

(A) She plans to end her career as a teacher.
(B) She enjoys talking about chess with others.
(C) She has **resided** in **Birchgrove** City over **fifteen years**.
(D) She has read many books written by European writers.

1-16 동의어 찾기 문제는 진짜 동의어를 찾는 것이 아니다.

① 보기의 대부분은 실제 동의어들이다.
② 단순히 같은 뜻을 찾는 것이 아니라 본문의 문맥에 어울리는 단어로 교체하는 것이 핵심이다.
③ 사전적 의미의 동의어가 아니라 본문에서 해석되는 의미를 찾는다.

시험에 이렇게 나온다

Questions 16-19 refer to the following article.

Books loved for good

March 18 – In West Randwick town, Jennie Walsh, who has been teaching European literature at Birchgrove City College for fifteen years, is perhaps better known as the owner of the region's oldest bookstore, The Lance Reading Place. The store is also famous for its unusual features such as its selection of rare books and only opens for business on Sundays. Obviously, orders placed by online or telephone from private collectors, museums, and universities are the bookstore's main source of revenue while walk in sales account only for a small part of Ms. Walsh's business.

On Saturday, Lance Reading Place is going to celebrate its fiftieth anniversary. "When my father, Horace, started this business many years ago on South Clovery Avenue, several blocks from here, he may never have expected that it would still be in business five decades later." Ms. Walsh said. Its original sign is still displayed over the entrance.

The exterior keeps the front porch atmosphere like a normal house with a swing, a rocking chair and benches. A corner of the store is full of books about chess, an everlasting passion of the Walsh family. On Friday afternoons, the store becomes a place for a casual social club. Apparently, the members are fascinated in literature, rare books, and chess.

Next month, Ms. Walsh will reach another milestone; she intends to retire as a professor. However, even though she is retiring, The Lance Reading Place is not going to extend its hours and still will be open only once a week. "My retirement from one job is not to allow more time for another." Ms. Walsh added. "Instead, I will be able to spend more time with my children and friends because I don't need to do any time consuming preparation for classes or tests."

18. The word "keeps" in paragraph 3, line 1 is closest in meaning to
(A) prevents
(B) maintains
(C) protects
(D) connects with

18번 문제 풀이 순서

STEP 1   영어 단어들은 한 단어가 여러 뜻을 가지며 여러 개의 동의어를 갖는다. keep도 '가지다, 유지하다, 계속하다, 소유하다, 보관하다, 보호하다' 등의 뜻이 있다.

STEP 2   keep이 해당 위치에서 어떤 의미로 쓰였는지를 먼저 확인한다.
The exterior <u>keeps</u> the front porch atmosphere like a normal house with a swing, a rocking chair and benches.
건물의 외관은 현관의 분위기를 보통의 집처럼 보이게 '유지해 준다'라고 언급하고 있다. '유지하다'의 의미로 keep이 사용되었으므로 (B)가 정답이다.

만점 필살기

동의어 문제는 실제로 난이도가 상당히 높게 출제될 수 있다.

ex) The cafe is located at the <u>**right**</u> edge of the water.
(A) one side
(B) correct
(C) exact
(D) claim

STEP 1   실제 right은 보기의 의미를 모두 가지고 있다.
(A) 오른쪽   (B) 맞는, 올바른   (C) 정확한   (D) 주장

STEP 2   '카페가 바로 물가에 있다'에서 right은 '바로 이곳, 바로 여기' 등의 강조의 의미이다.
즉, right here나 right now와 같은 의미로 쓰인 것이다. 이때 right here = exactly here / right now = exactly now가 된다. 정답은 (C) exact이다. 만약 '오른쪽'에 있다고 한다면 on the right side of가 되어야 한다.

1-17 보기 문장 중에 한 단어 오류를 찾아라.

① 보기 중에 오답인 문장은 한 단어씩의 오류를 포함하고 있다.
② 객관적인 분석 과정을 통해 보기에서 오류를 찾는 능력을 묻는다.
③ 대략적인 내용으로 답을 찾는 것이 아니라 꼼꼼하게 정보를 처리하는 것이 중요하다.

시험에 이렇게 나온다

Questions 16-19 refer to the following article.

Books loved for good

March 18 – In West Randwick town, Jennie Walsh, who has been teaching European literature at Birchgrove City College for fifteen years, is perhaps better known as the owner of the region's oldest bookstore, The Lance Reading Place. The store is also famous for its unusual features such as its selection of rare books and only opens for business on Sundays. Obviously, orders placed by online or telephone from private collectors, museums, and universities are the bookstore's main source of revenue while walk in sales account only for a small part of Ms. Walsh's business.

On Saturday, Lance Reading Place is going to celebrate its fiftieth anniversary. "When my father, Horace, started this business many years ago on South Clovery Avenue, several blocks from here, he may never have expected that it would still be in business five decades later." Ms. Walsh said. Its original sign is still displayed over the entrance.

The exterior keeps the front porch atmosphere like a normal house with a swing, a rocking chair and benches. A corner of the store is full of books about chess, an everlasting passion of the Walsh family. On Friday afternoons, the store becomes a place for a casual social club. Apparently, the members are fascinated in literature, rare books, and chess.

Next month, Ms. Walsh will reach another milestone; she intends to retire as a professor. However, even though she is retiring, The Lance Reading Place is not going to extend its hours and still will be open only once a week. "My retirement from one job is not to allow more time for another." Ms. Walsh added. "Instead, I will be able to spend more time with my children and friends because I don't need to do any time consuming preparation for classes or tests."

19. What is mentioned about The Lance Reading Place?
(A) Its sales may have increased significantly.
(B) It opens every weekday.
(C) Its children's book section will be expanded.
(D) Its current business hours will be unchanged.

19번 문제 풀이 순서

STEP 1   마지막 문제는 마지막 단락에 주로 답이 있다.

STEP 2   사실인 것을 묻는 문제는 보기를 먼저 정리한다.
(A) sales / increased
(B) every weekday
(C) children's book / expanded
(D) current business hours / unchanged

STEP 3 먼저 본문에서 키워드들을 검색한다. 본문 중의 키워드와 보기를 비교하여 오류 부분을 찾아 오답을 소거한 후에 정답을 찾는다.

생각의 순서 MAPPING

Books loved for good

March 18 – In West Randwick town, Jennie Walsh, who has been teaching European literature at Birchgrove City College for fifteen years, is perhaps better known as the owner of the region's oldest bookstore, **The Lance Reading Place.** The store is also famous for its unusual features such as its selection of rare books and **only opens** for business on **Sundays**.

(B) 일요일에만 오픈을 하므로 주중에 문을 연다는 내용은 오답이다.

Obviously, orders placed by online or telephone from private collectors, museums, and universities are the bookstore's main source of revenue while walk in sales account only for a small part of Ms. Walsh's business.

(A) 수입은 언급되지만 증가는 언급되지 않았다.

On Saturday, Lance Reading Place is going to celebrate its fiftieth anniversary. "When my father started this business ma_____ on South Clovery Avenue, several blocks from here, he may never have expected that it would

토요일은 영업이 아니라 행사이다.

still be in business five decades later." Ms. Walsh said. Its original sign is still displayed over the entrance.

The exterior keeps the front porch atmosphere like a normal house with a swing, a rocking chair and benches. A corner of the store is full of books about chess, an everlasting passion of the Walsh family. On **Friday** afternoons, the store becomes a place for a casual social club. Appa_____ lite_____

(D) 금요일에는 영업이 아니라 모임이 있는 것이므로 영업시간의 변화는 없다.

Next month, Ms. Walsh will reach another milestone; she intends to retire as a professor. However, even though she is retiring, The Lance Reading Place is **not going to extend its hours** and still will be open only once a week. "My retirement from one job is not to allow more time for another." Ms. Walsh added. "Instead, I will be able to spend more time with my **children** and friends because I don't need to do any_____ for classes o_____

(C) children은 언급되지만 책에 대한 언급은 없다.

19. What is mentioned about **The Lance Reading Place?**
(A) Its sales may have ~~increased significantly~~.
(B) It opens ~~every weekday~~.
(C) Its children's book section will be ~~expanded~~.
(D) Its current business hours will be unchanged.

1-18 답은 순서대로 배치된다.

① 전체 본문의 내용을 한번에 모두 기억해서 답을 찾으려고 하면 오히려 더 혼란스럽다.
② 문제 중에 키워드나 역접의 단어를 본문에서 검색하면 그 근처에 답이 있다.

시험에 이렇게 나온다

Questions 20-23 refer to the following article.

Tuesday, May 11

Sylvester Cinema on Devin Road will be closed to the public at the beginning of next month, yet this beautiful structure won't be unavailable for very long. The structure has been sold to Shawn Theater Group (STG), owned by John Cooper.

According to STG Vice President Loretta Spencer, the group has a plan to renovate the structure before it starts its operation. She claimed that all of the equipment such as screens, sound systems, and seats in the cinema will be replaced. — [1] — "Still," Ms. Spencer added, "One of the Sylvester Cinema's old projectors will be kept so as to continue to show classic pieces in their original format to the public."

Formerly, the Sylvester Cinema focused on showing artistic, noncommercial, and international movies. — [2] —. The previous owner, Mr. J.Terry, who retired recently, wanted to make the Sylvester Cinema the best place for artistic movies. For over a decade, it seemed successful, but the number of customers has dropped significantly in the past few years and the owner made the decision to sell the cinema. — [3] —.

"It wasn't easy for me to make a such decision," said Mr. J.Terry, "I already miss not only the cinema, but also everyone working with me. However, it's great that STG will revitalize the old cinema."

Under its new management, the cinema is planning to continue to show artistic films occasionally, as well as mainstream ones in order to bring more people to the cinema.

The cinema is scheduled to reopen to the public on August 5. Besides, the annual film festival focusing on classical pieces will be continuously hosted by the cinema starting September 11 for two weeks. Nothing about the event will be changed except one thing. It will not be called Sylvester Film Festival, but the Shawn Theater Group Movie Festival. — [4] —.

20. What is indicated about the Sylvester Cinema?
(A) It will reopen next month.
(B) Its customers will miss Mr. J.Terry's performance.
(C) Its equipment will be replaced soon.
(D) It will show only artistic movies.

21. According to the article, what was hard for Mr. J.Terry?
(A) Locating the most suitable equipment
(B) Selecting artistic films for his cinema
(C) Determining to put the cinema on sale
(D) Finding a place for his retirement party

20번 문제 풀이 순서

STEP 1 첫 번째 문제의 답은 90% 이상 지문의 상단부에 있다.

STEP 2 indicate, 즉 사실인 것을 묻는 문제는 보기의 키워드들을 먼저 확인한다.
(A) reopen / next month
(B) customers / miss Mr. J.Terry's performance
(C) equipment / replaced
(D) only artistic movies

STEP 3 지문의 앞부분에서 보기에 있는 키워드는 replaced이다.
두 번째 단락에서 all of the equipment such as screens, sound systems, and seats in the cinema will be replaced. 극장 내의 화면, 음향 시스템, 좌석과 같은 모든 기구들이 교체될 것이라고 나와 있다. 따라서 (C)가 정답이다.

21번 문제 풀이 순서

STEP 1 두 번째 문제의 답은 90% 이상 지문의 중반부에 있다.

STEP 2 문제의 키워드는 hard이다. 답은 반드시 키워드를 중심으로 위아래 두 줄에 위치한다.

STEP 3 본문의 중반부에서 It wasn't easy for me to make a such decision을 찾는다.

STEP 4 not easy = hard 키워드의 위아래 두 줄에서 답을 검색한다.
본문의 but the number of customers has dropped significantly in the past few years and the owner made a decision to sell the cinema. "It wasn't easy for me to make a such decision," said Mr. J. Terry에서 이전 소유주인 J. Terry 씨가 극장을 팔기로 결정을 내리는 것이 쉽지 않았음을 언급하고 있다. 따라서 정답은 (C)이다.

생각의 순서 MAPPING

Tuesday, May 11

Sylvester Cinema on Devin Road will be closed to the public at the beginning of next month, yet this beautiful structure won't be unavailable for very long. The structure has been sold to Shawn Theater Group (STG), owned by John Cooper.

According to STG Vice President Loretta Spencer, the group has a plan to renovate the structure before it starts its operation. She claimed that **20.** all of the **equipment** such as screens, sound systems, and seats in the cinema will be **replaced**. — [1] — "Still," Ms. Spencer added, "One of the Sylvester Cinema's old projectors will be kept so as to continue to show classic pieces in their original format to the public."

Formerly, the Sylvester Cinema focused on showing artistic, noncommercial, and international movies. — [2] —. The previous owner, Mr. J.Terry, who retired recently, wanted to make the Sylvester Cinema the best place for artistic movies. For over a decade, it seemed successful, **but** the number of customers has dropped significantly in the past few years and the owner **made the decision to sell the cinema**.
— [3] —

21. "It **wasn't easy** for me to **make a such decision**," said **Mr. J.Terry**, "I already miss not only the cinema, but also everyone working with me. However, it's g... old cinema."

Under its new m... planning to cont... occasionally, as well as mainstream ones in order to bring more people to the cinema.

- not easy = hard
- such decision은 앞에서 언급한 극장을 팔겠다는 결정

The cinema is scheduled to reopen to the public on August 5. Besides, the annual film festival focusing on classical pieces will be continuously hosted by the cinema starting September 11 for two weeks. Nothing about the event will be changed except one thing. It will not be called Sylvester Film Festival, but the Shawn Theater Group Movie Festival. — [4] —.

1-19 사람 이름은 항상 중요한 keyword이다.

① 비즈니스 문서는 커뮤니케이션의 정확성이 중요하다. 특히 다수의 이름이 등장하거나 다수의 사람들이 주고받는 문서에서 혼란이 없도록 하기 위해 등장인물간의 관계나 각자의 주장들을 이해하는 능력이 중요하다.

② 문서상에 다수의 사람들이 등장하는 경우, 사람들의 직업이나 요구 사항들을 따로 정리하면서 문서를 읽어야 한다. 특히 I/You/제3자 등의 관계를 파악하면서 내용을 정리해야 한다.

시험에 이렇게 나온다

Questions 20-23 refer to the following article.

Tuesday, May 11

Sylvester Cinema on Devin Road will be closed to the public at the beginning of next month, yet this beautiful structure won't be unavailable for very long. The structure has been sold to Shawn Theater Group (STG), owned by John Cooper.

According to STG Vice President Loretta Spencer, the group has a plan to renovate the structure before it starts its operation. She claimed that all of the equipment such as screens, sound systems, and seats in the cinema will be replaced. — [1] —. "Still," Ms. Spencer added, "One of the Sylvester Cinema's old projectors will be kept so as to continue to show classic pieces in their original format to the public."

Formerly, the Sylvester Cinema focused on showing artistic, noncommercial, and international movies. — [2] —. The previous owner, Mr. J.Terry, who retired recently, wanted to make the Sylvester Cinema the best place for artistic movies. For over a decade, it seemed successful, but the number of customers has dropped significantly in the past few years and the owner made the decision to sell the cinema. — [3] —.

"It wasn't easy for me to make a such decision," said Mr. J.Terry, "I already miss not only the cinema, but also everyone working with me. However, it's great that STG will revitalize the old cinema."

Under its new management, the cinema is planning to continue to show artistic films occasionally, as well as mainstream ones in order to bring more people to the cinema.

The cinema is scheduled to reopen to the public on August 5. Besides, the annual film festival focusing on classical pieces will be continuously hosted by the cinema starting September 11 for two weeks. Nothing about the event will be changed except one thing. It will not be called Sylvester Film Festival, but the Shawn Theater Group Movie Festival. — [4] —.

22. Who is Ms. Spencer?
(A) A constructor
(B) A business owner
(C) An executive
(D) An engineer

22번 문제 풀이 순서

STEP 1 특정 사람의 직업이나 관련 정보를 묻는 경우에는 먼저 본문에 등장하는 인물들을 정리해 두어야 한다.

STEP 2 본문 중에 구체적인 정보를 포괄적으로 설명한 답을 찾아야 한다.

STEP 3 혼동을 줄 만한 단어들을 본문에서 찾아 확보한 후 사람들의 이름과 직업을 연결한다.

생각의 순서 MAPPING

Tuesday, May 11

Sylvester Cinema on Devin Road will be closed to the public at the beginning of next month, yet **this beautiful structure** won't be unavailable for very long. The structure has been sold to **Shawn Theater Group (STG), owned by John Cooper**.

> John Cooper의 직업이 (B) A business owner이다.

According to STG **Vice President Loretta Spencer**, the group has a plan to renovate the cinema before it starts **its operation**.

> 키워드 Ms. Spencer

Most of the equipment such as screens, sound systems, and seats in the cinema will be replaced. — [1] — "Still," Ms. Spencer added, "One of the Sylvester Cinema's old projectors will be kept so as to continue to show classic pieces in their original format to the public."

Formerly, the Sylvester Cinema focused on showing artistic, noncommercial, and international movies. — [2] —. **The previous owner, Mr. J.Terry**, who retired recently, wanted to make the Sylvester Cinema the best place.

> J.Terry의 직업이 (B) A business owner이다.

For over a decade, it seemed successful, but the number of customers has dropped significantly in the past few years and the owner made the decision to sell the cinema. — [3] —.

"It wasn't easy for me to make a such decision," said Mr. J.Terry, "I already miss not only the cinema, but also everyone working with me. However, it's great that STG will revitalize the old cinema."

Under its new management, the cinema is planning to continue to show artistic films occasionally, as well as mainstream ones in order to bring more people to the cinema.

The cinema is scheduled to reopen to the public on August 5. Besides, the annual film festival focusing on classical pieces will be continuously hosted by the cinema starting September 11 for two weeks. Nothing about the event will be changed except one thing. It will not be called Sylvester Film Festival, but the Shawn Theater Group Movie Festival. — [4] —.

22. Who is Ms. Spencer?

(A) A constructor
(B) A business owner
(C) An executive
(D) An engineer

> vice president의 포괄적인 직책명은 '이사, 경영진, 임원'이다.

1-20 '문맥' 추가 문제는 위치와 연결어가 관건이다.

① 본문 중에 하나의 '문장(sentence)'을 추가하는 문제이다.
② 주어진 문장은 해석상으로는 전체 본문 중에 어디에 들어가더라도 말이 된다.
③ 해석상 말이 되는 위치가 답은 아니다.
　따라서 문장이 들어가기 위해서는 해당 위치 위아래로 연결어가 확보되는 것이 관건이다.
④ 비즈니스 문서는 한 가지 정보를 한번에 같이 언급한다.
　따라서 문단별로 주제어를 확보하고 관련 주제에 맞는 위치에 문장을 추가한다.

시험에 이렇게 나온다

Questions 20-23 refer to the following article.

Tuesday, May 11

Sylvester Cinema on Devin Road will be closed to the public at the beginning of next month, yet this beautiful structure won't be unavailable for very long. The structure has been sold to Shawn Theater Group (STG), owned by John Cooper.

According to STG Vice President Loretta Spencer, the group has a plan to renovate the structure before it starts its operation. She claimed that all of the equipment such as screens, sound systems, and seats in the cinema will be replaced. — [1] —. "Still," Ms. Spencer added, "One of the Sylvester Cinema's old projectors will be kept so as to continue to show classic pieces in their original format to the public."

Formerly, the Sylvester Cinema focused on showing artistic, noncommercial, and international movies. — [2] —. The previous owner, Mr. J.Terry, who retired recently, wanted to make the Sylvester Cinema the best place for artistic movies. For over a decade, it seemed successful, but the number of customers has dropped significantly in the past few years and the owner made the decision to sell the cinema. — [3] —.

"It wasn't easy for me to make a such decision," said Mr. J.Terry, "I already miss not only the cinema, but also everyone working with me. However, it's great that STG will revitalize the old cinema."

Under its new management, the cinema is planning to continue to show artistic films occasionally, as well as mainstream ones in order to bring more people to the cinema.

The cinema is scheduled to reopen to the public on August 5. Besides, the annual film festival focusing on classical pieces will be continuously hosted by the cinema starting September 11 for two weeks. Nothing about the event will be changed except one thing. It will not be called Sylvester Film Festival, but the Shawn Theater Group Movie Festival. — [4] —.

23. In which of the positions marked [1], [2], [3], and [4] does the following sentence best belong to?

"The lobby on the ground floor is going to be removed."

(A) [1]
(B) [2]
(C) [3]
(D) [4]

23번 문제 풀이 순서

STEP 1 주어진 문장의 키워드를 확보한다.
The **lobby** on the ground floor is going to be **removed**.에서 키워드는 lobby / removed이다.
1층에 로비는 없어질 것이다.

STEP 2 빈칸 앞뒤에 문맥을 파악하고 The lobby 또는 removed가 언급되거나 유사한 정보들이 있는 문단을 찾는다.

---

all of the equipment such as screens, sound systems, and seats in the cinema will be replaced. — [1] —.

장비가 교체되거나 유지되는 것을 언급하고 있다.

Cinema focused on showing artistic, noncommercial, and international movies. — [2] —.

상영하는 영화의 종류에 대해 설명하고 있다.

----

the number of customers has dropped significantly in the past few years and the owner made a decision to sell the cinema. — [3] —.

판매량 저하와 매각에 대한 언급을 한다.

It will not be called Sylvester Film Festival, but the Shawn Theater Group Movie Festival. — [4] —.

행사의 이름에 대한 설명을 하고 있다.

STEP 3 '장비/교체'에 대한 정보를 언급하고 있는 [1]번 위치에 추가되어야 한다.

1-21 동의어는 문맥상 대체할 수 있는 단어를 찾는 것이다.

① 영어 단어는 하나의 의미만이 아니라 대부분 여러 가지 의미와 품사를 갖는다.
② 보기에서 일차원적으로 같은 의미의 단어를 찾는 것이 아니라 그 단어의 다양한 의미 중에서 본문의 상황에 맞는 의미를 선택해야 한다.

시험에 이렇게 나온다

Questions 24-26 refer to the following article.

The Stuart Park to be Refurbished
By Forrest Paul

Camden (August 21) - A resolution to refurbish the ten-year-old Stuart Park has been unanimously approved by Camden Town Council. This initiative has been considered since originally proposed four years ago. However, it was not approved until Rick Shalib was officially appointed as mayor. "I promised the town that my first priority in office would be to put the project into action, and I intend to keep my word." he said in an interview. — [1] —.

When the park was completed, its four kilometer trail-lined with trees along a stream seemed to serve as a place for Camden residents' walk. But it did not last long because people found that the place is not the best choice for their kids. — [2] —.

"We often come to the path to take a walk, but our children would feel like playing with a ball," said one of the town residents, Alvin Rice. "There is not enough space for our kids to run and play freely. And since it doesn't have enough tables or benches, the park is not appropriate for a picnic lunch." — [3] —.

A series of tasks will be required to make a spacious green spot available for various outdoor activities. Picnic tables, benches, and a playground with an outdoor football field and a basketball court would be great additions. — [4] —. These were requested by one of the town's sport groups for those wishing to exercise at any time of the day. The overall refurbishment process will be done during the winter season, and the park will be set for the public in the coming spring.

24. What is suggested about the park's refurbishment?
(A) It is scheduled to start the coming spring.
(B) None of the council members disagreed to it.
(C) It needs more than a year to be done.
(D) Mayor Shalib proposed it a long time ago.

25. The word "initiative" in paragraph 1, line 4, is closest in meaning to
(A) start
(B) advantage
(C) action
(D) plan

24번 문제 풀이 순서

STEP 1 첫 번째 문제의 답은 90% 이상 지문의 상단부에 답이 있다.

STEP 2 'suggest' 사실인 것을 묻는 문제는 보기의 키워드들을 먼저 확인한다.
   (A) start / coming spring
   (B) None / members / disagreed
   (C) a year / done
   (D) Mayor / proposed

STEP 3 본문의 상단부에서 보기의 키워드들을 검색한다.

The Stuart Park to be Refurbished
By Forrest Paul

Camden (August 21) - A resolution to refurbish the ten-year-old Stuart Park has been unanimously approved by Camden Town Council. This initiative has been considered since originally proposed four years ago. However, it was not approved until Rick Shalib was officially appointed as mayor. "I promised the town that my first priority in office would be to put the project into action, and I inted to keep my word." he said in an interview. — [1] —.

(A) start / coming spring (언급 없음)
(B) None / members / disagreed
(C) a year / done
(D) Mayor / proposed (4년 전에 proposed 되었던 것은 맞지만 Shalib 시장이 제안한 것이 아님)

답 근거 단어
unanimously : 만장일치로
council의 모든 member들이 동의했다는 의미이다. 즉, 아무도 반대한 사람이 없다는 것이 답이 된다.

최신 함정 유형

보기에 한 단어씩은 모두 본문 중에 언급되기 때문에 세심하게 봐야 한다. 보기에서 일부는 맞는 내용이지만 한 두 단어의 오류를 추가하여 오답을 제시하기 때문에 보기를 꼼꼼히 살펴 오류 요소를 제거한 후에 정답을 선택해야 한다.

25번 문제 풀이 순서

STEP 1 initiative는 여러 가지 의미가 있다.
   ① 결단력
   ② 목표를 이루기 위한 계획(plan)
   ③ 주도(권) (control) ex. take the initiative 주도권을 가지다

STEP 2 단순히 initiative와 같은 의미를 찾는 것이 아니라 해당 문장에서 그 의미를 바꿔 쓸 수 있는 대체어를 찾는다.
   This initiative has been considered since originally proposed four years ago.
   이 initiative는 원래 4년 전에 제안된 이래로 고려되었다.

STEP 3 '계획'이라는 의미로 (D) plan이 정답이다.
   this initiative가 가리키는 것은 앞서 Town Council에서 만장일치로 승인이 된 해결 방안, 대책을 의미하는 A resolution (to refurbish the ten-year-old Stuart Park)을 의미한다.

1-22 '문맥' 추가 문제는 지시형용사, 지시대명사, 부사들이 답을 연결한다.

문맥 문제의 답을 결정하는 요인은 주로 다음의 세 가지이다.

① 지시형용사/지시대명사: 빈칸 위아래에서 해당 지시형용사나 대명사가 지칭하는 것을 찾아서 연결해야 한다.
② 연결어를 확보한다: 접속사/전치사/부사/접속부사들은 앞뒤 문맥의 연결 관계 즉, 추가, 역접, 대조, 인과, 순접 등의 관련성을 설명한다.
③ 주어진 지문에서의 키워드가 언급되어 있는 문단에 추가해야 한다. 한 가지 정보는 한 번만 언급되기 때문에 주어진 본문 중에 한 곳에서만 제시된다.

시험에 이렇게 나온다

Questions 24-26 refer to the following article.

The Stuart Park to be Refurbished
By Forrest Paul

Camden (August 21) - A resolution to refurbish the ten-year-old Stuart Park has been unanimously approved by Camden Town Council. This initiative has been considered since originally proposed four years ago. However, it was not approved until Rick Shalib was officially appointed as mayor. "I promised the town that my first priority in office would be to put the project into action, and I intend to keep my word," he said in an interview. — [1] —.

When the park was completed, its four kilometer trail-lined with trees along a stream seemed to serve as a place for Camden residents' walk. But it did not last long because people found that the place is not the best choice for their kids. — [2] —.

"We often come to the path to take a walk, but our children would feel like playing with a ball," said one of the town residents, Alvin Rice. "There is not enough space for our kids to run and play freely. And since it doesn't have enough tables or benches, the park is not appropriate for a picnic lunch." — [3] —.

A series of tasks will be required to make a spacious green spot available for various outdoor activities. Picnic tables, benches, and a playground with an outdoor football field and a basketball court would be great additions. — [4] —. These were requested by one of the town's sport groups for those wishing to exercise at any time of the day. The overall refurbishment process will be done during the winter season, and the park will be set for the public in the coming spring.

26. In which of the positions marked [1], [2], [3], and [4] does the following sentence best belong?

"And lampposts are planned to be installed along the park's path for evening visitors."

(A) [1]
(B) [2]
(C) [3]
(D) [4]

26번 문제 풀이 순서

STEP 1 주어진 문장의 키워드를 확보한다.

And lampposts are planned to be installed along the park's path for the evening visitors.
그리고 저녁에 이용하는 사람들을 위해 가로등은 산책로를 따라서 설치될 예정이다.

The Stuart Park to be Refurbished
By Forrest Paul

"I promised the town that my first priority in office would be to put the project into action, and I intend to keep my word." he said in an interview. — [1] —.

"이 계획을 실행에 옮기는 것을 가장 우선시할 것이라고 약속드립니다. 그리고 제가 한 약속을 지키기 위해서 노력할 것입니다."라고 인터뷰에서 말했습니다.

But it did not last long because people found that the place is not the best choice for their kids. — [2] —.

그러나 사람들이 이 장소가 아이들을 위한 최고의 선택이 아니라는 것을 알아차렸기 때문에 오랫동안 지속되지 않았습니다. — [2] —.

"~ And since it doesn't have enough tables or benches, the park is not appropriate for a picnic lunch." — [3] —.

그리고 충분한 의자와 테이블이 없기 때문에 공원은 소풍을 계획하는 데에 적합하지 않습니다." — [3] —.

A series of tasks will be required to make a spacious green spot available for various outdoor activities. Picnic tables, benches, and a playground with an outdoor football field and a basketball court would be great additions. — [4] —. These were requested by one of the town's sport groups for those wishing to exercise at any time of the day.

다양한 야외 활동을 할 수 있는 드넓은 공간이 확보되기 위해서는 일련의 작업이 필요합니다. 피크닉 테이블, 의자, 그리고 축구 경기장과 농구 코트를 갖춘 운동장은 좋은 추가 사항이 될 것입니다. — [4] —. 이것들은 언제나 운동을 하고 싶어 하는 사람들을 위해 마을의 스포츠 단체 중 한 곳이 요청했습니다.

STEP 2 빈칸의 문맥을 파악하여 [가로등 / 설치]에 관련된 내용을 찾는다. And라는 연결어가 있다는 것은 앞 문장에도 어떤 것들을 설치한다는 의미가 있어야 한다는 것이다.

[4]번 위치의 Picnic tables, benches, and playground with an outdoor football field and a basketball court would be great additions.
피크닉 테이블, 의자, 그리고 축구 경기장과 농구 코트를 갖춘 운동장은 좋은 추가 사항이 될 것입니다.
운동장이 설치될 계획이라는 것을 알 수 있다.

STEP 3 빈칸 앞뒤 혹은 연결어들을 파악한다.

[4]번 뒤에 언급된 These는 운동장과 가로등의 설치를 지칭한다.
문장의 마지막에 those wishing to exercise at any time of the day는 evening visitors를 포함한다.
따라서 답은 [4]번에 오게 된다.

문맥 추가 문제는 위아래 문맥을 연결해 주는 논리의 근거를 확보해야 한다.

① 주어진 본문의 키워드와 연결어(접속사, 전치사, 부사, 접속부사)들을 확보한다.
② 빈칸의 앞뒤에서 확인한 문맥의 연결 관계가 논리적으로 설명되는 문단이 답이 된다.

시험에 이렇게 나온다

Questions 27-29 refer to the following article.

Briefing on High Street Business

Keith's Bookstore has closed a deal to acquire the retail premises by its current space at 223 Bond Street in Victoria East. The well-known high street fixture will utilize the new premises for its needed expansion. — [1] —. "Since our store opened four years ago, our business has always been hitting the ground running." says Todd Sanders, cofounder and owner. "People said to us that small businesses like our bookstore are not as successful as they once were anymore." — [2] —. Sanders added, "The renovated Keith's Bookstore will be more spacious than the original one."

"The reopening ceremony will be held on June 25." said Sanders. — [3] —. "The extra space makes our customers as well as us very excited. — [4] —. It will allow us to hold more interesting events such as publication parties, book signings, and meetings with authors."

27. What is the article mainly about?
(A) A book signing event
(B) The launch of a publication
(C) Some changes to a local business
(D) A brief profile of a famous author

28. Who most likely is Mr. Sanders?
(A) A building inspector
(B) A famous writer
(C) An entrepreneur
(D) A news reporter

29. In which of the positions marked [1], [2], [3], and [4] does the following sentence best belong?
"We have proved that the opposite case exists."
(A) [1]
(B) [2]
(C) [3]
(D) [4]

27번 문제 풀이 순서

STEP 1 Why/discuss/about 등의 주제를 묻는 질문은 대부분 처음 3줄에 답이 있다.

Keith Bookstore has closed a deal to <u>acquire</u> the retail premises by its current space at 223 Bond Street in Victoria East.

STEP 2 본문의 내용은 구체적이지만 답은 포괄적으로 제시된다.
(A) A book ~~signing~~ event
(B) The launch of a ~~publication~~
(C) Some changes to a local business
(D) A brief profile of a ~~famous author~~

28번 문제 풀이 순서

STEP 1 문제 중에 사람 이름이 등장하면, I/You/고객/직원/제3자/글쓴이/인터뷰한 사람 등의 등장인물들을 정리한다. 특히 대명사를 주의한다.

28. Who most likely is Mr. Sanders?
(A) A building inspector
(B) A famous writer
(C) A entrepreneur
(D) A news reporter

> 지문에 등장하는 이름이 하나일 때는 그 사람의 직업에 관련된 표현들을 모아야 한다.

Briefing on High Street Business

Keith's Bookstore has closed a deal to acquire the retail premises by its current space at 223 Bond Street in Victoria East. The well-known high street fixture will utilize the new premises for its needed expansion. — [1] —. "Since our ago, our business the ground running." says Todd Sanders, cofounder and owner. "People said to us that small businesses like our bookstore is not as successful as it once was anymore." — [2] —. Sanders added, "The renovated Keith's Bookstore will be more spacious than the original one."

"The reopening ceremony will be held on June 25." said Sanders. — [3] —. "The extra space makes our customers as well as us very excited. — [4] —. It will allow us to hold more interesting events such as publication parties, book signings, and meetings with authors."

> 키워드 Mr. Sanders

29번 문제 풀이 순서

STEP 1 주어진 문장의 키워드를 확보한다.
We have **proved** that the **opposite case** exists.
우리는 반대 사례가 존재한다는 것을 증명했습니다.

STEP 2 빈칸의 앞뒤에서 반대의 내용이나 부정적인 내용이 연결되는 곳을 찾는다.

- 이 새 공간을 이용할 예정입니다. – [1] – 저희 서점이 4년 전에 개장된 이래로, 저희 사업은 항상 성공적 [긍정 + 긍정]
- 사람들은 저희 서점과 같은 작업 업체들은 예전처럼 더 이상 성공적이지 않다고 말했습니다." – [2] –. Sanders 는 덧붙였다, "보수된 Keith 서점은 원래보다 더 공간이 넓어질 것입니다." [부정 + 긍정] ▶정답
- "재개장 축하 행사는 6월 25일에 열릴 것입니다." – [3] –. 추가 공간은 저희 고객들을 매우 기쁘게 만들어 줄 것 입니다. [긍정 + 긍정]
- 저희 고객들을 매우 기쁘게 만들어 줄 것입니다 – [4] –. 이 공간은 저희가 출판 기념회, 책 사인회, 그리고 작가 와의 만남과 같은 흥미진진한 행사들을 개최하도록 해 줄 것입니다. [긍정 + 긍정]

STEP 3 성공하지 못할 것이라는 말에 대한 반대 사례(opposite case)를 보여 주었고 Keith's Bookstore는 더 넓어질 것이라는 내용이 되어야 하므로 [2]번 위치에 와야 한다.

1-24 온라인 채팅 '의도' 문제는 위아래 연결어가 있거나 전체적인 상황을 포괄적으로 묘사하는 것이 답이다.

① 주어진 문장과 단순히 같은 의미의 답을 찾는 것이 아니다.
② 보기 중에 주어진 표현과 같은 의미는 오히려 오답이다.
③ 해당 위치의 위아래 문맥을 파악하고 포괄적으로 답을 찾는 것이 관건이다.
④ 온라인 채팅의 대화에서는 등장인물들의 관계와 입장을 먼저 정리해야 한다.
ex) A: Did you finish writing the report? B: I had to attend a meeting.
    여기서 B와 같이 쓴 의미에 대한 정답은 give an excuse가 된다.

시험에 이렇게 나온다

Questions 30-31 refer to the following text message chain.

Lettie Arron [12:14 A.M.]
Mr. Wolfe, I sent you the updated contract by e-mail.
Did you get it?

Neal Wolfe [12:16 A.M.]
Yeah, I'm just looking at it now. Thank you for making those revisions.

Lettie Arron [12:17 A.M.]
No problem. Thanks for notifying me of the issue.
The contract now clearly indicates that $150 will be paid for an accepted article instead of $100.

Neal Wolfe [12:18 A.M.]
Excellent. I'm going to go over the details once again and sign it to mail it to you as soon as possible.

Lettie Arron [12:20 A.M.]
Thanks and please let me know if you need anything else. As you know we have a range of rental spaces and properties.

30. At 12:17 A.M., what does Ms. Arron mean when she writes, "No problem"?
(A) She has willingly fulfilled a request.
(B) She is still considering signing a contract.
(C) She is clear about the contract details.
(D) She was aware that an e-mail had already been sent.

30번 문제 풀이 순서

STEP 1 첫 번째 문제는 주로 지문의 상단부에 답이 있다.

STEP 2 문제를 분석하여 힌트의 위치와 문제 유형을 확인한다.

30. At 12:17 A.M. what does Ms. Arron mean when she writes, **"No problem"**?

| Lettie Arron | [12:17 A.M.] |

<u>No problem.</u> Thanks for notifying me of the issue.
The contract now clearly indicates that $150 will be paid for an accepted article instead of $100.

STEP 3 사람 이름을 정리하여 등장인물들의 관계를 정리한다.
Lettie Arron: 이메일을 보낸 사람, 교정을 한 사람
Neal Wolfe: 이메일을 받은 사람

> No problem이라는 표현은 주로
> 1. 상대의 제안/요청을 수락
> 2. 감사하다는 말에 대한 답변
> 3. 미안하다는 말에 대한 답변으로 사용한다. 하지만 시험에서는 실제 내용에서 어떤 의미를 갖는지를 묻는다.

STEP 4 보기의 키워드들을 정리한다.
(A) willingly fulfilled a request
(B) signing a contract
(C) clear / contract details
(D) aware / e-mail / sent

STEP 5 주어진 문장을 기준으로 위아래 본문의 내용을 파악한다.

생각의 순서 MAPPING

Lettie Arron   [12:14 A.M.]
Mr. Wolfe, <u>I sent you the updated contract by e-mail</u>.
Did you get it?

Neal Wolfe   [12:16 A.M.]
Yeah, I'm just looking at it now. <u>Thank you for making those revisions</u>.

Lettie Arron   [12:17 A.M.]
<u>No problem. Thanks for notifying me of the issue.</u>
The contract now clearly indicates that $150 will be paid for an accepted article instead of $100.

Neal Wolfe   [12:18 A.M.]
Excellent. I'm going to go over the details once again and sign it to mail it to you as soon as possible.

Lettie Arron   [12:20 A.M.]
Thanks and please let me know if you need anything else. As you know we have a range of rental spaces and properties.

❶ Lettie Arron: 이메일을 보낸 사람

❷ Neal Wolfe: 이메일을 받은 사람, You(Arron)에게 변경을 해 줘서 고맙다고 인사를 함

❸ Arron이 상대에게 알려줘서 고맙다고 답을 함

Arron이 계약서를 수정(revision)해 준 것에 대해 감사하다는 Wolfe의 말에, Arron이 No problem이라고 말했는데, 이는 Wolfe의 부탁을 Arron이 기꺼이 들어 줬고 그래서 자신도 명확해졌다는 의미이므로 정답은 (A)가 된다. (B) signing a contract나 (C)의 clear about the contract details, (D) e-mail had already been sent 등은 대화의 하단부에 모두 언급되지만 No problem과는 상관없는 내용이다. 이렇게 보기에 있는 내용이라 하더라도 해당 위치에 맞지 않는 정보는 오답이다.

1-25 online chat은 등장인물들의 관계도를 먼저 이해한다.

① 먼저 대화에 나오는 모든 등장인물들의 관계를 정리한다.
② I/You/제3자 각각의 직업을 확인한다.
③ 보기의 오답들이 본문 중에 언급되는 내용이기 때문에 혼동을 피하기 위해서는 미리 담당, 업무 진행 순서, 주체와 객체를 확인한다.

시험에 이렇게 나온다

Questions 30-31 refer to the following text message chain.

Lettie Arron   [12:14 A.M.]
Mr. Wolfe, I sent you the updated contract by e-mail. Did you get it?

Neal Wolfe   [12:16 A.M.]
Yeah, I'm just looking at it now. Thank you for making those revisions.

Lettie Arron   [12:17 A.M.]
No problem. Thanks for notifying me of the issue.
The contract now clearly indicates that $150 will be paid for an accepted article instead of $100.

Neal Wolfe   [12:18 A.M.]
Excellent. I'm going to go over the details once again and sign it to mail it to you as soon as possible.

Lettie Arron   [12:20 A.M.]
Thanks and please let me know if you need anything else. As you know we have a range of rental spaces and properties.

31. Where most likely does Ms. Arron work?
(A) A consulting firm
(B) A legal firm
(C) A bank
(D) A real estate agency

31번 문제 풀이 순서

STEP 1   등장인물은 모두 2명이다.
           Lettie Arron: 계약서를 보낸 사람
           Neal Wolfe: 계약서를 받은 사람

STEP 2   대화의 주제 파악과 업무의 진행 상황을 정리한다.
           Lettie Arron 계약서 수정
           → Neal Wolfe 계약서 검토 후 사인할 예정
           → Lettie Arron 감사 인사 + 임대 정보

STEP 3   마지막 문제의 답은 하단부에 위치한다.

생각의 순서 MAPPING

Lettie Arron   [12:14 A.M.]
Mr. Wolfe, I sent you the <u>updated contract by e-mail</u>. Did you get it?

Neal Wolfe   [12:16 A.M.]
Yeah, I'm just looking at it now. <u>Thank you for making those revisions</u>.

Lettie Arron   [12:17 A.M.]
<u>No problem. Thanks for notifying me of the issue.</u> The contract now clearly indicates that $150 will be paid for an accepted article instead of $100.

Neal Wolfe   [12:18 A.M.]
Excellent. I'm going to go over the details once again and sign it to mail it to you as soon as possible.

Lettie Arron   [12:20 A.M.]
Thanks and please let me know if you need anything else. As you know <u>we have a range of rental spaces and properties</u>.

❶ **Lettie Arron**: 이메일을 보낸 사람

❷ **Neal Wolfe**: 이메일을 받은 사람, You(Arron)가 변경을 해 줘서 고맙다고 인사를 함

❸ **Arron**이 상대에게 알려줘서 고맙다고 답을 함

❹ **Arron**이 더 많은 임대 장소와 건물들이 있다고 언급함

STEP 4   등장인물들의 직업을 정리한다.
Arron의 대사 중 I/We 등의 표현에서 많은 임대 장소와 건물을 가지고 있다는 말을 통해 (D) A real estate agency(부동산)에서 일하고 있음을 알 수 있다.

만점 필살기

John, we need your help. We should set tables for the banquet this evening. But I am currently preparing for a wedding in the garden. All the tables in the conference room should be decorated with ribbons which are in the basement. I have a key, so please take it and set up them.

Where will John go next?
(A) The garden
(B) The conference room
(C) The basement
(D) A banquet

▶ next는 대화가 끝나고 바로 다음 행동을 찾아야 한다. 대화에서 마지막에 열쇠를 받아가라고 하기 때문에 열쇠를 받기 위해 I가 있는 곳으로 먼저 와야 한다. 즉, garden에 와서 열쇠를 받아서 basement에 가서 리본을 챙겨서 conference room에 가서 의자들을 세팅해야 한다. 답은 (A) The garden이다.

John, we need your help. We should set tables for the <u>banquet</u> this evening. But I am currently preparing for a wedding <u>in the garden</u>. All the tables in the <u>conference room</u> should be decorated with ribbons which are <u>in the basement</u>. I have a key, so please take it and set up them.

1-26 online chat은 등장인물들의 담당 업무와 진행되는 일의 상황을 파악해야 한다.

① 대화 중에 누가 누구에게 어떤 업무를 지시했는가에 대한 사실 관계를 이해해야 한다.
② 현재 진행 상황과 문제점, 다음에 할 일 등에 대한 정보를 정리해야 한다.

시험에 이렇게 나온다

Questions 32-33 refer to the following text message chain.

Julia Ross [10:36 A.M.]
Is it okay to begin the presentation before you arrive? The client is already here.

Jesus Ruiz [10:38 A.M.]
Yes, please go ahead. I think I won't be able to make it in time.

Julia Ross [10:40 A.M.]
All right then, I'll start with the overview and move onto the discussion on the new features of our product. You should arrive here no later than 11:00, right?

Jesus Ruiz [10:41 A.M.]
Sure, and you will do a great job.

Julia Ross [10:42 A.M.]
Yeah, but I think you had better present the expense savings. It isn't really my field.

Jesus Ruiz [10:44 A.M.]
No problem. I'll be there as soon as I can.

32. At 10:38 A.M., what most likely does Mr. Ruiz mean when he writes, "Yes, please go ahead"?
(A) He wants some figures to be forwarded to him.
(B) He wants Ms. Ross to stick to schedule.
(C) He thinks a short break should be added.
(D) He is unhappy with a scheduling conflict.

33. According to Ms. Ross, what is Mr. Ruiz most familiar with?
(A) Sales
(B) Design
(C) Finance
(D) Shipping

32번 문제 풀이 순서

STEP 1 "Yes, please go ahead"
의도 문제는 주어진 표현과 같은 뜻을 찾는 것이 아니라 본문에서 위아래 문맥을 포괄적으로 설명하는 것이 답이 된다. 따라서 위아래 문맥을 보면,

당신이 도착하기 전에 발표를 시작해도 괜찮을까요? 고객이 이미 도착했습니다.
네, 시작해 주세요. 저는 제시간에 도착하지 못할 것 같아요.

Julia Ross [10:36 A.M.]
Is it okay to begin the presentation before you arrive? The client is already here.

Jesus Ruiz [10:38 A.M.]
Yes, please go ahead. I think I won't be able to make it in time.

STEP 2   답은 포괄적으로 paraphrasing되기 때문에 오류를 먼저 제거하고 답을 선택한다.
(A) He wants some ~~figures to be forwarded~~ to him. [수치 전송]
(B) He wants Ms. Ross to stick to schedule.
  [자신은 참석을 못하니 일정대로 진행하라는 의미로 정답]
(C) He thinks ~~a short break~~ should be added. [쉬는 시간]
(D) He is ~~unhappy~~ with a scheduling conflict. [불만]

33번 문제 풀이 순서

STEP 1   문제의 키워드를 잡고 유형을 파악한다.
  Ms. Ross의 말에서 답을 찾을 수 있으며 Mr. Ruiz가 무엇에 정통한지 분야나 직업을 묻는 문제이다.

STEP 2   온라인 대화에서 화자들의 직업은 가장 중요한 정보이다. 등장하는 사람들의 이름과 대명사를 이용해 직업을 정리해 두는 연습을 해야 한다.

STEP 3   등장인물은 모두 2명이다.
  Julia Ross : 제품의 특징 설명 → sales나 제품 개발 관련 분야
  Jesus Ruiz : 비용 절감에 대한 설명 → 회계나 재무 관련 분야

Julia Ross [10:40 A.M.]
All right then, I'll start with the overview and move onto the discussion on the new features of our product. You should arrive here no later than 11:00, right?

Jesus Ruiz [10:41 A.M.]
Sure, and you will do a great job.

> Ms. Ross가 Ruiz를 you라고 지칭했기 때문에 Mr. Ruiz가 하는 일이 비용 절감과 관련된 일이라는 것을 알 수 있다. 정답은 (C) Finance이다.

Julia Ross [10:42 A.M.]
Yeah, but I think you had better present the expense savings. It isn't really my field.

1-27 3인 이상이 등장하는 online chat

① 등장인물이 3인 이상이 되면 대화를 이끌어가는 한 명과 나머지 인물들의 입장과 요구 사항들을 정리해 두어야 한다. 대화를 이끌어가는 한 명과 나머지 인물들간의 대화에 집중해야 한다.
② 누가 누구에게 말을 하고 어떻게 대화가 이어지는지 진행 사항에 대해 묻기 때문에 대화상의 요구와 부탁 관계를 이해해야 한다.

시험에 이렇게 나온다

Questions 34-37 refer to the following online chat discussion.

Deanna Schultz [2:32 P.M.] In order to prepare for next week's branch managers' meeting, I have to arrange transportation from the airport. So, everyone needs to provide me your flight information. It is the first time we hold a meeting like this, and everything should be organized properly.

Lynn Santos [2:33 P.M.] It's unbelievable. If I use a car, will the travel costs be reimbursed to me? I tried to book a flight from New York, but all the seats have been sold out already.

Celia Sharp [2:34 P.M.] I have booked a seat on Leroy Airlines, flight 31, arriving in Washington, DC from San Francisco at 7:10 A.M.

Deanna Schultz [2:35 P.M.] Oh, my! That's bad news. I'd better check that for you.

Seth Stanley [2:35 P.M.] All the flights from Detroit were fully booked as well. So I'm going to catch a bus to New Jersey to take a plane from there, getting in at 7:05 A.M. I barely managed to make a reservation for the last seat to Washington, DC.

Deanna Schultz [2:37 P.M.] I just checked the policy that driving to any event over 60 miles away does not qualify for reimbursement. And there is no available flight from any airport in the cities nearby at the moment. Why don't you consider catching a train? You'd better make a reservation as soon as possible and notify me of the travel arrangements.

Lynn Santos [2:38 P.M.] That might be possible. I will do that.

Deanna Schultz [2:40 P.M.] Mr. Sharp and Ms. Stanley, grateful for the information. Taxis will be arranged to wait for your arrivals.

34. At 2:33 P.M., what most likely does Ms. Santos mean when she writes, "It's unbelievable"?
(A) She thought the meeting had been put off to next week.
(B) She was not able to book her flight ticket.
(C) She did not expect that Ms. Schultz would ask about her travel destination.
(D) She had not been informed of free transportation from the airport.

35. At 2:35 P.M., what will Ms. Schultz check?
(A) Available transportation options from the airport
(B) Information on Mr. Sharp's travel arrangement
(C) The company policy for reimbursement
(D) A discounted flight ticket from New York

34번 문제 풀이 순서

STEP 1 의도 문제는 주어진 표현과 같은 뜻을 찾는 것이 아니라 본문의 위아래 문맥을 포괄적으로 설명하는 것이 답이 된다. 따라서 문맥을 보면,

It's **unbelievable**. If I use a car, will the travel costs be reimbursed to me? <u>I tried to book a flight from New York, but</u> all the seats have been sold out already.

믿을 수 없어요. 만약 제가 차량을 이용하면, 여행 경비는 환급 받을 수 있나요? 저는 뉴욕에서 출발하는 비행기를 예약하려고 했지만, 모든 좌석이 전부 매진되었어요.

STEP 2 보기에서 오류 내용을 제거한다.
(A) She thought ~~the meeting had been put off~~ to next week.
(B) She was <u>not</u> able to <u>book her flight ticket</u>.
(C) She did not expect that Ms. Schultz would ask about her travel ~~destination~~.
(D) She had not been informed of ~~free transportation from the airport~~.

35번 문제 풀이 순서

STEP 1 온라인 대화에서는 누가 요구했으며, 무엇이 문제이며, 다음 행동이 무엇인지를 순차적으로 정리하고 이해하는 것이 중요하다.

STEP 2 대화를 이끌어 가는 중요 인물은 Deanna Schultz이며 그 외 나머지 세 사람의 입장이 나오고 있다.

STEP 3 해당 대사가 누구의 부탁에 이어지는지, 혹은 어떻게 진행되었는지를 확인해야 한다.
At 2:35 P.M., what will Ms. Schultz check?

Lynn Santos [2:33 P.M.] It's unbelievable. <u>If I **use a car**, will the **travel costs** be **reimbursed** to me?</u> I tried to book a flight from New York, but all the seats have been sold out already.   ❶ 문의 사항

Celia Sharp [2:34 P.M.] I have booked a seat on Leroy Airlines, flight 31, arriving in Washington, DC from San Francisco at 7:10 A.M.

키워드

Deanna Schultz [2:35 P.M.] Oh my! That's bad news. <u>I'd better **check that** for you</u>.

Seth Stanley [2:35 P.M.] All the flights from Detroit were fully booked as well. So I'm going to catch a bus to New Jersey to take a plane from there, getting in at 7:05 A.M. I barely managed to make a reservation for the last seat to Washington, DC.   ❷ 확인사항

Deanna Schultz [2:37 P.M.] <u>I just checked the **policy** that **driving** to any event over 60 miles away does not qualify for **reimbursement**</u>. And there is no available flight from any airport in the cities nearby at the moment. Why don't you consider catching a train? You'd better make a reservation as soon as possible and notify me of the travel arrangements.

STEP 4 키워드인 check 뒤에 한 번 더 나오면서 답이 등장한다.
<u>I just checked the policy that driving ~ for reimbursement</u>.
따라서 정답은 reimbursement에 대한 회사의 정책을 언급한 (C)이다.

1-28 미래의 계획은 상대방 대사에서 권유/제안으로 답이 제시되기도 한다.

① 업무에 관련된 내용을 읽고 어떻게 대처할 것인가를 묻는 문제로, 주로 지문의 마지막에 등장한다. 특정 조건이나 가정 하에 제안이나 요청 또는 무엇을 하기 위한 수단이나 방법을 물어보는 내용으로, 앞으로 어떤 일이 발생할지 미래 사실을 묻는 문제이기도 하다.
② 일반적인 미래의 일정은 본인의 대사에 답이 있지만 상대방 대사에서 ask, require, suggest, need 등의 동사를 사용해서 문제에 제시된 인물에게 요청을 하는 표현으로 답이 제시되기도 한다.

시험에 이렇게 나온다

Questions 34-37 refer to the following online chat discussion.

Deanna Schultz [2:32 P.M.] In order to prepare for next week's branch managers' meeting, I have to arrange transportation from the airport. So, everyone needs to provide me your flight information. It is the first time we hold a meeting like this, and everything should be organized properly.

Lynn Santos [2:33 P.M.] It's unbelievable. If I use a car, will the travel costs be reimbursed to me? I tried to book a flight from New York, but all the seats have been sold out already.

Celia Sharp [2:34 P.M.] I have booked a seat on Leroy Airlines, flight 31, arriving in Washington, DC from San Francisco at 7:10 A.M.

Deanna Schultz [2:35 P.M.] Oh my! That's bad news. I'd better check that for you.

Seth Stanley [2:35 P.M.] All the flights from Detroit were fully booked as well. So I'm going to catch a bus to New Jersey to take a plane from there, getting in at 7:05 A.M. I barely managed to make a reservation for the last seat to Washington, DC.

Deanna Schultz [2:37 P.M.] I just checked the policy that driving to any event over 60 miles away does not qualify for reimbursement. And there is no available flight from any airport in the cities nearby at the moment. Why don't you consider catching a train? You'd better make a reservation as soon as possible and notify me of the travel arrangements.

Lynn Santos [2:38 P.M.] That might be possible. I will do that.

Deanna Schultz [2:40 P.M.] Mr. Sharp and Ms. Stanley, grateful for the information. Taxis will be arranged to wait for your arrivals.

36. What is suggested about the branch managers?
(A) They will arrive from the same city.
(B) They will arrange their own taxi from the airport.
(C) They need to make a presentation at the meeting this year.
(D) They are having a meeting in Washington, DC.

37. How most likely will Ms. Santos get to the branch managers' meeting?
(A) She will ride a bus.
(B) She will catch a train.
(C) She will use an airline.
(D) She will take her own car.

36번 문제 풀이 순서

STEP 1   indicate/imply/suggest는 제안을 묻는 것이 아니라 '사실인 것'을 찾는 문제이다.

STEP 2   순서대로 답을 찾고 지문의 하단부까지 모두 검색하고 나면 다시 상단부로 올라가서 키워드를 검색한다. 문제 중에 키워드는 branch managers이다.

> **Deanna Schultz [2:32 P.M.]** In order to prepare for next week's **branch managers' meeting,** I have to arrange transp~~~~~~~~~~~~~~~~~~~~~~ provide me your flight information. ~~~~~~~~~~~~~~~~~~~ everything should be organized pro~~~~~~
>
> *branch managers' meeting을 위해 타는 비행기의 도착지는 arriving in Washington, DC 이기 때문에 답은 (D)가 된다. from은 출발지이다.*
>
> **Lynn Santos [2:33 P.M.]** It's unbelievable. If I use a car, will the travel costs be reimbursed to me? I tried to book a flight from New York, but all the seats have been sold out already.
>
> **Celia Sharp [2:34 P.M.]** I have booked a seat on Leroy Airlines, flight 31, **arriving in Washington,** DC from San Francisco at 7:10 A.M.

37번 문제 풀이 순서

STEP 1   수단이나 방법을 묻는 문제는 주로 하단부에 등장한다.

STEP 2   지문의 하단부에서 '~을 해야 한다', '~을 하기를 바란다' 등의 표현이 나오고 질문에 언급된 사람이 그렇게 하겠다고 답하는 부분을 찾아야 한다.

> **Deanna Schultz [2:37 P.M.]** I just checked the policy that driving to any event over 60 miles away does not qualify for reimbursement. And there is no available flight from any airport in the cities nearby at the moment. **Why don't you consider catching a train?** You'd better make a reservation as soon as possible and notify me of the travel arrangements.
>
> **Lynn Santos [2:38 P.M.]** That might be possible. I will do that.

STEP 3   '기차를 타고 오는 것은 어떤가요? 가능한 빨리 예약을 해서 저에게 여행편을 알려 주세요.'
Ms. Santos는 기차를 타고 갈 것이라는 (B)가 정답이다.

STEP 4   미래 일정을 제시하는 표현
           Please let me know ~   ~를 알려주세요
           You should/must/have to do ~   ~하셔야 합니다
           You are asked/requested/instructed/invited to do ~   ~을 해야 합니다
           Rearrange his personal finances. (명령문)   그 사람의 개인 자산을 재조정하세요.
           Why don't you ~? (제안)   ~하지 않으시겠어요?
           We want/recommend/suggest/ask/require + you to do   당신이 ~하실 것을 요청합니다
           If you have any questions ~   ~하는 데 궁금한 게 있으시면
           If you are interested in ~   ~하는 데 관심이 있으시면

CHAPTER 2
DOUBLE PASSAGE

CHAPTER 2
ACTUAL TEST

Questions 01-05 refer to the following notice and page from a brochure.

Joel Bookstore
Autumn Selection Brochure

Information for Customers:

Please look through our new brochure. Starting on page 4, in our Food and Drink section, you will find titles of interest for professional chefs and food lovers in both commercial and private kitchens. Our Travel and Tourism section on page 6 includes travel guides and phrase books to assist you wherever you visit this autumn. For all the latest on commercial and residential construction, see our selection of Design and Architecture titles (page 8). Renowned experts highlight the most recent business trends in the Management and Business section with the Sales and Marketing Encyclopedia publicly recognized for the best seller of the year beginning on page 10.

Only some part of our latest acquisitions are shown in this brochure. For more information on our entire range of titles, visit www.joelbookstore.com. Anyone in the Paddington area is advised to stop by our store for a great deal of extra reading not accessible on our website.

Joel Bookstore

New Generation Business Management
By Frederick Wells and Lance Williamson

Condition: Quite good with some wear to edges and corners. £26.85

Good for both business owners and students. The authors well combine theoretical principles with real-life instances through practical case studies. This valued book highlights not only sound business management theories but also effective applications.

The Sales and Marketing Encyclopedia
By Leroy Snyder

Condition: Fair with some signs of cover wear. £33.75

This book is definitely a must-have for all novices, entering the world of business, with its over 3,100 definitions of essential terms in sales and marketing.

The Nuts and Bolts of Accounting for Small Business Owners
By Clarence Russell

Condition: Almost new. £35.50

A must-read book for those running small companies and wishing to handle their own accounting and tax matters.

Finance Analysis Textbook
By Neal Cowden

Condition: Excellent with few signs of use. £34.85

Through interesting cartoons illustrating key points, and readable and clear contents of how to analyze and manage finances are introduced. Instructors are welcome to copy pages to use for class activities.

Joel Bookstore

01. According to the notice, what book most likely is available from Joel Bookstore?
(A) A training manual for amateur cooks
(B) A guide to top attractions in Asia
(C) A novel about time travel
(D) A well-known illustrator's autobiography

02. In the notice, the word "deal" in paragraph 2, line 3, is closest in meaning to
(A) handle
(B) amount
(C) contract
(D) trade

03. What most likely is true about Joel Bookstore?
(A) It publishes monthly brochures.
(B) It offers online discounts.
(C) It has many branches.
(D) It carries secondhand books.

04. What is NOT indicated in the descriptions of the books on the brochure page?
(A) Images to explain key points
(B) Cases drawn from the real business world
(C) Data for opening a new business
(D) Material allowed to be reproduced

05. Who received an award?
(A) Mr. Cowden
(B) Ms. Snyder
(C) Mr. Wells
(D) Mr. Russell

Questions 06-10 refer to the following advertisement and e-mail.

Winnipeg Transport Solutions

Winnipeg Transport Solutions is Winnipeg's most reputable, privately owned rental agency. Various types of vehicles are offered at the most affordable prices possible. If you find any other rental companies offering a lower rate, we are willing to match that rate and give you a discount voucher for a future rental.

The following are available vehicles for rent.

Price per Day	Detail	Type of Car
$48	Suitable for 6 people (4-door car) Able to load 3 large suitcases and 2 small bags	Premium
$32	Suitable for 6 people (4-door car) Able to load 2 large suitcases and 1 small bag	Standard
$24	Suitable for 5 people (2-door car) Able to load 1 large suitcase and 2 small bags	Compact
$19	Suitable for 5 people (2-door car) Able to load 1 large suitcase and 1 small bag	Economy

If you make a payment in person at our register counter, the prices indicated above will be applied. You can find more details about the features of each of the vehicles and reduced rates on our website at www.winnipegtransportsolutions.com. If you want even more savings, March and April are the best time as an extra 15% discounted price will be offered.

FROM	alfonsosteele@stewart.net
TO	vehiclereservation@winnipegtransportsolutions.com
DATE	February 23
SUBJECT	Rental Inquiry

Hello,

I am planning to go on a business trip scheduled for the beginning of next month, so I have tried to make a reservation for a vehicle on your website. I would like to make our trip a comfortable one with my five coworkers traveling with me, which made me choose to rent a 4-door vehicle. And, it should not be more than $ 40 since our budget is rather limited. However, I cannot complete the booking process because some information related to the car pick-up and drop-off location and some equipment I need is not clearly explained or maybe I may not be able to find it on the website. Will there be an extra fee if I drop the car off at any of your Rosser or Carlin branch instead of driving it back to the branch in Dugald where I will pick up the car? Also, I intend to add a navigation system to the car as it will be my first trip to Winnipeg.
If this is all possible, please let me know how much would the rent be.

Thank you in advance,

Glen Tran

06. What is NOT mentioned in the advertisement?
(A) How much each vehicle's rental fee is
(B) How many people can ride in each vehicle
(C) How much fuel each vehicle uses
(D) How much space for luggage in each vehicle is

07. What type of vehicle does Mr. Tran most likely rent?
(A) Economy
(B) Compact
(C) Standard
(D) Premium

08. What is suggested about Winnipeg Transport Solutions?
(A) A cash deposit is required to make online reservations.
(B) A new branch has recently opened in Dugald.
(C) It operates more than one branch in different locations.
(D) Business people are its primary customers.

09. What is indicated about Mr. Tran?
(A) He will have his own car equipped with a navigation system.
(B) He will be able to rent a car at a reduced rate.
(C) He often goes on business trips with his colleagues.
(D) He has been in Winnipeg on his business before.

10. According to the e-mail, what is the information that Mr. Tran cannot find?
(A) The types of the vehicles the company offers
(B) The availability of certain equipment
(C) The company's branch locations
(D) The company's operating hours

Questions 11-15 refer to following e-mails.

TO	b.vargas@leopt.net
FROM	l.vasquez@angieelectronicmarketing.com
DATE	Tuesday, August 7
SUBJECT	Angie Electronic Marketing tech support

Dear Mr. Bessie,

I would like to thank you again for applying to Angie Electronic Marketing. We were very impressed by the interview with you last Friday and are happy to ask you to join our technical support department. As you are aware, the responsibilities you will take on involve visiting our customers to assist with issues on their hardware as well as software systems. Your extensive experience in computer technology will be a valuable asset, since it is essential that you have clear understanding of technical details of the products we manufacture and can utilize this information effectively to support your customers.

Your first day will be September 12 with hands-on training at our main office in Tottenham, London. The exact time has not been decided yet, and for people who do not live in London, we need to find an appropriate time that works for as many people as possible. Please let us know which time on the date you would like.

This is a part-time position, and with the exception of the training programs we provide, jobs will be performed remotely over the hours you select. As mentioned, the pay rate varies in accordance with the level of each assignment's complexity. Our head of personnel, Alicia Wagner, will contact you in a few days for all the necessary forms you need to fill in.

We are expecting to work with you soon!

Leslie Vasquez
Angie Electronic Marketing

TO	All the new members of Tech Support
FROM	l.vasquez@angieelectronicmarketing.com
DATE	Wednesday, August 8
SUBJECT	AEM training

Dear new Tech Support team members,

We have set the schedule for the training session in the afternoon on the date based on your responses. Please be advised that the training will be held from 1 P.M. to 6 P.M. Anyone living outside London should arrive an hour before the session and we will arrange lunch for you with some of the technicians who are working with us currently if you would like. All expenses related your travel will be covered by us. Further information about this will be provided later. For now, I would just like to make sure that you put the schedule on your calendar.

Leslie Vasquez
Angie Electronic Marketing

11. What is the purpose of Mr. Vasquez's e-mail to Mr. Bessie?

(A) To negotiate a pay rate
(B) To give technical support
(C) To offer him a job
(D) To promote a training event

12. What detail is Mr. Bessie required to provide?

(A) A reference from his current employer
(B) Details of some technical issues
(C) His availability for an event
(D) His previous experience

13. What is suggested about the Tech Support staff?

(A) They used to work together.
(B) Their pay rates are not the same.
(C) They will work in a building.
(D) Their travel expenses are not reimbursed.

14. Why will Ms. Wagner contact Mr. Bessie?

(A) To arrange transportation
(B) To ask for employment documents
(C) To clarify some qualifications
(D) To explain an employee policy

15. What will Mr. Bessie most likely do at 12 P.M. on September 12?

(A) Hand in an assignment
(B) Arrive in Tottenham
(C) Take part in a training session
(D) Meet with Ms. Wagner

Questions 16-20 refer to the following website and announcement.

---

http:www.Albertastate.com

| Home | Dining | Hiking | Shopping | Featured Areas |

Alberta State's Areas

The Lake Area
Various communities of musicians and artists are vibrantly working on their art pieces in this area. There are many galleries and museums to visit which host special exhibitions all year around. There are a diverse range of musical entertainments offered at The Trevor Arena in Edson Square. It has plenty of seats, and performances are free of charge.

The South End
This area is famous for its colorful nightlife as well as its quality and tasty eateries along Leduc Avenue. Many premises in the area are well known for serving a wide range of exotic cuisines.

The Historic Zone
It boasts not only the oldest, but also the most fascinating structures and places in the county, with the Old State Train Station and Wade's Monument Tower. The Tour Bureau in the city center can arrange guided tours. Horse-drawn carriage tours in Min street can also make your visit the most memorable one.

Drayton Valley
It is representative of the natural environment of Alberta State. The Alberta State National Glass House can highlight its four seasons at any time of the year. By using cable cars, visitors can enjoy exquisite views of the valley.

Public Announcement: The Alberta Street Parade

Next Friday beginning at 4 P.M. at the Wade's Monument Tower, the Alberta Street Parade, one of the most popular annual events, will start.
Like previous years, all parade teams will get together and march up and down Jose Road and turn onto Sherri Street. The route of this parade reaches Edson Square and a local yet famous musician group, Gayle Rock Band, is planning to perform at 8 P.M. at the Trevor Arena after the parade. There will be an award ceremony to recognize the top entries from the parade. Due to temporary road closures for the parade, street parking will not be available and citizens are advised to detour around the road and street in the proximity of the parade route. Using public transportation is highly recommended by the city officials, and also bus and tram operating hours will be extended to 1 A.M.

16. Who most likely will visit the website?
(A) Property developers
(B) Tourists to Alberta State
(C) Parade organizers
(D) City officials

17. According to the website, what can be found in the South End?
(A) Horse-drawn carriage tours
(B) Excellent natural views
(C) Famous architectural sites
(D) A selection of dining places

18. What is NOT indicated about Alberta State?
(A) It is famous for its natural beauty.
(B) It is home to active historians.
(C) A parade is held there each year.
(D) Carriage tours can be found there.

19. What is suggested about the musical performance after the parade?
(A) Only professional musicians can participate in it.
(B) Its admission is free to the public.
(C) Drayton Valley was the original place for it.
(D) It features more than one band.

20. What suggestion is made in the announcement?
(A) To book a ticket for a rock performance
(B) To use Jose Road for the best view of the event
(C) To visit Wade's Monument Tower that has been completed
(D) To use public transportation to reduce congestion

2-01 본문 중에 구체적인 단서들을 모아서 포괄적인 답을 찾는다.

① 각 문서의 앞부분을 skimming한다.
② 문제를 분석하여 답의 위치/풀이 전략/키워드를 확보한다.
③ 먼저 사람 이름을 찾아 I/You를 분류한다.
④ 보기의 내용을 본문에서 검색하며 풀이한다.
⑤ 반드시 하나 이상의 문제가 두 문서를 동시에 이용해서 풀도록 출제된다.
⑥ 전체 문단을 한번에 읽지 말고 나누어서 해당 문제와 함께 읽는다.

시험에 이렇게 나온다

Questions 01-05 refer to the following notice and page from a brochure.

Joel Bookstore
Autumn Selection Brochure

Information for Customers:

Please look through our new brochure. Starting on page 4, in our Food and Drink section, you will find titles of interest for professional chefs and food lovers in both commercial and private kitchens. Our Travel and Tourism section on page 6 includes travel guides and phrase books to assist you wherever you visit this autumn. — 중략 —

Only some part of our latest acquisitions are shown in this brochure. For more information on our entire range of titles, visit www.joelbookstore.com. Anyone in the Paddington area is advised to stop by our store for a great deal of extra reading not accessible on our website.

New Generation Business Management
By Frederick Wells and Lance Williamson

Condition: Quite good with some wear to edges and corners. £26.85

Good for both business owners and students. The authors well combine theoretical principles with real-life instances through practical case studies. This valued book highlights not only sound business management theories but also effective applications.

The Sales and Marketing Encyclopedia
By Leroy Snyder

Condition: Fair with some signs of cover wear. £33.75

This book is definitely a must-have for all novices, entering the world of business, with its over 3,100 definitions of essential terms in sales and marketing.

The Nuts and Bolts of Accounting for Small Business Owners
By Clarence Russell

Condition: Almost new. £35.50

A must-read book for those running small companies and wishing to handle their own accounting and tax matters.

Finance Analysis Textbook
By Neal Cowden

Condition: Excellent with few signs of use. £34.85

Through interesting cartoons illustrating key points, and readable and clear contents of how to analyze and manage finances are introduced. Instructors are welcome to copy pages to use for class activities.

---

01. According to the notice, what book most likely is available from Joel Bookstore?
(A) A training manual for amateur cooks
(B) A guide to top attractions in Asia
(C) A novel about time travel
(D) A well-known illustrator's autobiography

02. In the notice, the word "deal" in paragraph 2, line 3, is closest in meaning to
(A) handle
(B) amount
(C) contract
(D) trade

01번 문제 풀이 순서

STEP 1 본문을 읽기 전에 반드시 문제를 먼저 분석해야 한다. 문제는 다음의 세 가지를 알려준다.
① 답의 위치 ② 문제 풀이 전략 ③ 키워드

01. According to the notice, what book most likely is available from Joel Bookstore?
- According to the notice로 보아 첫 번째 문서에 답이 있다.
- 다섯 문제 중 첫 번째 문제는 주로 첫 번째 문서 상단부에 정답 힌트가 나온다.

STEP 2 보기의 키워드들을 상단부에서 검색하고 오류가 있는 보기를 소거한다.
(A) A ~~training manual~~ for ~~amateur~~ cooks [training manual, amateur 언급 없음]
(B) A guide to top attractions in Asia
(C) A novel about ~~time~~ travel [시간 여행 소설은 언급 없음]
(D) A well-known ~~illustrator's autobiography~~ [삽화가의 자서전 언급 없음]

Joel Bookstore
Autumn Selection Brochure

Information for Customers:

Please look through our new brochure. Starting on page 4, in our Food and Drink section, you will find titles of interest for professional chefs and food lovers in both commercial and private kitchens. Our Travel and Tourism section on page 6 includes travel guides and phrase books to assist you wherever you visit this autumn.

STEP 3 본문의 내용은 항상 paraphrasing이 된다.
wherever you visit this autumn에서 '어디든지'라고 했기 때문에 Asia의 attractions(유명 방문 명소들)를 소개하는 가이드 책자를 구매할 수 있음을 알 수 있다.

02번 문제 풀이 순서

STEP 1 보기의 단어들은 모두 deal과 동의어이다.
(A) handle = deal with 처리하다   (B) amount = deal 양
(C) contract 계약   (D) trade = deal 거래

Joel Bookstore
– 중략 –
Only some part of our latest acquisitions are shown in this brochure. For more information on our entire range of titles, visit www.joelbookstore.com. Anyone in the Paddington area is advised to stop by our store for a great deal of extra reading not accessible on our website.

STEP 2 동의어 찾기 문제는 단순히 같은 뜻을 찾는 것이 아니다. 보기 중에서 본문의 문맥상 대체할 수 있는 단어를 선택한다.
for a great deal of extra reading not accessible on our website. '웹사이트에서 이용할 수 없는 많은 읽을거리'에서 deal은 '많음, 양'의 뜻으로 사용되었다. 따라서 '양'의 뜻인 (B)가 정답이다.

2-02 4가지 항목이 있는 문서는 공통 정보를 찾는 문제가 출제된다.

① 문제를 통해 답이 있는 문서를 알 수 있다.
② 4가지 항목이 있는 표, 전단지, 일정표, 광고 등에서는 4가지 항목의 공통점 혹은 다른 점, 특정한 키워드 관련 정보, 변경이나 오류를 묻는 문제가 출제된다.

시험에 이렇게 나온다

Questions 01-05 refer to the following notice and page from a brochure.

Joel Bookstore
Autumn Selection Brochure

Information for Customers:

Please look through our new brochure. Starting on page 4, in our Food and Drink section, you will find titles of interest for professional chefs and food lovers in both commercial and private kitchens.

New Generation Business Management
By Frederick Wells and Lance Williamson

Condition: Quite good with some wear to edges and corners. £26.85

Good for both business owners and students. The authors well combine theoretical principles with real-life instances through practical case studies. This valued book highlights not only sound business management theories but also effective applications.

The Sales and Marketing Encyclopedia
By Leroy Snyder

Condition: Fair with some signs of cover wear. £33.75

This book is definitely a must-have for all novices, entering the world of business, with its over 3,100 definitions of essential terms in sales and marketing.

The Nuts and Bolts of Accounting for Small Business Owners
By Clarence Russell

Condition: Almost new. £35.50

A must-read book for those running small companies and wishing to handle their own accounting and tax matters.

Finance Analysis Textbook
By Neal Cowden

Condition: Excellent with few signs of use. £34.85

Through interesting cartoons illustrating key points, and readable and clear contents of how to analyze and manage finances are introduced. Instructors are welcome to copy pages to use for class activities.

03. What most likely is true about Joel Bookstore?
(A) It publishes monthly brochures.
(B) It offers online discounts.
(C) It has many branches.
(D) It carries secondhand books.

04. What is NOT indicated in the descriptions of the books on the brochure page?
(A) Images to explain key points
(B) Cases drawn from the real business world
(C) Data for opening a new business
(D) Material allowed to be reproduced

03번 문제 풀이 순서

STEP 1   문제에 Joel Bookstore가 언급되었기 때문에 전체 본문에서 보기의 내용을 하나씩 확인해야 한다.

보기의 키워드를 두 번째 문서에 제시된 4가지 항목에서 검색한다.
(A) monthly [언급되지 않음]   (B) online discounts [웹주소가 나오긴 하지만 discount 내용은 없음]
(C) many branches [언급되지 않음]   (D) secondhand books

STEP 2   본문 중에 monthly/online discounts/many branches는 언급되지 않는다.

본문 중 4가지 항목에서 공통적으로 condition(상태)이라는 단어가 나오고, wear(낡은), almost new 등의 표현이 나온다. 따라서 답은 (D) secondhand books이다.

New Generation Business Management
By Frederick Wells and Lance Williamson

Condition: Quite good with some wear to edges and corners. £26.85

Good for both business owners and students. The authors well combine theoretical principles with real-life instances through practical case studies. This valued book highlight 04. (B) sound business management theories but also effective applications.

The Sales and Marketing Encyclopedia
By Leroy Snyder

Condition: Fair with some signs of cover wear. £33.75

This book is definitely a must-have for all novices, entering the world of business, with its over 3,100 definitions of essential terms in sales and marketing.

The Nuts and Bolts of Accounting for Small Business Owners
By Clarence Russell

Condition: Almost new. £35.50

A must-read book for those running small companies and wishing to handle their own accounting and tax matters.

Finance Analysis Textbook
By Neal Cowden

Condition: Excellent with few signs of use. £34.85   04. (A)

Through interesting cartoons illustrating key points, and readable and clear contents of how to analyze and manage finances are introduced. Instructors are welcome to copy pages to use for class activities.   04. (D)

04번 문제 풀이 순서

STEP 1   문제에 the brochure가 언급되었기 때문에 답은 두 번째 문서에서 찾아야 하며, Not Question은 보기의 키워드를 본문에서 하나씩 소거해야 한다.

(A) Images to explain key points
(B) Cases drawn from the real business world
(C) Data for opening a new business
(D) Material allowed to be reproduced

STEP 2   Not Question은 보기의 키워드 중 본문에서 검색되지 않는 것이 답이 된다.

images, cases, allowed to be reproduced는 위에서 보는 바와 같이 언급되어 있으므로 소거하고, 언급되지 않은 (C) Data for opening a new business가 정답이다.

2-03 5문제 중 반드시 한 문제 이상은 두 문서를 동시에 이용해야 답이 나온다.

① Double Passage는 반드시 두 문서를 동시에 이용해야 풀리는 문제가 출제된다.
② 문제의 키워드와 보기의 내용이 각각 다른 문서에 나오는 경우는 두 문서를 동시에 파악해야 한다.

시험에 이렇게 나온다

Questions 01-05 refer to the following note and page from a brochure.

Joel Bookstore
Autumn Selection Brochure

— 중략 —

For all the latest on commercial and residential construction, see our selection of Design and Architecture titles (page 8). Renowned experts highlight the most recent business trends in the Management and Business section with The Sales and Marketing Encyclopedia publicly recognized for the best seller of the year beginning on page 10.

Only some part of our latest acquisitions are shown in this brochure. For more information on our entire range of titles, visit www.joelbookstore.com. Anyone in the Paddington area is advised to stop by our store for a great deal of extra reading not accessible on our website.

New Generation Business Management
By Frederick Wells and Lance Williamson

Condition: Quite good with some wear to edges and corners. £26.85

Good for both business owners and students. The authors well combine theoretical principles with real-life instances through practical case studies. This valued book highlights not only sound business management theories but also effective applications.

The Sales and Marketing Encyclopedia
By Leroy Snyder

Condition: Fair with some signs of cover wear. £33.75

This book is definitely a must-have for all novices, entering the world of business, with its over 3,100 definitions of essential terms in sales and marketing.

The Nuts and Bolts of Accounting for Small Business Owners
By Clarence Russell

Condition: Almost new. £35.50

A must-read book for those running small companies and wishing to handle their own accounting and tax matters.

Finance Analysis Textbook
By Neal Cowden

Condition: Excellent with few signs of use. £34.85

Through interesting cartoons illustrating key points, and readable and clear contents of how to analyze and manage finances are introduced. Instructors are welcome to copy pages to use for class activities.

---

05. Who received an award?
(A) Mr. Cowden
(B) Ms. Snyder
(C) Mr. Wells
(D) Mr. Russell

05번 문제 풀이 순서

STEP 1 문제의 키워드인 award는 첫 번째 문서에 관련 내용이 나오고, 보기의 제시어인 사람 이름은 모두 두 번째 문서에 있다.

이 경우에는 두 문서를 동시에 이용해야 한다. 첫 번째 지문에서 award의 의미인 recognized for the best seller of the year에 있는 또 다른 키워드(The Sales and Marketing Encyclopedia)를 두 번째 문제에서 검색한다.

STEP 2 두 번째 문서에서 확보된 책(The Sales and Marketing Encyclopeia)의 작가 이름을 찾는다.

Joel Bookstore
Autumn Selection Brochure

– 중략 –

For all the latest on commercial and residential construction, see our selection of Design and Architecture titles (page 8). Renowned experts highlight the most recent business trends in the Management and Business section with The Sales and Marketing Encyclopedia publicly **recognized for the best seller of the year** beginning on page 10.

❶ award

Only some part of our latest acquisitions are shown in this brochure. For more information on our entire range of titles, visit www.joelbookstore.com. Anyone in the Paddington area is advised to stop by our store for a great deal of extra reading not accessible on our website.

New Generation Business Management
By Frederick Wells and Lance Williamson

Condition: Quite good with some wear to edges and corners. £26.85

Good for both ❷ 연결 키워드 확보 students. The authors well combine theoretical principles with real-life instances through practical case studies. This valued book highlights not only sound business management theories but also effective applications.

The Sales and Marketing Encyclopedia
By Leroy Snyder

Condition: Fair with some signs of cover wear. £33.75

This book is definitely a must-have for all novices, entering the world of business, with its over 3,100 definitions of essential terms in sales and marketing.

The Nuts and Bolts of Accounting for Small Business Owners
By Clarence Russell

Condition: Almost new. £35.50

A must-read book for those running small companies and wishing to handle their own accounting and tax matters.

Finance Analysis Textbook
By Neal Cowden

Condition: Excellent with few signs of use. £34.85

Through interesting cartoons illustrating key points, and readable and clear contents of how to analyze and manage finances are introduced. Instructors are welcome to copy pages to use for class activities.

STEP 3 보기 중에 또 다른 키워드인 The Sales and Marketing Encyclopedia의 저자인 (B) Ms. Snyder가 상을 받았다는 것을 알 수 있다.

2-04 표나 시각 자료 등에는 직접적인 답이 많지 않다.

① 시각 자료는 답을 선택할 수 있는 근거를 제공하는 역할을 하기 때문에 이를 통해 직접적으로 답을 찾을 수 있는 문제는 한 문제 정도만 배치된다.
② 두 문서 중 하나에 시각 자료가 나오면 두 문서 연계 문제의 출제 비중이 크다.
③ 문제를 본격적으로 풀기 전에 두 문서의 앞부분을 키워드 위주로 정리한다.
④ 특정 사람이 등장하는 문서와 불특정 다수를 대상으로 하는 문서는 그 사람에게 해당하는 정보를 적용해야 한다.

시험에 이렇게 나온다

Questions 06-10 refer to the following advertisement and e-mail.

Winnipeg Transport Solutions

Winnipeg Transport Solutions is Winnipeg's most reputable, privately owned rental agency. Various types of vehicles are offered at the most affordable prices possible. If you find any other rental companies offering a lower rate, we are willing to match that rate and give you a discount voucher for a future rental.

The following are available vehicles for rent.

Price per Day	Detail	Type of Car
$48	Suitable for 6 people (4-door car) Able to load 3 large suitcases and 2 small bags	Premium
$32	Suitable for 6 people (4-door car) Able to load 2 large suitcases and 1 small bag	Standard
$24	Suitable for 5 people (2-door car) Able to load 1 large suitcase and 2 small bags	Compact
$19	Suitable for 5 people (2-door car) Able to load 1 large suitcase and 1 small bag	Economy

---

FROM   alfonsosteele@stewart.net
TO   vehiclereservation@winnipegtransportsolutions.com
DATE   February 23
SUBJECT Rental Inquiry

Hello,

I am planning to go on a business trip scheduled for the beginning of next month, so I have tried to make a reservation for a vehicle on your website. I would like to make our trip a comfortable one with my five coworkers traveling with me, which made me choose to rent a 4-door vehicle. And, it should not be more than $ 40 since our budget is rather limited.

---

06. What is NOT mentioned in the advertisement?
(A) How much each vehicle's rental fee is
(B) How many people can ride in each vehicle
(C) How much fuel each vehicle uses
(D) How much space for luggage in each vehicle is

07. What type of vehicle does Mr. Tran most likely rent?
(A) Economy
(B) Compact
(C) Standard
(D) Premium

06번 문제 풀이 순서

STEP 1   Not Question은 보기의 키워드를 먼저 정리하고 본문을 검색한다.

문제 중에 advertisement '광고'라는 단어가 있기 때문에 첫 번째 지문을 검색한다.

(A) rental fee
(B) many people can ride
(C) How much fuel
(D) How much space for luggage

Winnipeg Transport Solutions

Winnipeg Transport Solutions is Winnipeg's most reputable, privately owned rental agency. Various types of vehicles are offered at the most affordable prices possible. If you find any other rental companies offering a lower rate, we are willing to match that rate and give you a discount voucher for a future rental.

(A) rental fee are available vehicles for rent.

Price per Day	Detail **(B) how many people**	e of Car
$48	Suitable for 6 people (4-door car) Able to load 3 large suitcases and 2 small bags	Premium
$32	Suitable for 6 people (4-door car) Able to load 2 large suitcases and 1 small bag **(D) room for luggage**	

07번 문제 풀이 순서

STEP 1   두 문서를 동시에 이용하는 연계 문제 유형
문제에서 제시된 사람 Mr. Tran은 두 번째 문서에 있다. 반면에 첫 번째 문서는 광고로서 일반적인 내용만을 언급하고 있다. 이 경우에는 특정 사람이 언급된 문서에서 조건을 정리하여 첫 번째 문서에서 답을 선택해야 한다.

STEP 2   두 번째 문서에서 Mr. Tran이 원하는 조건을 먼저 정리한다.

Hello,
I am planning to go on a business trip scheduled for the beginning of next month, so I have tried to make a reservation for a vehicle on your website. I would like to make our trip a comfortable one with **my five coworkers** traveling with me, which made me choose to rent **a 4-door vehicle**. And, it should **not be more than $40** since our budget is rather limited.

$32	Suitable for **6 people (4-door car)** Able to load 2 large suitcases and 1 small bag	Standard

STEP 3   첫 번째 문서에서 비용이 40달러 이하이고 4도어이며 5명이 탈 수 있는 차를 찾아야 한다. 따라서 답은 (C) Standard이다.

두 문서를 동시에 이용하는 연계 문제 유형 1

① 사람 이름은 가장 중요한 keyword이다. 두 문서의 각 주어, 목적어, 제3자를 확보해 둔다.
② 두 문서에서 각각 I/You의 관계를 이해해야 한다. from/sign한 사람은 I에 해당되며 to/dear는 You에 해당한다.

시험에 이렇게 나온다

Questions 06-10 refer to the following advertisement and e-mail.

Winnipeg Transport Solutions

Winnipeg Transport Solutions is Winnipeg's most reputable, privately owned rental agency. Various types of vehicles are offered at the most affordable prices possible. If you find any other rental companies offering a lower rate, we are willing to match that rate and give you a discount voucher for a future rental.

The following are available vehicles for rent.

Price per Day	Detail	Type of Car
$48	Suitable for 6 people (4-door car) Able to load 3 large suitcases and 2 small bags	Premium
$32	Suitable for 6 people (4-door car) Able to load 2 large suitcases and 1 small bag	Standard
$24	Suitable for 5 people (2-door car) Able to load 1 large suitcase and 2 small bags	Compact
$19	Suitable for 5 people (2-door car) Able to load 1 large suitcase and 1 small bag	Economy

If you make a payment in person at our register counter, the prices indicated above will be applied. You can find more details about the features of each of the vehicles and reduced rates on our website at www.winnipegtransportsolutions.com. If you want even more savings, March and April are the best time as an extra 15% discounted price will be offered.

FROM   alfonsosteele@stewart.net
TO   vehiclereservation@winnipegtransportsolutions.com
DATE   February 23
SUBJECT Rental Inquiry

Hello,

I am planning to go on a business trip scheduled for the beginning of next month, so I have tried to make a reservation for a vehicle on your website. I would like to make our trip a comfortable one with my five coworkers traveling with me, which made me choose to rent a 4-door vehicle. And, it should not be more than $ 40 since our budget is rather limited. However, I cannot complete the booking process because some information related to the car pick-up and drop-off location and some equipment I need is not clearly explained or maybe I may not be able to find it on the website. Will there be an extra fee if I drop the car off at any of your Rosser or Carlin branch instead of driving it back to the branch in Dugald where I will pick up the car? Also, I intend to add a navigation system to the car as it will be my first trip to Winnipeg.
If this is all possible, please let me know how much would the rent be.

Thank you in advance,

Glen Tran

---

08. What is suggested about Winnipeg Transport Solutions?
(A) A cash deposit is required to make online reservations.
(B) A new branch has recently opened in Dugald.
(C) It operates more than one branch in different locations.
(D) Business people are its primary customers.

08번 문제 풀이 순서

STEP 1 두 문서가 문제의 키워드인 Winnipeg Transport Solutions에 관한 것이다. 다섯 문제 중 세 번째 문제는 두 번째 문서에 답이 있을 확률이 높다.
suggest/indicate/imply 문제는 보기의 키워드를 정리하여 본문에서 검색한다.

(A) A cash deposit / online reservations [첫 번째 광고 지문에서 웹주소는 있지만 deposit은 언급 없음]
(B) A new branch / Dugald
(C) More than one branch / different locations
(D) Business people / primary customers

STEP 2 두 번째 지문에서 to와 from을 확인하여 I와 You를 찾아 놓는다.
Winnipeg Transport Solutions는 TO에 있기 때문에 You에 해당한다. 따라서 두 번째 문서에서 You를 찾는다.

Winnipeg Transport Solutions

Winnipeg Transport Solutions is Winnipeg's most reputable, privately owned rental agency. **Various types of vehicles** are offered at the most affordable prices possible. If you find any other rental companies offering a lower rate, we are willing to match ~~~ for a future rental.

> 타겟 대상은 주로 광고의 상단부에 나온다.
> (D) 다양한 유형의 차량으로 Business people에만 한정되지 않는다.

The following are available vehicles for rent.

Price per Day	Detail	Type of Car
$48	Suitable for 6 people (4-door car) Able to load 3 large suitcases and 2 small bags	Premium
$32	Suitable for 6 people (4-door car) Able to load 2 large suitcases and 1 small bag	Standard
$24	Suitable for 5 people (2-door car) Able to load 1 large suitcase and 2 small bags	Compact
$19	Suitable for 5 people (2-door car) Able to load 1 large suitcase and 1 small bag	Economy

If you **make a payment** in person at our register counter, the prices indicated above will be applied. You can find more details about the features of each of the vehicles and reduced rates on our website at www.winnipegtransportsolutions.com. If you want even more savings, March and April are the best time as an extra 15% discounted price will b~~~

> 주문 방법/결제는 하단부에 나온다. (A) payment를 언급하지만 cash deposit의 내용은 없다.

FROM   alfonsosteele@stewart.net
TO   vehiclereservation@winnipegtransportsolutions.com
DATE   February 23
SUBJECT   Rental Inquiry

Hello,
– 중략 –
However, I cannot complete the booking process because some information related to the car pick-up and drop-off location and some equipment I need is not clearly explained or maybe I not be able to find it on the website. Will there be an extra fee if I drop the car off at any of **your Rosser** or **Carlin branch** instead of driving it back to the **branch in Dugald** where I will pick up the car? Also, I intend to add a naviga~~~
If this is all possible, please let me kno~~~

Thank you in advance,

Glen Tran

> (B) Dugald 지점은 차를 인수 받게 될 지점이며 최근에 오픈했다는 내용은 없다.

> your라는 표현 뒤에 2개의 지점이 나오기 때문에 지점이 최소 2개 이상이라는 것을 알 수 있다. 따라서 하나 이상의 지점이 여러 장소에서 운영되고 있다는 (C)가 정답이다.

두 문서를 동시에 이용하는 연계 문제 유형 2

① 일정상의 변경이나 가격 할인, 혜택 조건들을 적용하여 풀어야 하는 문제들이다.
② 한 문서가 할인이나 멤버십 자격 조건 등을 보여 주면 나머지 문서에서 특정 인물의 조건과 연계해서 답을 찾아야 한다.
③ but, unfortunately, however 뒤에는 답과 관련된 내용이 있다.

시험에 이렇게 나온다

Questions 06-10 refer to the following advertisement and e-mail.

Winnipeg Transport Solutions

Winnipeg Transport Solutions is Winnipeg's most reputable, privately owned rental agency. Various types of vehicles are offered at the most affordable prices possible. If you find any other rental companies offering a lower rate, we are willing to match that rate and give you a discount voucher for a future rental.

The following are available vehicles for rent.

Price per Day	Detail	Type of Car
$48	Suitable for 6 people (4-door car) Able to load 3 large suitcases and 2 small bags	Premium
$32	Suitable for 6 people (4-door car) Able to load 2 large suitcases and 1 small bag	Standard
$24	Suitable for 5 people (2-door car) Able to load 1 large suitcase and 2 small bags	Compact
$19	Suitable for 5 people (2-door car) Able to load 1 large suitcase and 1 small bag	Economy

If you make a payment in person at our register counter, the prices indicated above will be applied. You can find more details about the features of each of the vehicles and reduced rates on our website at www.winnipegtransportsolutions.com. If you want even more savings, March and April are the best time as an extra 15% discounted price will be offered.

FROM   alfonsosteele@stewart.net
TO   vehiclereservation@ winnipegtransportsolutions.com
DATE   February 23
SUBJECT Rental Inquiry

Hello,

I am planning to go on a business trip scheduled for the beginning of next month, so I have tried to make a reservation for a vehicle on your website. I would like to make our trip a comfortable one with my five coworkers traveling with me, which made me choose to rent a 4-door vehicle. And, it should not be more than $ 40 since our budget is rather limited. However, I cannot complete the booking process because some information related to the car pick-up and drop-off location and some equipment I need is not clearly explained or maybe I may not be able to find it on the website. Will there be an extra fee if I drop the car off at any of your Rosser or Carlin branch instead of driving it back to the branch in Dugald where I will pick up the car? Also, I intend to add a navigation system to the car as it will be my first trip to Winnipeg.
If this is all possible, please let me know how much would the rent be.

Thank you in advance,

Glen Tran

---

09. What is indicated about Mr. Tran?
(A) He will have his own car equipped with a navigation system.
(B) He will be able to rent a car at a reduced rate.
(C) He often goes on business trips with his colleagues.
(D) He has been in Winnipeg for his business before.

10. According to the e-mail, what is the information that Mr. Tran cannot find?
(A) The type of the vehicles the company offers
(B) The availability of certain equipment
(C) The company's branch locations
(D) The company's operating hours

09번 문제 풀이 순서

STEP 1 Mr. Tran은 두 번째 문서에서 I에 해당한다.

STEP 2 '할인'에 대한 정보는 대부분 두 문서를 동시에 이용해야 답이 나온다.

Winnipeg Transport Solutions

Winnipeg Transport Solutions is Winnipeg's most reputable, privately owned rental agency. Various types of vehicles are offered at the most affordable prices possible. If you find any other rental companies offering a lower rate, we are willing to match that rate and give you a discount voucher for a future rental.

— 중략 —

If you make a payment in person at our register counter, the prices indicated above will be applied. You can find more details about the features of each of the vehicles and reduced rates on our website at www.winnipegtransportsolutions.com. If you want even more savings, ③ March and April are the best time as an **extra 15% discounted price** will be offered.

FROM   alfonsosteele@stewart.net
TO   vehiclereservation@winnipegtransportsolutions.com
DATE   ① **February 23**
SUBJECT   Rental Inquiry

Hello,

I am planning to go on a business trip scheduled ② for the beginning of next month, so I have tried to make a reservation for a vehicle ~~~~~~ with my five coworkers traveling with ~~~~~~~~~~~~~~~~~~~~~~~~~~~~~~~~~~ not be more than $40 since our bu~~~~~~~~~~~~~~~~~~~~~~~~~~~~~~~~~~~~ cess because some information relat~~~~~~~~~~~~~~~~~~~~~~~~~~~~~~~~~~~ need is not clearly explained or mayb~~~~~~~~~~~~~~~~~~~~~~~~~~~~~~~~~~~ drop the car off at any of your Rosser or Carlin branch instead of driving it back to the branch in Dugald where I will pick up the car? Also, I intend to add a navigation system to the car as it will be my first trip to Winnipeg.

If this is all possible, please let me know how much would the rent be.

Thank you in advance
Glen Tran

> 2월 23일에 메일을 보내면서, 다음 달 초에 출장 갈 때 쓸 차량을 임차하려고 했음을 언급하고 있다. 그리고 첫 번째 지문에서 3월에는 추가 할인이 있을 것이라고 언급하므로, **Tran** 씨가 절감된 비용으로 차를 빌릴 수 있을 것이라는 내용의 **(B)**가 정답이다.

10번 문제 풀이 순서

STEP 1 According to the e-mail, – 두 번째 문서에 답이 있다.

STEP 2 Mr. Tran cannot find – I가 찾을 수 없는 것을 언급한 부분을 찾는다.
일반적으로 부정적인 단어 cannot 등이 키워드가 된다.

Hello,

I am planning to go on a business trip scheduled for the beginning of next month, so I have tried to make a reservation for a vehicle on your website. I would like to make our trip a comfortable one with my five coworkers traveling with me, which made me choose to rent a 4-door vehicle. And, it should not be more than $40 since our budget is rather limited. However, I cannot complete the booking process because some information related to the car pick-up and drop-off location and some equipment I need is not clearly explained or maybe I may not be able to find it on the website. Will there be an extra fee if I drop the car off at any of your Rosser or Carlin branch instead of driving it back to the branch in Dugald where I will pick up the car? Also, I intend to add a navigation system to the car as it will be my first trip to Winnipeg.

If this is all possible, please let me know how much would the rent be.

Thank you in advance
Glen Tran

STEP 3 Tran 씨는 the car pick-up and drop-off location and some equipment(차량을 픽업하고 반납할 장소, 일부 장비)에 대한 정보를 웹사이트에서 찾지 못했다고 하므로 정답은 (B)이다.

수동태형 문제는
상대방이 작성한 문서에 답이 있다.

① 특정인이 원하는 것을 묻는 문제의 경우 당사자가 사인한 문서에 답이 있다.
② 수동태형 문제의 경우에는 다른 사람이 작성한 문서에서 답을 찾아야 한다.
③ 두 문서의 I/You를 확보하고 앞부분을 skimming한다.

시험에 이렇게 나온다

Questions 11-15 refer to following e-mails.

To: b.vargas@leopt.net
From: l.vasquez@angieelectronicmarketing.com
Date: Tuesday, August 7
Subject: Angie Electronic Marketing tech support

Dear Mr. Bessie,

I would like to thank you again for applying to Angie Electronic Marketing. We were very impressed by the interview with you last Friday and are happy to ask you to join our technical support department. As you are aware, the responsibilities you will take on involve visiting our customers to assist with issues on their hardware as well as software systems.

– 중략 –

Your first day will be September 12 with hands-on training at our main office in Tottenham, London. The exact time has not been decided yet, and for people who do not live in London, we need to find an appropriate time that works for as many people as possible. Please let us know which time on the date you would like.

To: All new members of Tech Support
From: l.vasquez@angieelectronicmarketing.com
Date: Wednesday, August 8
Subject: AEM training

Dear new Tech Support team members,

We have set the schedule for the training session in the afternoon on the date based on your responses. Please be advised that the training will be held from 1 P.M. to 6 P.M. Anyone living outside London should arrive an hour before the session and we will arrange lunch for you with some of the technicians who are working with us currently if you would like.

---

11. What is the purpose of Mr. Vasquez's e-mail to Mr. Bessie?
(A) To negotiate a pay rate
(B) To give technical support
(C) To offer him a job
(D) To promote a training event

12. What detail is Mr. Bessie required to provide?
(A) A reference from his current employer
(B) Details of some technical issues
(C) His availability for an event
(D) His previous experience

11번 문제 풀이 순서

STEP 1 처음 2줄을 skimming하여 주요 정보와 대략의 상황을 파악한다.

STEP 2 첫 번째 문제인 글의 목적은 대부분 지문 상단부에 답이 있다.
일반적으로는 첫 번째 지문의 I would like to/I am writing to/I want you to/I want to ask you to 등의 표현은 목적을 나타낸다. 여기서는 (we) are happy to ask you to join our technical support department에서 답을 알 수 있다.

STEP 3 본문은 구체적이지만 답은 포괄적이므로 정답은 (C) '그에게 일자리를 제공하기 위해'가 된다.

12번 문제 풀이 순서

STEP 1 Mr. Bessie가 수신자로 나와 있는 첫 번째 지문을 확인해야 한다.
What detail is Mr. Bessie required to provide?에서 Mr. Bessie가 '요구 받는 것'을 찾아야 한다. 이렇게 수동태로 문제가 제시되는 경우에는 본인이 작성한 문서에서 I was asked 등의 표현을 찾아야 하거나 상대방이 작성한 문서에서 I ask you 등으로 답이 나올 확률도 높다. 즉, 상대방인 Leslie Vasquez가 작성한 첫 번째 문서에서 I(Leslie Vasquez)가 You(Mr. Bessie)에게 요구하는 것을 찾아야 한다.

STEP 2 요구 사항 문제는 주로 중하단부에서 Please, Why don't you, You should 등의 표현을 찾아야 한다.
본문 중에 '당신이 ~을 해 달라'는 표현은 Please let us know which time on the date you would like. 가 유일하다.

Dear Mr. Bessie, 받는 이: You

I would like to thank you again for applying to Angie Electronic Marketing. We were very impressed by the interview with you last Friday and are happy to ask you to join our technical support department. As you are aware, the responsibilities you will take on involve visiting our customers to assist with issues on their hardware as well as software systems. Your extensive experience in computer technology will be a valuable asset, since it is essential that you have clear understanding of the technical details of the products we manufacture and can utilize this information effectively to support our customers.

Your first day will be September 12 with hands-on training at our main office in Tottenham, London. The exact time has not been decided yet, and for people who do not live in London, we need to find an appropriate time that works for as many people as possible. **Please** let us know which time on the date you would like.

STEP 3 사람에 대해 availability를 쓰면 그 사람이 '~을 할 수 있거나 누군가를 만날 수 있는 시간'이라는 의미이다.
본문에서는 training을 받는 날짜에 몇 시가 좋은지에 대해 대답해 줄 것을 요청 받고 있다. 따라서 정답은 (C) His availability for an event이다.

키워드를 이용하는 문제

① 문제에서 제시하는 키워드들을 최대한 이용한다. 키워드가 어느 문서에서 제시되는지를 먼저 확인한다.
② 답은 키워드 근처에 있다.

시험에 이렇게 나온다

Questions 11-15 refer to following e-mails.

To: b.vargas@leopt.net
From: l.vasquez@angieelectronicmarketing.com
Date: Tuesday, August 7
Subject: Angie Electronic Marketing tech support

Dear Mr. Bessie,

I would like to thank you again for applying to Angie Electronic Marketing. We were very impressed by the interview with you last Friday and are happy to ask you to join our technical support department. As you are aware, the responsibilities you will take on involve visiting our customers to assist with issues on their hardware as well as software systems.

– 중략 –

This is a part-time position, and with the exception of the training programs we provide, jobs will be performed remotely over the hours you select. As mentioned, the pay rate varies in accordance with the level of each assignment's complexity. Our head of personnel, Alicia Wagner, will contact you in a few days for all the necessary forms you need to fill in.

We are expecting to work with you soon!

To: All new members of Tech Support
From: l.vasquez@angieelectronicmarketing.com
Date: Wednesday, August 8
Subject: AEM training

Dear new Tech Support team members,

We have set the schedule for the training session in the afternoon on the date based on your responses. Please be advised that the training will be held from 1 P.M. to 6 P.M. Anyone living outside London should arrive an hour before the session and we will arrange lunch for you with some of the technicians who are working with us currently if you would like.

---

13. What is suggested about the technical support staff?
(A) They used to work together.
(B) Their pay rates are not the same.
(C) They will work in a building.
(D) Their travel expenses are not reimbursed.

14. Why will Ms. Wagner contact Mr. Bessie?
(A) To arrange transportation
(B) To ask for employment documents
(C) To clarify some qualifications
(D) To explain an employee policy

13번 문제 풀이 순서

STEP 1 Suggest 문제이고, 키워드는 technical support staff이다. technical support staff 또는 유사 키워드는 첫 번째 지문에 있다.
보기의 키워드를 첫 번째 지문에서 technical support staff 근처의 내용에서 검색해야 한다.

STEP 2 보기의 키워드를 분석한다.
(A) used to work together, (B) Their pay rates, (C) work in a building, (D) travel expenses를 본문에서 찾아 표시한다.

Dear Mr. Bessie,

I would like to thank you again for applying to Angie Electronic Marketing. We were very impressed by the interview with you last Friday and are happy to ask you to join our **technical support** department. As you are aware, the responsibilities you will take on involve visiting our customers to assist with issues on their hardware as well as software systems. Your extensive experience in computer technology will be a valuable asset, since it is essential that you have clear understanding of the technical details of the products we manufacture and can utilize this information effectively to support our customers.

Your first day will be September 12 with hands-on training at our main office in Tottenham, London. The exact time has not been decided yet, and for people who do not live in London, we need to find an appropriate time that works for as many people as possible. Please let us know which tim

[13번 pay rate을 제외한 나머지 보기는 본문 중에 언급되지 않는다. 따라서 정답은 (B)이다.]

This is a part-time position, and with t[...] jobs will be performed remotely over the hours you select. As mentioned, the **pay rate varies** in accordance with the level of each assignment's complexity. Our head of **personnel**, **Alicia Wagner**, will contact you in a few days for **all the necessary forms you need to fill in.** [14번 키워드]

We are expecting to work with you soon!

14번 문제 풀이 순서

STEP 1 키워드는 Ms. Wagner contact이다. I/You가 아닌 제3자이다.

STEP 2 Ms. Wagner는 첫 번째 문서에 등장하며, 미래에 대한 정보나 연락 방법 등과 관련된 정보는 하단부에 나온다.

STEP 3 Alicia Wagner, will contact you in a few days for all the necessary forms you need to fill in. – 인사부장인 Wagner 씨가 Bessie에게 문서 작업을 요청하기 위해 연락을 할 것이라 언급하고 있다. 따라서 정답은 (B)이다.

(A) To arrange ~~transportation~~
(B) To ask for employment documents = all the necessary forms
(C) To clarify some ~~qualifications~~
(D) To explain an ~~employee policy~~

두 문서를 동시에 이용하는 연계 문제 유형 3

① 해당 위치를 검색하면 답이 없고 그 위치에 또 다른 키워드를 남기므로 다른 문서에서 키워드를 찾아야 한다.

시험에 이렇게 나온다

Questions 11-15 refer to following e-mails.

To: b.vargas@leopt.net
From: l.vasquez@angieelectronicmarketing.com
Date: Tuesday, August 7
Subject: Angie Electronic Marketing tech support

Dear Mr. Bessie,

I would like to thank you again for applying to Angie Electronic Marketing. We were very impressed by the interview with you last Friday and are happy to ask you to join our technical support department. As you are aware, the responsibilities you will take on involve visiting our customers to assist with issues on their hardware as well as software systems. Your extensive experience in computer technology will be a valuable asset, since it is essential that you have clear understanding of the technical details of the products we manufacture and can utilize this information effectively to support our customers.

Your first day will be September 12 with hands-on training at our main office in Tottenham, London. The exact time has not been decided yet, and for people who do not live in London, we need to find an appropriate time that works for as many people as possible. Please let us know which time on the date you would like.

This is a part-time position, and with the exception of the training programs we provide, jobs will be performed remotely over the hours you select. As mentioned, the pay rate varies in accordance with the level of each assignment's complexity. Our head of personnel, Alicia Wagner, will contact you in a few days for all the necessary forms you need to fill in.

To: All new members of Tech Support
From: l.vasquez@angieelectronicmarketing.com
Date: Wednesday, August 8
Subject: AEM training

Dear new Tech Support team members,

We have set the schedule for the training session in the afternoon on the date based on your responses. Please be advised that the training will be held from 1 P.M. to 6 P.M. Anyone living outside London should arrive an hour before the session and we will arrange lunch for you with some of the technicians who are working with us currently if you would like. All expenses related your travel will be covered by us. Further information about this will be provided later. For now, I would just like to make sure that you put the schedule on your calendar.

15. What will Mr. Bessie most likely do at 12 P.M. on September 12?
(A) Hand in an assignment
(B) Arrive in Tottenham
(C) Take part in a training session
(D) Meet with Ms. Wagner

15번 문제 풀이 순서

STEP 1 다섯 문제 중에서 반드시 한 문제 이상 두 문서를 동시에 이용하여 푸는 문제가 출제된다.

STEP 2 문제의 키워드는 September 12이며, 시간을 나타내는 at 12 P.M. 관련 내용이 두 번째 문서에 있다.

To: b.vargas@leopt.net
From: l.vasquez@angieelectronicmarketing.com
Date: Tuesday, August 7
Subject: Angie Electronic Marketing tech support

Dear Mr. Bessie,
— 중략 —

❶ 키워드 9월 12일

Your first day will be **September 12** with hands-on **training** at our main office in **Tottenham, London**. The exact time has not been decided yet, and for people who do not live in London, we need to find an appropriate time that works for as many people as possible. Please let us know which time on the date you would like.

> 시간이 정해지지 않았고 언제가 좋은지를 알려 달라는 말을 통해서 Mr. Bessie가 London에 살고 있지 않음을 알 수 있다.

From: l.vasquez@angieelectronicmarketing.com
Date: Wednesday, August 8
Subject: AEM training

Dear new Tech Support team members,

❷ 연결 키워드
training이 9월 12일에 Tottenham에서 있을 것이다.

We have set the schedule for the **training session** in the afternoon on the date **based on your responses**. Please be advised that the training will be held from **1 P.M. to 6 P.M.** Anyone living outside London should **arrive an hour before the session** and we will arrange lunch for you with some of the technicians who are working with us currently if you would like.

❸ 키워드 12시
London 밖에 거주하는 사람은 12시까지 도착해야 한다.

STEP 3 첫 번째 지문에서 시간이 나오지 않고 training이라는 또 다른 키워드를 남긴다.

STEP 4 두 번째 지문에서 training을 찾으면 시간은 정확하게 at 12 P.M.이 언급되어 있지는 않다.

> 이런 경우 시간 관련 내용들을 연결하여 답을 찾는다. the training will be held from 1 P.M. to 6 P.M. Anyone living outside London should arrive an hour before the session에서 훈련이 9월 12일 오후 1시부터 오후 6시까지 열릴 것이며, 훈련이 시작하기 한 시간 전인 12시에 훈련 받을 장소인 Tottenham에 도착해 있어야 함을 언급하고 있다. 따라서 정답은 (B)이다.

2-10 두 문서를 동시에 이용하는 연계 문제 유형 4

① Not Question 유형 중에는 보기의 내용을 두 문서에서 모두 검색해야 하는 문제들이 있다.
② 문제의 키워드가 알려주는 범위에 없는 내용은 또 다른 문서에서 답을 찾는다.
③ 지문이 4가지 항목으로 구성되어 있다면 각각의 첫 줄을 skimming한다.

시험에 이렇게 나온다

Questions 16-20 refer to the following website and announcement.

http:www.Albertastate.com

| Home | Dining | Hiking | Shopping | Featured Areas |

Alberta State's Areas

The Lake Area
Various communities of musicians and artists are vibrantly working on their art pieces in this area. There are many galleries and museums to visit which host special exhibitions all year around. There are a diverse range of musical entertainments offered at The Trevor Arena in Edson Square. It has plenty of seats, and performances are free of charge.

The South End
This area is famous for its colorful nightlife as well as its quality and tasty eateries along Leduc Avenue. Many premises in the area are well known for serving a wide range of exotic cuisines.

The Historic Zone
It boasts not only the oldest, but also the most fascinating structures and places in the county, with the Old State Train Station and Wade's Monument Tower. The Tour Bureau in the city center can arrange guided tours. Horse-drawn carriage tours in Min street can also make your visit the most memorable one.

Drayton Valley
It is representative of the natural environment of Alberta State. The Alberta State National Glass House can highlight its four seasons at any time of the year. By using cable cars, visitors can enjoy exquisite views of the valley.

Public Announcement: The Alberta Street Parade

Next Friday beginning at 4 P.M. at the Wade's Monument Tower, the Alberta Street Parade, one of the most popular annual events, will start.
Like previous years, all parade teams will get together and march up and down Jose Road and turn onto Sherri Street. The route of this parade reaches Edson Square and a local yet famous musician group, Gayle Rock Band, is planning to perform at 8 P.M. at the Trevor Arena after the parade. There will be an award ceremony to recognize the top entries from the parade. Due to temporary road closures for the parade, street parking will not be available and citizens are advised to detour around the road and street in the proximity of the parade route. Using public transportation is highly recommended by the city officials, and also bus and tram operating hours will be extended to 1 A.M.

---

16. Who most likely will visit the website?
(A) Property developers
(B) Tourists to Alberta State
(C) Parade organizers
(D) City officials

17. According to the website, what can be found in the South End?
(A) Horse-drawn carriage tours
(B) Excellent natural views
(C) Famous architectural sites
(D) A selection of dining places

18. What is NOT indicated about Alberta State?
(A) It is famous for its natural beauty.
(B) It is home to active historians.
(C) A parade is held there each year.
(D) Carriage tours can be found there.

16번 문제 풀이 순서

STEP 1 Who most likely will visit the website?는 첫 번째 지문에 답이 있다.

STEP 2 4가지 항목의 공통점을 찾는다.
The Lake Area : There are many galleries and museums to visit which host special exhibitions
The South End : nightlife as well as its quality and tasty eateries
The Historic Zone : most fascinating structures and places in the county
Drayton Valley : cable cars, visitors can enjoy exquisite views of the Valley

STEP 3 본문은 구체적이지만 답은 항상 포괄적이다.
웹사이트는 Alberta 주의 명소들에 대해 소개하고 있다. 따라서 웹사이트에 방문하는 사람들은 Alberta 주 관광객이라는 것을 알 수 있으므로 정답은 (B)이다.

17번 문제 풀이 순서

STEP 1 According to the website라고 했으므로 첫 번째 지문에 답이 있으며 키워드는 the South End이다.

> **The South End**
> This area is famous for its colorful nightlife as well as its quality and tasty eateries along Leduc Avenue. Many premises in the area are well known for serving a wide range of exotic cuisines.

(A) Horse-drawn ~~carriage tours~~ : The Historic Zone   **(D) A selection of dining places**
(B) Excellent ~~natural~~ views : Drayton Valley
(C) Famous ~~architectural sites~~ : The Historic Zone

18번 문제 풀이 순서

STEP 1 Not Question은 보기의 내용들을 본문에서 검색하여 검색된 정보는 소거하고 검색되지 않는 보기를 답으로 한다.

STEP 2 키워드는 Alberta State이다.
그런데 이 키워드는 두 문서에 모두 등장한다. 따라서 두 문서를 모두 이용해서 답을 찾아야 한다.
(A) It is famous for its natural beauty.
(B) It is home to active historians.
(C) A parade is held there each year.
(D) Carriage tours can be found there.

> **The Historic Zone**
> It boasts not only the oldest, but also the most fascinating structures and places in the county, with the Old State Train Station and Wade's Monument Tower. The Tour Bureau in the city center can arrange guided tours. Horse-drawn carriage tours in Min street can also make your visit the most memorable one.
>
> **Drayton Valley**
> It is representative of the natural environment of Alberta State. The Alberta State National Glass House can highlight its four seasons at any time of the year. By using cable cars, visitors can enjoy exquisite views of the valley.

> **Public Announcement: The Alberta Street Parade**
> Next Friday beginning at 4 P.M. at the Wade's Monument Tower, the Alberta Street Parade, one of the most popular annual events, will start.

STEP 3 Albertta State가 역사가들의 고향이라는 내용은 언급되지 않았으므로 정답은 (B)이다.

2-11 요구와 제안은 하단부에 답이 있다.

① 권유나 제안, 부탁, 요구 등은 지문의 하단부에 답이 있다.
② What is suggested는 언급된 것, 사실인 것을 묻고, What suggestion은 요구나 제안을 묻는 것이다.

시험에 이렇게 나온다

Questions 16-20 refer to the following website and announcement.

http:www.Albertastate.com

| Home | Dining | Hiking | Shopping | **Featured Areas** |

Alberta State's Areas

The Lake Area
Various communities of musicians and artists are vibrantly working on their art pieces in this area. There are many galleries and museums to visit which host special exhibitions all year around. There are a diverse range of musical entertainments offered at The Trevor Arena in Edson Square. It has plenty of seats, and performances are free of charge.

The South End
This area is famous for its colorful nightlife as well as its quality and tasty eateries along Leduc Avenue. Many premises in the area are well known for serving a wide range of exotic cuisines.

The Historic Zone
It boasts not only the oldest, but also the most fascinating structures and places in the county, with the Old State Train Station and Wade's Monument Tower. The Tour Bureau in the city center can arrange guided tours. Horse-drawn carriage tours in Min street can also make your visit the most memorable one.

Drayton Valley
It is representative of the natural environment of Alberta State. The Alberta State National Glass House can highlight its four seasons at any time of the year. By using cable cars, visitors can enjoy exquisite views of the valley.

Public Announcement: The Alberta Street Parade
Next Friday beginning at 4 P.M. at the Wade's Monument Tower, the Alberta Street Parade, one of the most popular annual events, will start.
Like previous years, all parade teams will get together and march up and down Jose Road and turn onto Sherri Street. The route of this parade reaches Edson Square and a local yet famous musician group, Gayle Rock Band, is planning to perform at 8 P.M. at the Trevor Arena after the parade. There will be an award ceremony to recognize the top entries from the parade. Due to temporary road closures for the parade, street parking will not be available and citizens are advised to detour around the road and street in the proximity of the parade route. Using public transportation is highly recommended by the city officials, and also bus and tram operating hours will be extended to 1 A.M.

19. What is suggested about the musical performance after the parade?
(A) Only professional musicians can participate in it.
(B) Its admission is free to the public.
(C) Drayton Valley was the original place for it.
(D) It features more than one band.

20. What suggestion is made in the announcement?
(A) To book a ticket for a rock performance
(B) To use Jose Road for the best view of the event
(C) To visit Wade's Monument Tower that has been completed
(D) To use public transportation to reduce congestion

19번 문제 풀이 순서

STEP 1 키워드 musical performance/after the parade는 두 문서에 모두 등장한다.

Alberta State's Areas

The Lake Area — (C) performance가 열리는 장소
Various communities of musicians and artists are vibrantly working on their art pieces in this area. There are many galleries and museums to visit which host special exhibitions all year around. There are a diverse range of musical entertainments offered at The "Trevor Arena" in Edson Square. It has plenty of seats, and performances are **free of charge**.

Public Announcement: The Alberta Street Parade — ❷ 연결 키워드

Next Friday beginning at 4 P.M. at the Wade's Monument Tower, the Alberta Street Parade, one of the most popular annual events, will start.
Like previous years, all parade teams will get together and march up and down Jose Road and turn onto Sherri Street. The route of this parade reaches Edson Square and a local yet famous musician group, **Gayle Rock Band**, is planning to **perform** at 8 P.M. at the **"Trevor Arena" after the parade**. There will be an award ceremony to recognize the top entries from the parade. Due to temporary road closures for the parade, street parking will not be available and citizens are advised to detour around the road and street in the proximity of the parade route. Using public transportation is highly recommended by the city officials, and also bus and tram operating hours will be extended to 1 A.M.

(A), (D) local band로 Gayle Rock Band가 공연을 한다.

❶ 키워드 perform / after the parade

STEP 2
(A) ~~Only~~ professional musicians can participate in it.
(B) Its admission is free to the public.
(C) ~~Drayton Valley~~ was the original place for it.
(D) It features ~~more than one band~~.

STEP 3
두 번째 지문의 The route of this parade reaches Edson Square and a local yet famous musician group, Gayle Rock Band, is planning to perform at 8 P.M. at the Trevor Arena after the parade.에서 퍼레이드가 끝난 뒤 음악 공연이 있을 예정인데, 장소가 Trevor Arena로 언급되었다. 그런데 첫 번째 지문의 There are a diverse range of musical entertainments offered at The Trevor Arena in Edson Square. It has plenty of seats, and performances are free of charge.에서 Trevor Arena에서는 무료 공연이 열린다고 언급되고 있다. 따라서 (B)가 정답이다.

20번 문제 풀이 순서

STEP 1 문제가 announcement를 지칭했기 때문에 답은 두 번째 문서에 있다.

STEP 2 What suggestion은 요구나 제안을 묻는 것으로 본문의 하단부에 답이 있다.

Like previous years, all parade teams will get together and march up and down Jose Road and turn onto Sherri Street. The route of this parade reaches Edson Square and a local yet famous musician group, Gayle Rock Band, is planning to perform at 8 P.M. at the Trevor Arena after the parade. There will be an award ceremony to recognize the top entries from the parade. **Due to temporary road closures for the parade, street parking will not be available and ① citizens are advised to detour** around the road and street in the proximity of the parade route. **② Using public transportation is highly recommended** by the city officials, and also bus and tram operating hours will be extended to 1 A.M.

STEP 3 권유, 제안의 표현에는 recommend, advice 등이 있다.

① citizens are advised to detour around the road and street in the proximity of the parade route.와 ② Using public transportation is highly recommended by the city officials에서 퍼레이드로 인해 일시적으로 도로가 폐쇄될 예정이어서 우회도로 이용과 대중교통 이용이 권고된다는 내용이 언급되고 있다. 따라서 대중교통을 이용하라는 내용의 (D)가 정답이다.

CHAPTER 3
TRIPLE PASSAGE

CHAPTER 3

ACTUAL TEST

Questions 01-05 refer to the following credit card statement and e-mails.

Cameron Terry Page 2
Account number: 7878-98575-04-352134-23432   May 3 – June 2
Purchase

AMOUNT	PLACE	DATE
35.45	Randal Bistro	May 4
37.15	Terrance Women's Store	May 5
27.20	Inez Fresh Restaurant	May 7
25.35	Swanson Café	May 13
41.50	Leslie Souvenir	May 16
52.70	Angie Eatery	May 29
100.55	Tucker Office Stationery	June 1

TO	customercare@lesliesouvenir.com
FROM	cameronterry@skynet.com
DATE	June 6
SUBJECT	incorrect amount charged

To whom it may concern

This is regarding a payment charged to my credit card by Leslie Souvenir. I had put in an order for a pair of gloves by telephone and was charged £41.50, although the price indicated in the online brochure is £35.50. The standard delivery fee is £6.00. However, my order was over £30.00, which means the delivery fee should be waived as your website shows. It would be great if you investigate this error and issue a refund of £6.00 to me, which caused the overcharge on my purchase.

Sincerely,
Cameron Terry

TO	cameronterry@skynet.com
FROM	rickywebb@lesliesouvenir.com
DATE	June 7
SUBJECT	inquiry about the overcharge

Dear Ms. Terry,

Your e-mail of June 6, inquiring about the overcharged amount on your credit card, has been investigated. First of all, we sincerely apologize for the inconvenience. There might have been a misunderstanding that the amount was for gift-wrapping your item as you requested; an extra charge for the gift wrapping service has been added. You can see it in the attached order form you completed. A clear notice for the service should have been listed. I apologize again. However, we would like to provide you with a £5.50 credit on this purchase or a £12 discount on a future order [over £35]. We will process it as soon as you let us know which offer you would like. We always appreciate your business with us and expect to serve you again in the near future.

Best regards,

Ricky Webb
Sales Manager

01. What did Ms. Terry use her credit card for most often in May?
(A) Stationery
(B) Dining
(C) Souvenir
(D) Apparel

02. When did Ms. Terry place her order form by telephone?
(A) May 13
(B) May 16
(C) June 1
(D) June 6

03. In the first e-mail, the word "indicated" in line 2 is closest in meaning to
(A) highlighted
(B) examined
(C) listed
(D) drawn

04. How much does the gift wrapping cost?
(A) £6
(B) £5.50
(C) £10
(D) £12

05. What did Mr. Webb want to ask Ms. Terry?
(A) Whether she will use a service again
(B) Where to send her the gift
(C) What type of compensation she wants
(D) When to contact her

Questions 06-10 refer to the following e-mail, notice, and order form.

TO	Edwin Mendoza
FROM	Clifford Mason
SUBJECT	Delivery Company
DATE	April 1

Hello Ms. Mendoza,

Thank you for signing up for consignment sale of our various fresh fruits and vegetables we grow here on our own farm specialized in greenhouse cultivation. I am confident that not only you but also your customers will be satisfied with the produce provided by our farm.

The area in which your shop is located is quite new to us, so we have high expectations about entering a new market with our quality produce. However, there is an issue with the delivery service based in Chichester we currently use, since they do not provide service to Eastbourne. If you have a preference for any particular company, please let us know. We will be happy to work with them so as to provide our produce as soon as possible. Thanks in advance for any suggestions you can provide.

Sincerely,

Clifford Mason

Green Life Grocery Mart
New Additions This Week!

Produce from Dereck Family Farm April 27

Dear Customers,

We are delighted to inform you that we have the newest additions in the fresh produce section. There has been high demand among our patrons for local produce which has just been freshly harvested. Dereck Greenhouse Farm, located just about a couple of hours from here, in Brighton will fully satisfy our customers' needs.

√ white Radish (bunch)
√ carrots
√ lettuces and cabbages
√ berries (raspberries, blueberries)
√ courgettes

In the summer, a more range of fruits from Sunny Field Orchard in Portsmouth will be carried. If there is any question you would like inquire about, please do not hesitate.

Order Form
Dereck Family Farm

Name	Green Life Grocery Mart
Date of order	April 30
Arrival Date	May 4

Details of order:
Repeat the same order as last week's with some changes below.
- Lettuces and cabbages needed this week
- Rather than a bunch of radishes in a bag, please ship them in a crate.
(as shown in your brochure)

P.S. Regarding the new shipping company, Cecil Shipping, they are quite good. The items were in good condition, the delivery people were polite and very kind, and not to mention the truck with produce we ordered arrived on time.

Name: Edwin Mendoza Purchasing Manager
Signature: *Edwin Mendoza*

---

06. What is the main reason Mr. Mason sent the e-mail?
(A) To promote new merchandise
(B) To solicit a recommendation
(C) To notify a shipping estimate
(D) To announced a procedure change

07. Where is Green Life Grocery Mart located?
(A) In Chichester
(B) In Brighton
(C) In Portsmouth
(D) In Eastbourne

08. According to the notice, what is suggested about Dereck Family Farm produce?
(A) It is scheduled to be available beginning summer.
(B) It is going to be sold at reduced rates.
(C) It is cultivated relatively close to the grocery mart.
(D) It is much cheaper than that of other farms.

09. What will Green Life Grocery Mart probably receive on May 4?
(A) Cucumber
(B) Lettuces
(C) Cabbages
(D) Carrots

10. What does Mr. Mendoza indicate in the order form?
(A) Some produce he ordered did not arrived in time.
(B) The berries are popular among customers.
(C) He tends to care about the packing method.
(D) The new delivery people from Cecil Shipping were not courteous.

Questions 11-15 refer to the following coupon, memo, and e-mail.

Money-saving Coupon
Good for one day only

END-OF-SEASON SALE
Valid on Saturday, June 19

- One discounted clearance product: Up to 50% off
- One regular-priced product: Up to 30% off

All of Antton Lilia Co's products are available including jackets, T-shirts, coats, pants, accessories, footwear, and more. Business hours will be extended for the event from 9:30 A.M. to 10:00 P.M.

Other promotional offers cannot be applied with this coupon. Althea, Estela, or Alyce brands are not subject to this special offer. A customer can use only one coupon. Refunds, exchanges, and store credits are not applicable on the clearance products.

Antton Lilia Co.

TO	All Antton Lilia staff members
FROM	Mary Smith, Sales Manager
DATE	June 18
RE	Upcoming sale event

We have an urgent issue which requires our immediate attention. The coupon printed in The Noreen's Daily neglected to mention that products available under the brand name Yesenia are not included in the sale on regularly priced products. Thus, please give our apologies, explaining the matter, to anyone trying to buy a product of this specific brand. But, don't forget to inform them that as a courtesy, the discount will nevertheless be honored.

In addition, three more sales representatives will be needed from 2:00 P.M to 8:00 P.M. because there may be more shoppers than usual coming after seeing the promotion in the media. So, please inform me as soon as possible if you would like to work for extra hours in the afternoon and evening on the day.

Thank you in advance.

FROM	<cusomercare@anttonlilia.co.us>
TO	Jerome Warren <troynave@supermail.co.us>
DATE	June 19, 4:43 P.M.
SUBJECT	Receipt for your purchase

Dear Mr. Warren,

Upon your request, the following is the digital receipt from Antton Lilia Co.

Item	Price	Quantity
Marvin leather jacket Promotional discount 50% Price of the item	$350.00 -$175.00 $175.00	1
Yesenia winter boots Promotional discount 30% Price of the item	$120.00 -$36.00 $84.00	1
Lance fur scarf	$28.00	1
Total Total saved	$287.00 $211.00	

Amount charged to JeelBR credit card   XXXX XXXX XXXX 4032
Thanks for your purchase at Antton Lilia.

11. In the coupon, what was suggested about the event on June 19?
(A) The business will stay open longer hours.
(B) Customers will be able to get coupons at the register.
(C) Returned items will be fully refunded.
(D) New shipments will be delivered to the shop.

12. According to the memo, what are sales representatives asked to do?
(A) Ask customers to join a membership
(B) Encourage customers to complete a survey
(C) Notify their willingness to work for an additional shift
(D) Start work earlier than usual

13. How much was originally charged to Ms. Warren's credit card?
(A) $ 323.00
(B) $ 287.00
(C) $ 175.00
(D) $ 295.00

14. What did Ms. Warren probably NOT receive when she bought the winter boots?
(A) An explanation
(B) An apology
(C) A gift certificate
(D) A discount

15. What is indicated about Ms. Warren?
(A) She paid for her items with cash.
(B) She is a regular shopper at Antton Lilia.
(C) She bought a regular-priced product.
(D) She recently started her new job.

표나 그래프 등 시각 자료는 다른 문서와 연결하여 답을 찾는 문제가 주로 출제된다.

① 보기에 있는 정보들과 문제의 키워드가 연결되지 않으면 두 문서를 이용해서 답을 찾아야 한다.
② 표에 있는 관련 정보들을 다른 지문들에서 모아서 답을 찾아야 한다.

시험에 이렇게 나온다

Questions 01-05 refer to the following credit card statement and e-mails.

Cameron Terry Page 2
Account number: 7878-98575-04-352134-23432   May 3 – June 2

Purchase

AMOUNT	PLACE	DATE
35.45	Randal Bistro	May 4
37.15	Terrance Women's Store	May 5
27.20	Inez Fresh Restaurant	May 7
25.35	Swanson Café	May 13
41.50	Leslie Souvenir	May 16
52.70	Angie Eatery	May 29
100.55	Tucker Office Stationery	June 1

To: customercare@lesliesouvenir.com
From: cameronterry@skynet.com
Date: June 6
Subject: incorrect amount charged

To whom it may concern

I'm writing regarding a payment charged to my credit card by Leslie Souvenir. I had put in an order for a pair of gloves by telephone and was charged £41.50, although the price indicated in the online brochure is £35.50. The standard delivery fee is £6.00. However, my order was over £30.00, which means the delivery fee should be waived as your website shows. It would be great if you investigate this error and issue a refund of £6.00 to me, which caused the overcharge on my purchase.

Sincerely,
Cameron Terry

To: cameronterry@skynet.com
From: rickywebb@lesliesouvenir.com
Date: June 7
Subject: inquiry about the overcharge

Dear Ms. Terry,

Your e-mail of June 6, inquiring about the overcharged amount on your credit card, has been investigated. First of all, we sincerely apologize for the inconvenience. There might have been a misunderstanding that the amount was for gift-wrapping your item as you requested; an extra charge for the gift wrapping service has been added. You can see it in the attached order form you completed. A clear notice for the service should have been listed. I apologize again. However, we would like to provide you with a £5.50 credit on this purchase or a £12 discount on a future order [over £35]. We will process it as soon as you let us know which offer you would like. We always appreciate your business with us and expect to serve you again in the near future.

Best regards,

Ricky Webb
Sales Manager

---

01. What did Ms. Terry use her credit card for most often in May?

(A) Stationery
(B) Dining
(C) Souvenir
(D) Apparel

02. When did Ms. Terry place her order form by telephone?

(A) May 13
(B) May 16
(C) June 1
(D) June 6

01번 문제 풀이 순서

STEP 1 문제의 키워드는 credit card / most often / May이다.
표나 목록, 일정표 등이 있는 경우는 구체적인 항목들을 모아서 신용카드를 자주 사용한 부분을 찾는다.

STEP 2 Bistro / Restaurant / Café / Eatery 등을 종합해 보면 가장 빈번한 사용은 '음식'이라는 것을 알 수 있으므로 정답은 (B)이다.

STEP 3 문제의 May 또한 중요한 키워드이다. $100 이상을 사용했던 Tucker Office Stationery의 경우는 June에 구매한 내역이므로 정답에서 제외한다.

02번 문제 풀이 순서

STEP 1 문제의 키워드는 Ms. Terry / order / by telephone이다. telephone은 두 번째 문서에 등장한다.

STEP 2 두 번째 지문의 I had put in an order for a pair of gloves by telephone and was charged £41.50를 확인한다.

STEP 3 키워드 근처에 답이 없는 경우는 또 다른 키워드를 남긴다. 여기서 또 다른 키워드는 £41.50이다.

STEP 4 첫 번째 문서의 £41.50를 찾아 보면 해당 단어가 Leslie Souvenir이다.
보기 중에서 날짜를 찾는 것이 관건이기 때문에 Leslie Souvenir 옆을 확인해 보면 (B) May 16이 답이 된다.

생각의 순서 MAPPING

Cameron Terry Page 2
Account number: 7878-98575-04-352134-23432   May 3 – June 2

Purchase

AMOUNT	PLACE	DATE
35.45	Randal Bistro	May 4
37.15	Terrance Women's Store	May 5
27.20	Inez Fresh Restaurant	May 7
25.35	Swanson Café	May 13
41.50	Leslie Souvenir	**May 16**
52.70	Angie Eatery	May 29
100.55	Tucker Office Stationery	June 1

To: customercare@lesliesouvenir.com
From: cameronterry@skynet.com
Date: June 6
Subject: incorrect amount charged

❷ 연결 키워드

To whom it may concern

I'm writing regarding a payment charged to my credit card by Leslie Souvenir. I had put in an order for a pair of gloves **by telephone** and was charged **£41.50**, although the price indicated in the online brochure is £35.50. The delivery fee is £6.00. However, my order was over £30.00, which means the delivery fee should be waived as your website shows. It would be great if you investigate this error and issue a refund of £6.00 to me, which caused the overcharge on my purchase.

❶ 키워드

Sincerely,
Cameron **Terry**

가격/비용/날짜 등을 묻는 문제는 본문에서 모든 정보를 찾아서 순서대로 배열한 후에 최종 답을 찾는다.

① 보기의 숫자들은 본문에 모두 제시되기 때문에 키워드와 관련된 숫자가 답이 된다.
② 할인이나 변경의 경우 계산을 해야 답이 나온다.

시험에 이렇게 나온다

Questions 01-05 refer to the following credit card statement and e-mails.

Cameron Terry Page 2
Account number: 7878-98575-04-352134-23432
May 3 – June 2

Purchase

AMOUNT	PLACE	DATE
35.45	Randal Bistro	May 4
37.15	Terrance Women's Store	May 5
27.20	Inez Fresh Restaurant	May 7
25.35	Swanson Café	May 13
41.50	Leslie Souvenir	May 16
52.70	Angie Eatery	May 29
100.55	Tucker Office Stationery	June 1

To: customercare@lesliesouvenir.com
From: cameronterry@skynet.com
Date: June 6
Subject: incorrect amount charged

To whom it may concern

I'm writing regarding a payment charged to my credit card by Leslie Souvenir. I had put in an order for a pair of gloves by telephone and was charged £41.50, although the price indicated in the online brochure is £35.50. The standard delivery fee is £6.00. However, my order was over £30.00, which means the delivery fee should be waived as your website shows. It would be great if you investigate this error and issue a refund of £6.00 to me, which caused the overcharge on my purchase.

Sincerely,
Cameron Terry

To: cameronterry@skynet.com
From: rickywebb@lesliesouvenir.com
Date: June 7
Subject: inquiry about the overcharge

Dear Ms. Terry,

Your e-mail of June 6, inquiring about the overcharged amount on your credit card, has been investigated. First of all, we sincerely apologize for the inconvenience. There might have been a misunderstanding that the amount was for gift-wrapping your item as you requested; an extra charge for the gift wrapping service has been added. You can see it in the attached order form you completed. A clear notice for the service should have been listed. I apologize again. However, we would like to provide you with a £5.50 credit on this purchase or a £12 discount on a future order [over £35]. We will process it as soon as you let us know which offer you would like. We always appreciate your business with us and expect to serve you again in the near future.

Best regards,

Ricky Webb
Sales Manager

---

03. In the first e-mail, the word "indicated" in line 2 is closest in meaning to
(A) highlighted
(B) examined
(C) listed
(D) drawn

04. How much does the gift wrapping cost?
(A) £6
(B) £5.50
(C) £10
(D) £12

03번 문제 풀이 순서

STEP 1 동의어 찾기 문제는 같은 뜻의 단어가 아니라 문맥상 대체할 수 있는 단어가 답이 된다.

STEP 2 단어가 포함된 지문의 although the price indicated in the online brochure is £35.50.에서 온라인 안내 책자에 '적힌' 가격이 35.50파운드라고 언급하고 있다.

STEP 3 '언급된'의 뜻으로서 indicated가 사용되었으므로 '보여 주다/말하다/쓰여 있다/제시하다' 등이 답이 된다.

STEP 4 '강조된/조사된/~에 실려 있는/그려진'이라는 의미 중에서 정답은 (C) listed '~에 실려 있는'이다.

04번 문제 풀이 순서

STEP 1 보기에 등장하는 숫자들을 모두 확보해 둔다.

STEP 2 문제의 키워드는 'gift-wrapping cost(선물 포장비)'이다. 선물 포장비는 세 번째 지문에서 등장한다. 하지만 이 단어 근처에는 답이 없다.

STEP 3 포장비 옆에는 misunderstanding / the amount라는 또 다른 키워드가 등장한다.

STEP 4 두 번째 문서 하단부에 배송비로 알고 환불을 요청한 금액 £6가 답이 된다.
(A) £6는 환불 요청액, (B) £5.50와 (D) £12는 회사가 제시하는 대안이다. (C) £10은 언급이 없다.

생각의 순서 MAPPING

To whom it may concern

I'm writing regarding a payment charged to my credit card by Leslie Souvenir. I had put in an order for a pair of gloves by telephone and was charged £41.50, although the price indicated in the online brochure is £35.50. The standard delivery fee is £6.00. However, my order was over £30.00, which means the delivery fee should be waived as your website shows. It would be great if you investigate this error and issue a ③ **refund of £6.00** to me, which caused the overcharge on m...

❸ 추가로 청구된 £6(배송비)에 대한 환불 요청

Dear Ms. Terry,

❷ 연결 키워드

Your e-mail June 6, inquiring about the **overcharged amount** on your credit card, has been investigated. First of all, we sincerely apologize for the inconvenience. There might have been a **misunderstanding** that **the amount** was for ① **gift-wrapping** your item ② **as you requested;** an **extra charge** for the gift wrapping service has been **added**. You can see it in the attach... should have been listed. I a... a £5.50 credit on this purch... process it as soon as you let us know which offer you would like. We always appreciate your business with us and expect to serve you again in the near future.

❶ 키워드
과잉 청구된 금액은 gift-wrapping을 요청하여 추가된 금액임

마지막 문제의 답은 주로 세 번째 문서에 등장한다.

① 단일 지문 문제와 마찬가지로 다중 지문의 문제들도 답은 순서대로 등장한다.

시험에 이렇게 나온다

Questions 01-05 refer to the following credit card statement and e-mails.

Cameron Terry Page 2
Account number: 7878-98575-04-352134-23432   May 3 – June 2

Purchase

AMOUNT	PLACE	DATE
35.45	Randal Bistro	May 4
37.15	Terrance Women's Store	May 5
27.20	Inez Fresh Restaurant	May 7
25.35	Swanson Café	May 13
41.50	Leslie Souvenir	May 16
52.70	Angie Eatery	May 29
100.55	Tucker Office Stationery	June 1

To: customercare@lesliesouvenir.com
From: cameronterry@skynet.com
Date: June 6
Subject: incorrect amount charged

To whom it may concern

I'm writing regarding a payment charged to my credit card by Leslie Souvenir. I had put in an order for a pair of gloves by telephone and was charged £41.50, although the price indicated in the online brochure is £35.50. The standard delivery fee is £6.00. However, my order was over £30.00, which means the delivery fee should be waived as your website shows. It would be great if you investigate this error and issue a refund of £6.00 to me, which caused the overcharge on my purchase.

Sincerely,
Cameron Terry

To: cameronterry@skynet.com
From: rickywebb@lesliesouvenir.com
Date: June 7
Subject: inquiry about the overcharge

Dear Ms. Terry,

Your e-mail of June 6, inquiring about the overcharged amount on your credit card, has been investigated. First of all, we sincerely apologize for the inconvenience. There might have been a misunderstanding that the amount was for gift-wrapping your item as you requested; an extra charge for the gift wrapping service has been added. You can see it in the attached order form you completed. A clear notice for the service should have been listed. I apologize again. However, we would like to provide you with a £5.50 credit on this purchase or a £12 discount on a future order [over £35]. We will process it as soon as you let us know which offer you would like. We always appreciate your business with us and expect to serve you again in the near future.

Best regards,

Ricky Webb
Sales Manager

---

05. What did Mr. Webb want to ask Ms. Terry?
(A) Whether she will use a service again
(B) Where to send her the gift
(C) What type of compensation she wants
(D) When to contact her

05번 문제 풀이 순서

STEP 1   문제의 키워드는 Mr. Webb / ask이다.
Mr. Webb이 Ms. Terry에게 쓴 마지막 지문을 확인해야 한다.

STEP 2   Mr. Webb은 마지막 지문의 I/We, 그리고 Ms. Terry는 You에 해당한다.

STEP 3   요청 사항은 지문의 하단부를 확인한다.
마지막 지문의 However, we would like to provide you with a £5.50 credit on this purchase or a £12 discount on a future order [over £35]. We will process it as soon as you let us know which offer you would like.에서 Webb 씨는 Terry 씨에게 두 가지의 보상 유형을 설명했고, 한 가지를 선택해 줄 것을 요청했다.

생각의 순서 MAPPING

To: cameronterry@skynet.com
From: rickywebb@lesliesouvenir.com
Date: June 7
Subject: inquiry about the overcharge

Dear **Ms. Terry**,   ❶ 받는 이: You

Your e-mail June 6, inquiring about the overcharged amount on your credit card, has been investigated. First of all, we sincerely apologize for the inconvenience. There might have been a misunderstanding that the amount was for gift-wrapping your item as you requested; an extra charge for the gift wrapping service has been added. You can see it in the attached order form you completed. A clear notice for the service should have been listed. I apologize again. **However, we would like to provide you with a £5.50 credit on this purchase or a £12 discount on a future order [over £35]. We will process it as soon as you let us know which offer you would like**. We always appreciate your business with us and expect to serve you again in the near future.

Best regards,

Ricky **Webb**   ❷ 보내는 이: I
Sales Manager

---

05. What did Mr. Webb want to ask Ms. Terry?
(A) ~~Whether~~ she will use a service again
(B) ~~Where~~ to send her the gift
(C) What type of compensation she wants
(D) ~~When~~ to contact her

목적이 앞부분에 없을 때는 하단부에 나오는 요구 사항에 답이 있다.

① 목적이나 주제를 묻는 문제는 주로 지문의 상단부에 목적이 언급되지만, 초반에 편지나 이메일을 보내게 된 배경 등을 설명할 때는 하단부에 요청 사항으로 목적이 등장한다.

시험에 이렇게 나온다

Questions 06-10 refer to the following e-mail, notice, and order form.

To: Edwin Mendoza
From: Clifford Mason
Subject: Delivery Company
Date: April 1

Hello Mr. Mendoza,

Thank you for signing up for consignment sale of the various fresh fruits and vegetables we grow here on our own farm specialized in greenhouse cultivation. I am confident that not only you but also your customers will be satisfied with the produce provided by our farm.

The area in which your shop is located is quite new to us, so we have high expectations about entering a new market with our quality produce. However, there is an issue with the delivery service based in Chichester we currently use, since they do not provide service to Eastbourne. If you have a preference for any particular company, please let us know. We will be happy to work with them so as to provide our produce as soon as possible. Thanks in advance for any suggestions you can provide.

Sincerely,

Clifford Mason

Green Life Grocery Mart
New Additions This Week!

Produce from Dereck Family Farm   April 27

Dear Customers,

We are delighted to inform you that we have the newest additions in the fresh produce section. There has been high demand among our patrons for local produce which has just been freshly harvested. Dereck Family Farm, located just a couple of hours from here, in Brighton will fully satisfy our customers' needs.

Order Form
Dereck Family Farm

Name	Green Life Grocery Mart
Date of order	April 30
Arrival Date	May 4

Details of order:
Repeat the same order as last week's with some changes below.
- Lettuces and cabbages needed this week
- Rather than a bunch of radishes in a bag, please ship them in a crate.
(as shown in your brochure)

---

06. What is the main reason Mr. Mason sent the e-mail?
(A) To promote new merchandise
(B) To solicit a recommendation
(C) To notify a delivery estimate
(D) To announce a procedure change

06번 문제 풀이 순서

STEP 1 첫 번째 문제는 대부분 첫 번째 지문에 답이 있다.
문제의 키워드는 reason/Mr. Mason/e-mail이다. Mr. Mason이 이메일을 쓰는 목적을 묻는 문제이다.

STEP 2 앞부분에서 상황 설명이 길게 나오는 경우에 목적은 하단부의 요구 사항이 있는 부분에 답이 나온다.

STEP 3 요구의 표현은 일반적으로 문서의 중후반부에 If ~/Please ~/명령문을 이용해 제시된다.

STEP 4 but, yet, however 등의 표현 뒤에 주로 답이 있다.

To: Edwin Mendoza
From: Clifford Mason
Subject: Delivery Company
Date: April 1

> 농장(farm)에서 새롭게 계약을 맺은 가게(mart)로 보내는 이메일

Hello **Mr. Mendoza**, — 받는 이: You

Thank you for signing up for consignment sale of the various fresh fruits and vegetables we grow here on our own farm specialized in greenhouse cultivation. I am confident that not only you but also your customers will be satisfied with the produce provided by our farm.

The area in which your shop is located is quite new to us, so we have high expectations about entering a new market with our quality produce. **However**, there is an issue with the delivery service based in Chichester we currently use, since they do not provide service to Eastbourne. **If you have a preference** for any particular company, **please let us know**. We will be happy to work with them so as to provide our produce as soon as possible. provide.

> Mason 씨는 Mendoza 씨에게 배송 회사를 추천해 줄 것을 요청하고 있다. 따라서 '추천을 얻기 위해서'라는 (B)가 정답이다.

Sincerely,

Clifford **Mason** — 보내는 이: I

STEP 5 보기 중에서 본문의 해당 위치에 언급되지 않은 것을 오답으로 소거한다.

(A) To promote ~~new merchandise~~
(B) To solicit a recommendation
(C) To notify a delivery ~~estimate~~
(D) To announce ~~a procedure change~~

보기가 모두 장소이거나 시간, 사람 이름 등이면 모두 본문에서 검색해 두어야 한다.

① 문제의 키워드를 중심으로 보기에 해당하는 명사들을 빠르게 찾는 것이 관건이다.
② 보기의 명사들이 키워드와 매칭되는지 확인한다.

시험에 이렇게 나온다

Questions 06-10 refer to the following e-mail, notice, and order form.

To: Edwin Mendoza
From: Clifford Mason
Subject: Delivery Company
Date: April 1

Hello Mr. Mendoza,

Thank you for signing up for consignment sale of the various fresh fruits and vegetables we grow here on our own farm specialized in greenhouse cultivation. I am confident that not only you but also your customers will be satisfied with the produce provided by our farm.

The area in which your shop is located is quite new to us, so we have high expectations about entering a new market with our quality produce. However, there is an issue with the delivery service based in Chichester we currently use, since they do not provide service to Eastbourne. If you have a preference for any particular company, please let us know. We will be happy to work with them so as to provide our produce as soon as possible. Thanks in advance for any suggestions you can provide.

Sincerely,

Clifford Mason

Green Life Grocery Mart
New Additions This Week!

Produce from Dereck Family Farm   April 27

Dear Customers,

We are delighted to inform you that we have the newest additions in the fresh produce section. There has been high demand among our patrons for local produce which has just been freshly harvested. Dereck Family Farm, located just a couple of hours from here, in Brighton will fully satisfy our customers' needs.

√ white radish (bunch)
√ carrots
√ lettuces and cabbages
√ berries (raspberries, blueberries)
√ courgettes

In the summer, a wider range of fruits from Sunny Field Orchard in Portsmouth will be carried. If there is any question you would like to inquire about, please do not hesitate.

Order Form
Dereck Family Farm

Name	Green Life Grocery Mart
Date of order	April 30
Arrival Date	May 4

Details of order:
Repeat the same order as last week's with some changes below.
- Lettuces and cabbages needed this week
- Rather than a bunch of radishes in a bag, please ship them in a crate.
(as shown in your brochure)

---

07. Where is Green Life Grocery Mart located?

(A) In Chichester   (B) In Brighton
(C) In Portsmouth   (D) In Eastbourne

07번 문제 풀이 순서

STEP 1 세 문서들의 관계를 먼저 정리해야 한다.
첫 번째 지문: 농장에서 마트로 보낸 편지
두 번째 지문: 마트에서 고객들에게 보낸 편지
세 번째 지문: 마트가 농장으로 보낸 주문서

STEP 2 세 문서의 주제와 진행 상황을 정리한다.

STEP 3 보기가 모두 장소이기 때문에 지문 중에 나오는 장소를 모두 검색한다.

To: **Edwin Mendoza**
From: Clifford Mason
Subject: Delivery Company
Date: April 1

> 농장에서 새롭게 계약을 맺은 마트로 보낸 이메일

Hello Mr. Mendoza,
— 중략 —
The area in which your shop is located is quite new to us, so we have high expectations about entering a new market with our quality produce. However, there is an issue with ① **the delivery service** based in **Chichester** we currently use, since they do not provide service to **Eastbourne**.

❶ 첫 번째 지문을 보면 농장에서 Green Life Mart(Eastbourne)로 delivery가 안 되기 때문에 의견을 달라고 한다.

Green Life Grocery Mart
New Additions This Week!

Produce from Dereck Family Farm

> 마트에서 고객에게 공지하는 내용

Dear Customers,

We are delighted to inform you that we have the newest additions in the fresh produce section. There has been high demand among our patrons for local produce which has just been freshly harvested. ② **Dereck Family Farm,** located just a couple of hours from here, **in Brighton** will fully satisfy our customers' needs.

❷ 두 번째 문서에서는 농장이 마트에서 두 시간 걸리는 Brighton에 있다고 언급한다.

— 중략 —
In the summer, a wider range of fruits from **Sunny Field Orchard in Portsmouth** will be carried. If there is any question you would like to inquire about, please do not hesitate.

Order Form
Dereck Family Farm

> 마트에서 농장으로 보내는 주문서

Name	Green Life Grocery Mart
Date of order	April 30
Arrival Date	May 4

Details of order:
Repeat the same order as last week's with some changes below.
- Lettuces and cabbages needed this week
- Rather than a bunch of radishes in a bag, please ship them in a crate. (as shown in your brochure)
— 중략 —
Name: Edwin Mendoza Purchasing Manager
Signature: *Edwin Mendoza*

STEP 4 마지막 정답 관련 정리

(A) In Chichester: 농장에서 기존에 이용하는 a delivery service company의 소재
(B) In Brighton: Dereck Family Farm의 소재
(C) In Portsmouth: Sunny Field Orchard의 소재
(D) In Eastbourne: Green Life Grocery Mart의 소재

3-06 Paraphrasing된 표현을 주의하라.

① paraphrasing은 단순히 같은 의미를 찾기보다는 해당 표현의 의도를 파악해야 한다.

시험에 이렇게 나온다

Questions 06-10 refer to the following e-mail, notice, and order form.

To: Edwin Mendoza
From: Clifford Mason
Subject: Delivery Company
Date: April 1

Hello Mr. Mendoza,

Thank you for signing up for consignment sale of the various fresh fruits and vegetables we grow here on our own farm specialized in greenhouse cultivation. I am confident that not only you but also your customers will be satisfied with the produce provided by our farm.

The area in which your shop is located is quite new to us, so we have high expectations about entering a new market with our quality produce. However, there is an issue with the delivery service based in Chichester we currently use, since they do not provide service to Eastbourne.

Green Life Grocery Mart
New Additions This Week!

Produce from Dereck Family Farm   April 27

Dear Customers,

We are delighted to inform you that we have the newest additions in the fresh produce section. There has been high demand among our patrons for local produce which has just been freshly harvested. Dereck Family Farm, located just a couple of hours from here, in Brighton will fully satisfy our customers' needs.

√ white radish (bunch)
√ carrots
√ lettuces and cabbages
√ berries (raspberries, blueberries)
√ courgettes

In the summer, a wider range of fruits from Sunny Field Orchard in Portsmouth will be carried. If there is any question you would like to inquire about, please do not hesitate.

Order Form
Dereck Family Farm

Name	Green Life Grocery Mart
Date of order	April 30
Arrival Date	May 4

Details of order:
Repeat the same order as last week's with some changes below.
- Lettuces and cabbages needed this week
- Rather than a bunch of radishes in a bag, please ship them in a crate.
(as shown in your brochure)

---

08. According to the notice, what is suggested about Dereck Family Farm produce?
(A) It is scheduled to be available from summer.
(B) It is going to be sold at reduced rates.
(C) It is cultivated relatively close to the grocery mart.
(D) It is much cheaper than that of other farms.

08번 문제 풀이 순서

STEP 1 According to the notice에서 두 번째 지문에 답이 있다는 것을 알 수 있다.

STEP 2 키워드는 Dereck Family Farm produce이다.

STEP 3 what is suggested와 같이 사실인 것을 찾는 문제는 보기를 먼저 정리하고 본문에서 키워드들을 검색해야 한다.

(A) summer
(B) reduced rates
(C) relatively close
(D) much cheaper

키워드

마트에서 고객에게 공지하는 내용

Green Life Grocery Mart
New Additions This Week!

Produce from Dereck Family Farm   April 27

Dear Customers,

We are delighted to inform you that we have the newest additions in the fresh produce section. There has been high demand among our patrons for local produce which has just been freshly harvested. <u>Dereck Family Farm, **located just a couple of hours** from here</u>, in Brighton will fully satisfy our customers' needs.

(C) relatively close
즉, just를 통해서 멀지 않고 비교적 가깝다는 의미를 나타낸다.

√ white radish (bunch)
√ carrots
√ lettuces and cabbages
√ berries (raspberries, blueberries)
√ courgettes

<u>In the **summer**, a wider range of fruits **from Sunny Field Orchard** in Portsmouth will be carried.</u> If there is any question you would like to inquire about, please do not hesitate.

(A) 여름에 대한 언급이 있지만 from Sunny Field Orchard이기 때문에 다른 농장이다.

STEP 4 (A) It is scheduled to be available from summer. [다른 농장에 대한 언급]
(B) It is going to be sold ~~at reduced rates~~. [가격 언급 없음]
(C) It is cultivated relatively close to the grocery mart.
(D) It is much ~~cheaper~~ than that of other farms. [가격 언급 없음]

3-07 문제가 주는 힌트나 지문 내에 답에 영향을 주는 모든 요소들을 이용한다.

① 시간을 의미하는 연결 키워드는 지문들의 작성 시기나 날짜, 일정 등을 따져야 한다.

시험에 이렇게 나온다

Questions 06-10 refer to the following e-mail, notice, and order form.

To: Edwin Mendoza
From: Clifford Mason
Subject: Delivery Company
Date: April 1

Hello Mr. Mendoza,

Thank you for signing up for consignment sale of the various fresh fruits and vegetables we grow here on our own farm specialized in greenhouse cultivation. I am confident that not only you but also your customers will be satisfied with the produce provided by our farm.

Green Life Grocery Mart
New Additions This Week!

Produce from Dereck Family Farm   April 27

Dear Customers,

We are delighted to inform you that we have the newest additions in the fresh produce section. There has been high demand among our patrons for local produce which has just been freshly harvested. Dereck Family Farm, located just a couple of hours from here, in Brighton will fully satisfy our customers' needs.

√ white radish (bunch)
√ carrots
√ lettuces and cabbages
√ berries (raspberries, blueberries)
√ courgettes

In the summer, a wider range of fruits from Sunny Field Orchard in Portsmouth will be carried. If there is any question you would like to inquire about, please do not hesitate.

Order Form
Dereck Family Farm

Name	Green Life Grocery Mart
Date of order	April 30
Arrival Date	May 4

Details of order:
Repeat the same order as last week's with some changes below.
- Lettuces and cabbages needed this week
- Rather than a bunch of radishes in a bag, please ship them in a crate.
(as shown in your brochure)

PS. Regarding the new shipping company, Cecil Shipping, they are quite good. The items were in good condition, the delivery people were polite and very kind, and not to mention the truck with produce we ordered arrived on time.

Name: Edwin Mendoza Purchasing Manager
Signature: *Edwin Mendoza*

---

09. What will Green Life Grocery Mart probably receive on May 4?
(A) Cucumbers   (B) Lettuces
(C) Cabbages   (D) Carrots

09번 문제 풀이 순서

STEP 1 품목이 나오는 문서는 두 번째와 세 번째 문서이다.
STEP 2 키워드가 May 4이기 때문에 세 번째 문서를 먼저 확인한다.

Green Life Grocery Mart
New Additions This Week!

〔마트에서 고객에게 공지하는 내용〕

Produce from Dereck Family Farm   April 27

Dear Customers,
We are delighted to inform you that we have the newest additions in the fresh produce section. There has been high demand among our patrons for local produce which has just been freshly harvested. Dereck Family Farm, located just a couple of hours from here, in Brighton will fully satisfy our customers' needs.

- √ white radish (bunch)
- √ carrots (D)
- √ lettuces and cabbages (B), (C)
- √ berries (raspberries, blueberries)
- √ courgettes

❸ 지난주 물품

In the summer, a wider range of fruits from Sunny Field Orchard in Portsmouth will be carried. If there is any question you would like to inquire about, please do not hesitate.

---

❷ 지난주 주문과 똑같은 내용이지만 with some changes below라고 했기 때문에 지난주 물품들을 먼저 확인해야 한다.

Order Form
Dereck Family Farm

〔마트에서 농장으로 보내는 주문서〕

Name	Green Life Grocery Mart
Date of order	April 30
Arrival Date	**May 4**

❶ 키워드 May 4

Details of order:
Repeat the same order as **last week's** with some changes below.
- Lettuces and cabbages needed this week
- Rather than a bunch of radishes in a bag, please ship them in a crate. (as shown in your brochure)

❹ 변경 사항 확인

PS. Regarding the new shipping company, Cecil Shipping, they are quite good. The items were in good condition, the delivery people were polite and very kind, and not to mention the truck with produce we ordered arrived on time.

Name: Edwin Mendoza Purchasing Manager
Signature: *Edwin Mendoza*

STEP 3
(A) ~~Cucumbers~~ [언급 없음]
(B) Lettuces
(C) Cabbages
(D) Carrots

세 번째 지문에서 lettuces와 cabbages는 이번 주에 필요한 것이라고 했으므로 May 4에 받는 물품이 아니다.

세 번째 문서의 변경 사항에 들어 있지 않으면서도 last week's order의 내용에 있는 것은 보기 중에 carrots이다. 따라서 정답은 (D)이다.

한 단어로만 답을 찾으려 하지 말고 구체적인 정보들을 모아서 포괄적인 답을 찾는다.

① 구체적인 정답 결정 단어들을 포괄할 수 있는 표현이 답이 된다.

시험에 이렇게 나온다

Questions 06-10 refer to the following e-mail, notice, and order form.

To: Edwin Mendoza
From: Clifford Mason
Subject: Delivery Company
Date: April 1

Hello Mr. Mendoza,

Thank you for signing up for consignment sale of the various fresh fruits and vegetables we grow here on our own farm specialized in greenhouse cultivation. I am confident that not only you but also your customers will be satisfied with the produce provided by our farm.

Green Life Grocery Mart
New Additions This Week!

Produce from Dereck Family Farm   April 27

Dear Customers,

We are delighted to inform you that we have the newest additions in the fresh produce section. There has been high demand among our patrons for local produce which has just been freshly harvested. Dereck Family Farm, located just a couple of hours from here, in Brighton will fully satisfy our customers' needs.

√ white radish (bunch)
√ carrots
√ lettuces and cabbages
√ berries (raspberries, blueberries)
√ courgettes

Order Form
Dereck Family Farm

Name	Green Life Grocery Mart
Date of order	April 30
Arrival Date	May 4

Details of order:
Repeat the same order as last week's with some changes below.
- Lettuces and cabbages needed this week
- Rather than a bunch of radishes in a bag, please ship them in a crate.
(as shown in your brochure)

PS. Regarding the new shipping company, Cecil Shipping, they are quite good. The items were in good condition, the delivery people were polite and very kind, and not to mention the truck with produce we ordered arrived on time.

Name: Edwin Mendoza Purchasing Manager
Signature: *Edwin Mendoza*

---

10. What does Mr. Mendoza indicate in the order form?

(A) Some produce he ordered did not arrived in time.
(B) The berries are popular among customers.
(C) He tends to care about the packing method.
(D) The new delivery people from Cecil Shipping were not courteous.

10번 문제 풀이 순서

STEP 1 키워드는 Mr. Mendoza / in the order form이므로 마지막 지문에서 답을 찾을 수 있다.
언급된 것이나 사실인 것을 찾는 문제 중에 특정 키워드가 없는 경우에는 답의 위치를 쉽게 잡아낼 수가 없다.

STEP 2 문제 중에 특정 사람 이름이 등장하고 그 사람이 언급한 것이나 요구한 것을 찾는 문제는 그 사람이 작성한 문서에 답이 있다.

STEP 3 마지막 문제의 답은 마지막 문서에 나오거나 마지막 문서에서 검색을 시작하여 다른 문서와 연계하여 풀어야 한다.

Order Form
Dereck Family Farm

Name	Green Life Grocery Mart
Date of order	April 30
Arrival Date	May 4

Details of order:
Repeat the same order as last week's with some changes below.
- Lettuces and cabbages needed this week
- Rather than a bunch of radishes **in a bag**, please ship them **in a crate**.
(as shown in your brochure)

(C) packing method

PS. Regarding the new shipping company, **Cecil Shipping, they are** quite good. The items were in good condition, the **delivery people** were polite and very kind, and not to mention the truck with produce we ordered arrived on time.

Name: Edwin Mendoza Purchasing Manager
Signature: *Edwin Mendoza*

(A) Some produce he ordered did ~~not arrived in time~~. [제시간에 도착했음]
(B) ~~The berries are popular~~ among customers. [berries에 대한 언급 없음]
(C) He tends to care about the **packing method.**
(D) The new delivery people from Cecil Shipping were ~~not courteous~~. [친절하다고 언급되어 있음]

STEP 4 본문의 구체적인 정보들을 모아보면 (C)가 답이라는 것을 알 수 있다.
in a bag / in a crate = packing method

문제 중에 키워드가 있으면 해당 지문에서 검색된 키워드 위주로 정보를 연결한다.

① 키워드를 중심으로 지문을 검색하고 paraphrasing 여부나 한 단어 오류 등에 주의해서 답을 선택한다.

시험에 이렇게 나온다

Questions 11-15 refer to the following coupon, memo, and e-mail.

Money-saving Coupon
Good for one day only

END-OF-SEASON SALE
Valid on Saturday, June 19

- One discounted clearance product: Up to 50% off
- One regular-priced product: Up to 30% off

All of Antton Lilia Co's products are available including jackets, T-shirts, coats, pants, accessories, footwear, and more. Business hours will be extended for the event from 9:30 A.M. to 10:00 P.M.

Other promotional offers cannot be applied with this coupon. Althea, Estela, or Alyce brands are not subject to this special offer. A customer can use only one coupon. Refunds, exchanges, and store credits are not applicable on the clearance products.

Antton Lilia Co.

To: All Antton Lilia staff members
From: Mary Smith, Sales Manager
Date: June 18

Re: Upcoming sale event

We have an urgent issue which requires our immediate attention. The coupon printed in The Noreen's Daily neglected to mention that products available under the brand name Yesenia are not included in the sale on regularly priced products. Thus, please give our apologies, explaining the matter, to anyone trying to buy a product of this specific brand. But, don't forget to inform them that as a courtesy, the discount will nevertheless be honored.

From: <cusomercare@anttonlilia.co.us>
To: Jerome Warren <troynave@supermail.co.us>
Date: June 19, 4:43 P.M.
Subject: Receipt for your purchase

Dear Ms. Warren,

Upon your request, the following is the digital receipt from Antton Lilia Co.

Item	Price	Quantity
Marvin leather jacket Promotional discount 50% **Price of the item**	$350.00 -$175.00 **$175.00**	1

11. In the coupon, what was suggested about the event on June 19?
(A) The business will stay open longer hours.
(B) Customers will be able to get extra coupons at the register.
(C) Returned items will be fully refunded.
(D) New shipments will be delivered to the shop.

11번 문제 풀이 순서

STEP 1   In the coupon이라고 문제가 지칭했기 때문에 답은 첫 번째 문서에 있다.

STEP 2   문제 중에 키워드는 event/June 19이다.

STEP 3   보기의 키워드들을 정리한다.
              (A) open longer hours
              (B) Customers / extra coupons
              (C) fully refunded
              (D) New shipments / to the shop

Money-saving Coupon
Good for one day only

END-OF-SEASON SALE
Valid on Saturday, **June 19**   ❶ 키워드: June 19

- One discounted clearance product: Up to 50% off
- One regular-priced product: Up to 30% off

All of Antton Lilia Co's products are available including jackets, T-shirts, coats, pants, accessories, footwear, and more. **Business hours will be extended** for the event from 9:30 A.M. to 10:00 P.M.

(A) open longer hours

Other promotional offers cannot be applied with **this coupon**. Althea, Estela, or Alyce brands are not subject to this special offer. A customer can use only one coupon. **Refunds**, exchanges, and store credits are **not applicable** on the clearance products.

(A) The business will stay open longer hours.
(B) Customers will be able to get ~~extra~~ coupons at the ~~register~~.
    [coupon은 언급되어 있지만 extra/register는 언급이 없음]
(C) Returned items will ~~be fully refunded~~. [본문에서는 환급 불가라고 언급됨]
(D) ~~New shipments~~ will be delivered to the shop. [신제품 입고에 대한 언급이 없음]

특정 명사가 지칭하는 대상을 확인하라.

① 해당 키워드를 찾고 문서 안에서 해당하는 대상이 누구인지를 확인해야 한다.

시험에 이렇게 나온다

Questions 11-15 refer to the following coupon, memo, and e-mail.

Money-saving Coupon
Good for one day only

END-OF-SEASON SALE
Valid on Saturday, June 19

- One discounted clearance product: Up to 50% off
- One regular-priced product: Up to 30% off

All of Antton Lilia Co's products are available including jackets, T-shirts, coats, pants, accessories, footwear, and more. Business hours will be extended for the event from 9:30 A.M. to 10:00 P.M.

Other promotional offers cannot be applied with this coupon. Althea, Estela, or Alyce brands are not subject to this special offer. A customer can use only one coupon.

To: All Antton Lilia staff members
From: Mary Smith, Sales Manager
Date: June 18

Re: Upcoming sale event

We have an urgent issue which requires our immediate attention. The coupon printed in The Noreen's Daily neglected to mention that products available under the brand name Yesenia are not included in the sale on regularly priced products. Thus, please give our apologies, explaining the matter, to anyone trying to buy a product of this specific brand. But, don't forget to inform them that as a courtesy, the discount will nevertheless be honored.

In addition, three more sales representatives will be needed from 2:00 P.M to 8:00 P.M. because there may be more shoppers than usual coming after seeing the promotion in the media. So, please inform me as soon as possible if you would like to work for extra hours in the afternoon and evening on the day.

Thank you in advance.

From: <cusomercare@anttonlilia.co.us>
To: Jerome Warren <troynave@supermail.co.us>
Date: June 19, 4:43 P.M.
Subject: Receipt for your purchase

Dear Ms. Warren,

Upon your request, the following is the digital receipt from Antton Lilia Co.

---

12. According to the memo, what are sales representatives asked to do?

(A) Ask customers to join a membership
(B) Encourage customers to complete a survey
(C) Notify their willingness to work for an additional shift
(D) Start work earlier than usual

12번 문제 풀이 순서

STEP 1 According to the memo라고 했기 때문에 두 번째 문서에 답이 있다.

STEP 2 키워드인 Sales representatives는 두 번째 문서(memo)의 수신자이다.
Sales manager가 물건 판매 시에 지침을 전달하고 3명의 sales representative가 더 필요할 것이라는 내용에서 확인할 수 있다.

STEP 3 요구/권유 등의 정보는 문서의 하단부에 If, Please, You should, I want you, 명령문 등의 표현에 나온다.

STEP 4 본문에서 요구 사항은 다음의 세 가지이다.
① 이 특정 브랜드의 제품을 구매하려는 고객님들에게 문제를 설명하고 사과의 말씀을 드리세요.
② 할인을 받을 수 있음을 예의상 고객님들에게 잊지 말고 알려주세요.
③ 추가로 근무를 하고 싶다면 가능한 빨리 저에게 알려주세요.

To: All Antton Lilia staff members
From: Mary Smith, Sales Manager
Date: June 18
Re: Upcoming sale event

We have an urgent issue which requires our immediate attention. The coupon printed in The Noreen's Daily neglected to mention that products available under the brand name Yesenia are not included in the sale on regularly priced products. ① **Thus, please give our apologies, explaining the matter, to anyone trying to buy a product of this specific brand.** But, ② **don't forget to inform them that as a courtesy, the discount will nevertheless be honored.**

In addition, three more sales representatives will be needed from 2:00 P.M. to 8:00 P.M. because there may be more shoppers than usual coming after seeing the promotion in the media.
③ **So, please inform me as soon as possible if you would like to work for extra hours in the afternoon and evening on the day.**

Thank you in advance.

STEP 5 이 중에 보기와 일치하는 내용은 ③이다.

(A) Ask customers to join a ~~membership~~
(B) Encourage customers to ~~complete a survey~~
(C) Notify their willingness to work for an additional shift
(D) Start work ~~earlier~~ than usual

STEP 6 please inform me ~에서 me는 이 문서를 작성한 사람 즉, From에 해당한다.
Mary Smith, Sales Manager에게 일을 하겠다는 결정을 알려달라는 의미이다.

차액/변경 사항들은 original과 new로 정보를 구분해 두어야 한다.

① 주로 originally, previously, formerly 등의 부사들과 자주 출제되며, 변경되는 사항과 문서간의 연결 키워드를 확인해야 한다.

시험에 이렇게 나온다

Questions 11-15 refer to the following coupon, memo, and e-mail.

Money-saving Coupon
Good for one day only

END-OF-SEASON SALE
Valid on Saturday, June 19

Antton Lilia Co.
To: All Antton Lilia staff members
From: Mary Smith, Sales Manager
Date: June 18

Re: Upcoming sale event

We have an urgent issue which requires our immediate attention. The coupon printed in The Noreen's Daily neglected to mention that products available under the brand name Yesenia are not included in the sale on regularly priced products. Thus, please give our apologies, explaining the matter, to anyone trying to buy a product of this specific brand. But, don't forget to inform them that as a courtesy, the discount will nevertheless be honored.

In addition, three more sales representatives will be needed from 2:00 P.M to 8:00 P.M. because there may be more shoppers than usual coming after seeing the promotion in the media. So, please inform me as soon as possible if you would like to work for extra hours in the afternoon and evening on the day.

From: <cusomercare@anttonlilia.co.us>
To: Jerome Warren <troynave@supermail.co.us>
Date: June 19, 4:43 P.M.
Subject: Receipt for your purchase

Dear Ms. Warren,

Upon your request, the following is the digital receipt from Antton Lilia Co.

Item	Price	Quantity
Marvin leather jacket Promotional discount 50% **Price of the item**	$350.00 -$175.00 **$175.00**	1
Yesenia winter boots Promotional discount 30% **Price of the item**	$120.00 -$36.00 **$84.00**	1
Lance fur scarf	$28.00	1
Total Total saved	$287.00 $211.00	

Amount charged to JeelBR credit card   XXXX XXXX XXXX 4032
Thanks for your purchase at Antton Lilia.

13. How much was originally charged to Ms. Warren's credit card?
(A) $323.00   (B) $287.00
(C) $175.00   (D) $295.00

13번 문제 풀이 순서

STEP 1 할인이나 혜택의 자격에 대해서는 두 문서를 연계하여 풀어야 하는 문제가 자주 등장한다.

STEP 2 특정한 사람이 지불해야 하는 금액은 그 사람의 조건과 다른 문서에서 제시되는 기준을 비교해야 답을 찾을 수 있다.

STEP 3 문제 중에 originally나 new 등의 표현이 나온다면 변경이 있었다는 뜻이기 때문에 과거의 정보와 현재/미래의 정보를 둘 다 찾아야 한다.

STEP 4 How much was originally charged ~?는 질문이 과거형이기 때문에 원래 청구되었어야 하는 금액이 현재의 가격($ 287.00)이 아님을 의미한다.

To: All Antton Lilia staff members
From: Mary Smith, Sales Manager

– 중략 –

> 매니저가 직원들에게 할인 공지가 잘못되었다고 전달하는 공지

We have an urgent issue which requires our immediate attention. The coupon printed in The Noreen's Daily neglected to mention that products available under the brand name **Yesenia are not included in the sale** on regularly priced products. Thus, please give our apologies, explaining the matter, to anyone trying to buy a product of this specific brand. But, don't forget to inform them that as a courtesy, the discount will nevertheless be honored.

Dear **Ms. Warren**,

> Ms. Warren에게 정정된 영수증을 보내는 이메일

Upon your request, the following is the digital receipt from Antton Lilia Co.

Item	Price	Quantity
Marvin leather jacket Promotional discount 50% **Price of the item**	$350.00 -$175.00 **$175.00**	1
Yesenia winter boots Promotional discount 30% **Price of the item**	$120.00 -$36.00 **$84.00**	1
Lance fur scarf	$28.00	1
Total Total saved	**$287.00** $211.00	

Amount charged to JeelBR credit card   XXXX XXXX XXXX 4032

STEP 5 두 번째 문서에서 Yesenia 브랜드 제품이 정상 가격 제품 할인에 포함되지 않는다고 했다.

따라서 원래 가격에 Yesenia winter boots는 할인이 되지 않은 가격이 적용되었어야 한다. 따라서 총 청구 금액은 $175 + $120(할인 미적용 금액) + $28 = $323.00이 된다.

할인의 조건/자격은 빈출 연계 문제이다. 문제의 키워드 옆에 답이 없다면 또 다른 키워드를 남긴다.

① 해당 지문에서 등장하는 키워드는 다른 문서에서 등장하는 또 다른 키워드가 있다. 다중 지문 문제를 풀 때는 문서간의 관계를 염두에 두고 푸는 것이 좋다.

시험에 이렇게 나온다

Questions 11-15 refer to the following coupon, memo, and e-mail.

Money-saving Coupon
Good for one day only

END-OF-SEASON SALE
Valid on Saturday, June 19

To: All Antton Lilia staff members
From: Mary Smith, Sales Manager
Date: June 18
Re: Upcoming sale event

We have an urgent issue which requires our immediate attention. The coupon printed in The Noreen's Daily neglected to mention that products available under the brand name Yesenia are not included in the sale on regularly priced products. Thus, please give our apologies, explaining the matter, to anyone trying to buy a product of this specific brand. But, don't forget to inform them that as a courtesy, the discount will nevertheless be honored.

In addition, three more sales representatives will be needed from 2:00 P.M to 8:00 P.M. because there may be more shoppers than usual coming after seeing the promotion in the media. So, please inform me as soon as possible if you would like to work for extra hours in the afternoon and evening on the day.

From: <cusomercare@anttonlilia.co.us>
To: Jerome Warren <troynave@supermail.co.us>
Date: June 19, 4:43 P.M.
Subject: Receipt for your purchase

Dear Ms. Warren,

Upon your request, the following is the digital receipt from Antton Lilia Co.

Item	Price	Quantity
Marvin leather jacket Promotional discount 50% **Price of the item**	$350.00 -$175.00 **$175.00**	1
Yesenia winter boots Promotional discount 30% **Price of the item**	$120.00 -$36.00 **$84.00**	1
Lance fur scarf	$28.00	1
Total Total saved	$287.00 $211.00	

Amount charged to JeelBR credit card   XXXX XXXX XXXX 4032
Thanks for your purchase at Antton Lilia.

---

14. What did Ms. Warren probably NOT receive when she bought the winter boots?

(A) An explanation   (B) An apology
(C) A gift certificate   (D) A discount

14번 문제 풀이 순서

STEP 1   Ms. Warren과 winter boots라는 키워드가 언급된 것은 마지막 지문이고 보기의 내용이 있는 것은 두 번째 지문이다.

STEP 2   문제의 키워드와 보기가 각각 다른 문서에 있을 때에는 두 문서를 연계하는 문제이다.

STEP 3   winter boots라는 단어 근처에는 답이 없고 또 다른 키워드인 Yesenia가 있다.

To: All Antton Lilia staff members
From: Mary Smith, Sales Manager
Date: June 18
Re: Upcoming sale event

We have an urgent issue which requires our immediate attention. The coupon printed in The Noreen's Daily neglected to mention that products available under the brand name ③ **Yesenia** are not included in the sale on regularly priced products. Thus, please give our (B) **apologies**, (A) **explaining** the matter, to anyone trying to buy a product of this specific brand. But, don't forget to inform them that as a courtesy, (D) **the discount** will nevertheless be honored.

In addition, three more sales representatives will be needed from 2:00 P.M to 8:00 P.M. because there may be more shoppers than usual coming after seeing the promotion in the media. So, please inform me as soon as possible if you would like to work for extra hours in the afternoon and evening on the day.

Dear ① **Ms. Warren**,

Upon your request, the following is the digital receipt from Antton Lilia Co.

Item	Price	Quantity
Marvin leather jacket Promotional discount 50% **Price of the item**	$350.00 -$175.00 **$175.00**	1
Yesenia ① **winter boots** Promotional discount 30% **Price of the item**		1
Lance fur scarf	$28.00	1
Total Total saved	$287.00 $211.00	
Amount charged to JeelBR credit card	XXXX XXXX XXXX 4032	

❶ 키워드 Ms. Warren / winter boots

❷ 키워드 옆에 답이 없다. 또 다른 키워드는 Yesenia이다.

STEP 4   보기 중에 두 번째 문서에서 언급되지 않은 것은 (C) A gift certificate이다.

특정인과 관련한 사실 확인 문제는 해당 지문과 연계 지문을 동시에 봐야 한다.

① 세 지문 중에 하나의 지문에만 언급되는 사람과 관련한 사실 확인 문제는 보기의 키워드를 통해 위치를 확인해야 한다. 이때 해당 지문뿐만 아니라 연계 지문의 내용이 보기의 키워드로 등장한다.

시험에 이렇게 나온다

Questions 11-15 refer to the following coupon, memo, and e-mail.

Money-saving Coupon
Good for one day only

END-OF-SEASON SALE
Valid on Saturday, June 19

- One discounted clearance product: Up to 50% off
- One regular-priced product: Up to 30% off

All of Antton Lilia Co's products are available including jackets, T-shirts, coats, pants, accessories, footwear, and more. Business hours will be extended for the event from 9:30 A.M. to 10:00 P.M.

Other promotional offers cannot be applied with this coupon. Althea, Estela, or Alyce brands are not subject to this special offer. A customer can use only one coupon. Refunds, exchanges, and store credits are not applicable on the clearance products.

To: All Antton Lilia staff members
From: Mary Smith, Sales Manager

– 중략 –

We have an urgent issue which requires our immediate attention.

From: <cusomercare@anttonlilia.co.us>
To: Jerome Warren <troynave@supermail.co.us>
Date: June 19, 4:43 P.M.
Subject: Receipt for your purchase

Dear Ms. Warren,

Upon your request, the following is the digital receipt from Antton Lilia Co.

Item	Price	Quantity
Marvin leather jacket Promotional discount 50% **Price of the item**	$350.00 -$175.00 **$175.00**	1
Yesenia winter boots Promotional discount 30% **Price of the item**	$120.00 -$36.00 **$84.00**	1
Lance fur scarf	$28.00	1
Total Total saved	$287.00 $211.00	

Amount charged to JeelBR credit card   XXXX XXXX XXXX 4032
Thanks for your purchase at Antton Lilia.

---

15. What is indicated about Ms. Warren?
(A) She paid for her items with cash.
(B) She is a regular shopper at Antton Lilia.
(C) She bought a regular-priced product.
(D) She recently started her new job.

15번 문제 풀이 순서

STEP 1 마지막 문제는 대부분 마지막 지문에 답이 있거나 마지막 지문에서 시작하여 다른 문서로 연계하여 해결한다.

From: <cusomercare@anttonlilia.co.us>
To: Jerome Warren <troynave@supermail.co.us>

— 중략 —

Dear Ms. Warren,

Upon your request, the following is the digital receipt from Antton Lilia Co.

Item	Price	Quantity
Marvin leather jacket Promotional discount 50% **Price of the item**	$350.00 -$175.00 **$175.00**	1
(C) Yesenia winter boots ① **Promotional discount 30%** **Price of the item**	$120.00 -$36.00 **$84.00**	1
Lance fur scarf	$28.00	1
Total Total saved	$287.00 $211.00	

Amount charged to JeelBR credit card   XXXX XXXX XXXX 4032
Thanks for your purchase at Antton Lilia.

STEP 2 마지막 문서에서 찾을 수 있는 오답들을 먼저 소거한다.

(A) She paid for her items ~~with cash~~.
(B) She is a ~~regular shopper~~ at Antton Lilia. [단골 고객이라는 언급은 없음]
(C) She bought a regular-priced product.
(D) She recently started her new job. [언급 없음]

STEP 3 마지막 지문에 있는 항목들은 Ms. Warren이 구입한 물건들과 가격들이다.
물건 항목들과 가격들에 대한 정보는 첫 번째 지문에 있다.

Money-saving Coupon
Good for one day only

END-OF-SEASON SALE

Valid on Saturday, June 19

- One **discounted clearance product: Up to 50% off**
- ② **One regular-priced product: Up to 30% off**

All of Antton ~~~~~~~~~~~~~~~~~~~~~~~~~~~~~~ rts, coats, pants, accessories, footwear, and ~~~~~~~~~~~~~~~~~~~~~~~~~~~~~ om 9:30 A.M. to 10:00 P.M.

> Yesenia winter boots를 30% 할인 받았고 Lance fur scarf를 정가에 구매했다는 것은 하나의 regular-priced product을 할인을 받았고 하나는 정상 가격에 구매했다는 것이다.

STEP 4 지문의 내용 중에 단골이라거나 새로운 일을 시작했다는 표현은 없다. 따라서 (C)가 답이 된다.

FINAL TEST
실전 모의고사

Questions 147-148 refer to the following advertisement.

Drop By and Enjoy

Genevieve Field

- More than 30 exciting outdoor rides
- More than 40 enjoyable games and activities with prizes
- A special indoor area only for children under 7
- The province's most extensive outdoor food and drink stands
- Fantastic music events including parades all year around

Genevieve Field is running throughout the year, Tuesday through Saturday. Admission passes are available online or at the main gate. Prices for groups can be applicable to parties of 10 or more.

147. What is being promoted?
(A) A food and beverage fair
(B) An amusement park
(C) A charitable activity
(D) A music performance

148. Who most likely is able to get a discount?
(A) Those buying admission passes online
(B) Those coming with kids under seven years old
(C) Those purchasing tickets as a group
(D) Those visiting more than three times a year

Questions 149-150 refer to the following webpage.

Business Answers

This is what we can provide

- Personalized software programs and on-site hardware including periodic care service (six-month contract required)
- Regular management of applications and databases including upgrades
- Data backup and recovery service as well as data storage
- A 24-hour customer service center for offering resolution of any issues without delay
- Our exclusive Business Remote Overseeing (BRO) system (access rights)

For our corporate clients like you

- Access to state of the art technology
- The less use, the less pay; thus cutting hardware and software expenses
- An ongoing streamlined billing procedure that can be paid up-front

149. What is one of the services provided by Business Answers?
(A) Comments on legal issues
(B) Accounting service
(C) Software improvement
(D) Building repair work

150. What is indicated about ongoing maintenance of computer equipment?
(A) It is conducted by external experts.
(B) It is intended for outdated computer system.
(C) It has to be contracted for at least six months.
(D) It is available only to new clients.

Questions 151-152 refer to the following letter.

Tim Moreno
4944 Westminster Avenue
Goreno Town, WC 99812

July 18

Neil O'Brien
223 Candice West Road
Estelle, RO 11212

Dear Mr. O'Brien

I would like to express my sincere gratitude to you for writing a professional reference letter for me. The reference letter supporting my application surely helped me a lot to be offered the job as business news analyst at TTM Station. The experience acquired while I worked with you, particularly through analyzing national and international economic trends, made me well prepared for this position. It would be interesting for you to know that my job here involves not only analyzing but also reporting business data in the new program. Again, I really appreciate your help.

Yours sincerely,
Tim Moreno
Tim Moreno

151. What is the purpose of Mr. Moreno's letter?
(A) To say how grateful he is
(B) To offer an employment opportunity
(C) To ask for economic analysis
(D) To make some information clear

152. What type of business is Mr. Moreno working for?
(A) A business school
(B) An employment agency
(C) A broadcasting company
(D) A business consulting organization

Questions 153-155 refer to following e-mail.

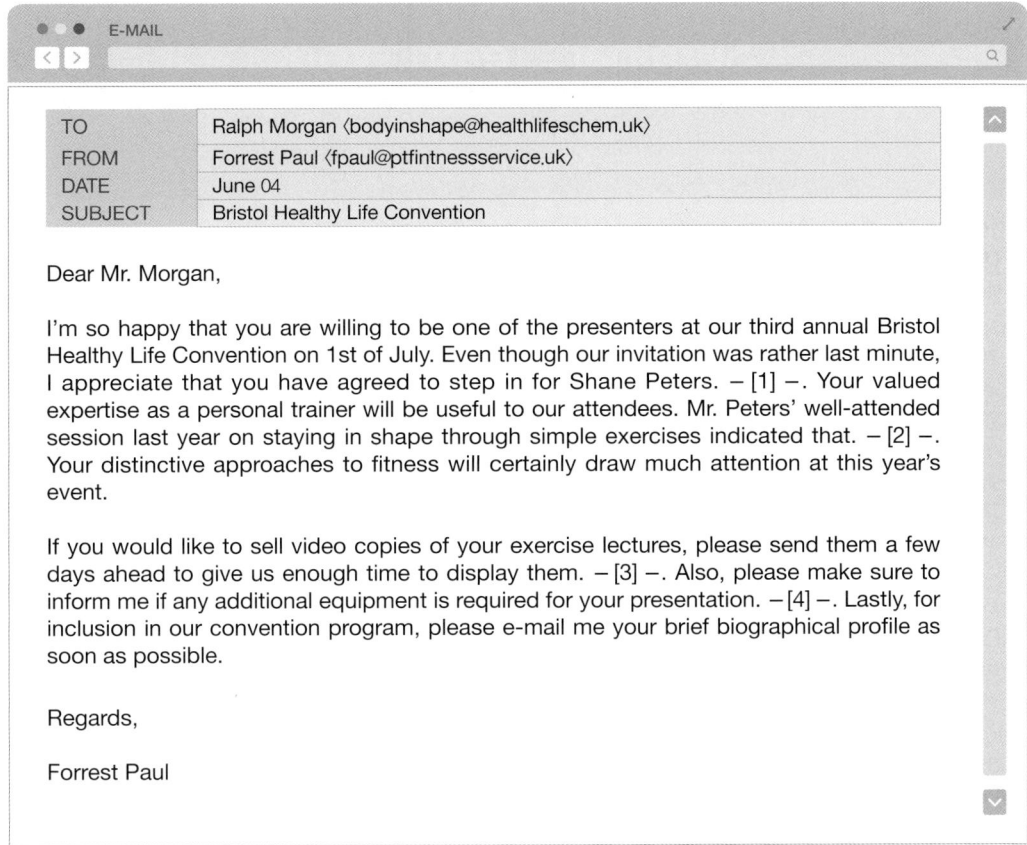

TO	Ralph Morgan <bodyinshape@healthlifeschem.uk>
FROM	Forrest Paul <fpaul@ptfintnessservice.uk>
DATE	June 04
SUBJECT	Bristol Healthy Life Convention

Dear Mr. Morgan,

I'm so happy that you are willing to be one of the presenters at our third annual Bristol Healthy Life Convention on 1st of July. Even though our invitation was rather last minute, I appreciate that you have agreed to step in for Shane Peters. – [1] –. Your valued expertise as a personal trainer will be useful to our attendees. Mr. Peters' well-attended session last year on staying in shape through simple exercises indicated that. – [2] –. Your distinctive approaches to fitness will certainly draw much attention at this year's event.

If you would like to sell video copies of your exercise lectures, please send them a few days ahead to give us enough time to display them. – [3] –. Also, please make sure to inform me if any additional equipment is required for your presentation. – [4] –. Lastly, for inclusion in our convention program, please e-mail me your brief biographical profile as soon as possible.

Regards,

Forrest Paul

153. What is indicated about Mr. Peters?
(A) He is studying to be a personal trainer.
(B) He has released an exercise video.
(C) He is a coworker of Mr. Morgan.
(D) He spoke at the convention last year.

154. What is the main reason Mr. Paul sent the e-mail?
(A) To ask Mr. Morgan to come to an event
(B) To request some personal information
(C) To solicit a recommendation from Mr. Morgan
(D) To require a time slot to be revised

155. In which of the positions marked [1], [2], [3], and [4] does the following sentence best belong?

"If you need it, there is visual equipment available to use such as a projector."

(A) [1]
(B) [2]
(C) [3]
(D) [4]

Questions 156-158 refer to the following agenda.

Seminar: Team Work
May 21
10:00 A.M. to 5:00 P.M.
$35 per person

10:00 A.M.: Getting Started
Deal with vital topics small businesses inevitably encounter. Not only set long and short term goals for your business, but also identify areas that need to be improved.

10:30 A.M.: Creating Fellowship
Get advice on ways to help foster an ambiance of staff members working together rather than competing with each other at all levels in your company.

12:10 P.M.: Break for Lunch
There are two options of complimentary entrees for participants: shrimp sandwiches with potato chips or corned-beef salad with mashed potatoes.

1:20 P.M.: Group Activities
Exercises for building good relationships, and cooperating with each other in both small and large teams. Work as a group with your teammates in order to create an ideal plan that can be used for your businesses.

3:30 P.M.: Assessment Techniques
Learn about methods for determining whether exercises for building a good relationship, and cooperating with each other result in the intended effect by setting clear criteria. Learn how common office software programs can be used to manage progress in your business.

156. For whom is the seminar most likely intended?
(A) Personnel experts
(B) Business reporters
(C) New staff at small businesses
(D) Owners of small companies

157. Which session deals with identifying objectives?
(A) Getting Started
(B) Creating Fellowship
(C) Group Activities
(D) Assessment Techniques

158. What is NOT suggested about the participants in the seminar?
(A) They may work as a team.
(B) They are offered a free lunch.
(C) They will learn new software.
(D) They need to pay a fee to attend.

Questions 159-160 refer to the following online chat discussion.

Jordan Walters 10:11 A.M.
I've never participated in an online training session before. The invitation e-mail I received indicates that I should click the Join button. Is that right?

Joel Woods 10:12 A.M.
Exactly! It will ask you to enter the access code: 2352525.

Jordan Walters 10:13 A.M.
Oh, dear. Maybe I did something wrong. It says "The code is not appropriate. Try again." Do I need to enter a different code?

Joel Woods 10:14 A.M.
I'd better check that for you.

Jordan Walters 10:15 A.M.
There might be a problem with the e-mail invitation I got.

Joel Woods 10:15 A.M.
No problem. I can give you a new access code. Please can you try 393910?

Jordan Walters 10:16 A.M.
Yeah, it does work.

Joel Woods 10:16 A.M.
That's good. Before you start, please make sure to click the mute button at the bottom of the screen on the first page of our training site to prevent any background noise from your side, but your computer speaker needs to be on so that you can hear the trainer.

159. At 10:15 A.M., what most likely does Mr. Woods mean when he says, "No problem"?
(A) He is impressed by Mr. Walters' knowledge.
(B) He has identified the cause of an issue.
(C) He is about to start a new system.
(D) He has been invited to an event by Mr. Walters.

160. What is suggested about Mr. Walters?
(A) He has recently purchased a new computer.
(B) He is not required to speak during the training.
(C) He does not have a proper computer speaker.
(D) He has accessed a wrong website.

Questions 161-163 refer to the following article.

Waiting for Your Insight: Survey of an Extra Shopping Place

An increasing number of Cotswolds residents' as well as many visitors' have expressed interest to town officials that there should be more shopping places. – [1] – Some have suggested constructing a third shopping mall in the next few years.

In order for town officials to learn the extent of the interest in an additional shopping place, a data-collection project has been scheduled to start on Tuesday, conducted by Anita Publicity Association, through the weekend when the current shopping areas in the town are normally overcrowded.

– [2] – Once the study is done, an updated receptive capacity of the current influx of visitors to the area will be provided so as to determine the feasibility of a new shopping mall construction project. – [3] –

"With the office and residential complex projects people in the area have seen over the past three years, the demand can be understood." the Planning Director anecdotally added. – [4] –

161. How many shopping malls are currently in Cotswolds?
(A) One
(B) Two
(C) Three
(D) Four

162. What is implied about the survey in the article?
(A) It will search for appropriate locations for a shopping mall.
(B) It will be led by Cotswolds' planning director.
(C) It will be filled out by Anita Publicity Association.
(D) It will identify the extent of the need for a shopping mall.

163. In which of the positions marked [1], [2], [3], and [4] does the following sentences best belong?

"However, hard data is needed to consider constructing another shopping mall."

(A) [1]
(B) [2]
(C) [3]
(D) [4]

Questions 164-167 refer to the following website.

Craig Moore
As Your View Matters

Over the past twenty five years, the Craig Moore Institution has been dedicated to collecting public opinions on various issues through polls. Based on telephone interviews, those living in specific polling areas, aged 18 years or older, are subject to all our polls. In order to give an equal opportunity of being contacted to everyone in the age group within a polling area, our own computer system chooses potential interviewees by randomly selecting contact information.

Please visit the Result of the New Polls page to see what people's general view is on contemporary issues in the world. Gathered results are released every week, and posted online to allow the public to access them. If you would like to look up the results of polls on a specific subject, see the Subject Direction page. If you intend to reproduce any graphics such as tables and charts designed by Craig Moore, go to the Permissions page which will provide you with an online form to fill in with information on where and how you are planning to use them. Usually, you will receive a response within a couple of days of submission.

164. The word "contemporary" In paragraph 2, line 2, is closest in meaning to
(A) trendy
(B) current
(C) habitual
(D) serious

165. What is indicated about poll respondents?
(A) They are intentionally selected.
(B) They are interviewed regularly.
(C) They are not interviewed in person.
(D) They are up to 18 years old.

166. What is NOT mentioned about the Craig Moore Institution?
(A) It updates its site regularly.
(B) It has its own computer software.
(C) It is looking for a new web designer.
(D) It permits people to use its data.

167. How can graphic information be used by the public?
(A) By sending a fax
(B) By making a phone call
(C) By submitting details in writing
(D) By leaving information online

Questions 168-171 refer to the following article.

Dawson City Welcomes Small Business Expert

Dawson City (June 11) – Franklin Willis, regarded as the "small business expert" by *Dawson City Chronicle*, has been invited as the keynote speaker at the fourth annual Dawson City Small Business Fair (DCSBF). The fair is scheduled to be held at the Dawson City Conference Center from July 1 through July 4. About 1,500 small business owners are expected to attend seminars and run their booths which can allow visitors to ask questions as well as collect information.

A DCSBF press release indicated that Mr. Willis will emphasize some of the tips covered in his popular book "Success Is Equal to Efforts" published a few months ago. Mr. Willis is confident that any new business scheme requires several key decisions to turn into a successful one. "Just creating goods you will sell won't make your business successful." Mr. Willis reflects his strong view in his book. "Creating goods people want to purchase is the key element. It is also a basic policy, and must be kept to succeed in business." Mr. Willis has been running his successful business in New York, in which he has lived with his family for the last 15 years.

"I was born and raised in Dawson City." Mr. Willis added. "I would like to help people in my home town live a successful life, so it is a good chance to do it by participating in the fair. Small business owners can find many outstanding opportunities to make their businesses prosper if they follow the important and clear directions I suggest, and these will definitely make many other small businesses successful."

Admission to the fair is $120. Tickets can be purchased through the fair's website at www.dawsoncityfair.com/gr.

168. What is the purpose of the article?
(A) To report a way to start a new small business
(B) To discuss new strategies to attract customers
(C) To announce an entrepreneur's visit to his home town
(D) To talk about the advantages of starting a small business

169. What is mentioned about Mr. Willis?
(A) He has led many seminars.
(B) He has published a book.
(C) He has won an award.
(D) He has never visited Dawson City.

170. What does Mr. Willis say is the key to success for entrepreneurs?
(A) Developing aggressive marketing strategies
(B) Obtaining merchandise that appeals to consumers
(C) Creating a way to make goods cost-effectively
(D) Having an outstanding manufacturing facility

171. Why does Mr. Willis wants to participate in the fair?
(A) To get some information for a report
(B) To hire highly qualified employees
(C) To improve his current business
(D) To help entrepreneurs in his hometown

Questions 172-175 refer to the following text message chain.

●●●○○

Eleanor Porter - 4 May, 11:15
Curtis, have you sent order #0022-B5 yet?
If you haven't, the client wanted us to add item #882-S1.

Curtis Ramos - 4 May, 11:18
That's a customized gold bracelet, right? The process for engraving a client's personalized message on an item normally needs at least 2 days.

Eleanor Porter - 4 May, 11:19
Is it possible to get it done more quickly? The client wants it sooner than that.

Curtis Ramos - 4 May, 11:21
I'd better talk with a person from the engraving division.

Curtis Ramos - 4 May, 11:23
Francies, could you do an urgent work on a bracelet? The model number is #882-S1, which is for order #0022-B5.

Francies Rojas - 4 May, 11:24
How soon does it need to be completed? Would a day be okay?

Eleanor Porter - 4 May, 11:25
Great, that will work. Thanks both of you for help!

172. What kind of products does the business carry?
(A) Packaging
(B) Jewelry
(C) Clothing
(D) Gravestones

173. What does the client ask to do?
(A) Get a refund
(B) Update an order
(C) Revise a shipping address
(D) Try a different packaging method

174. Why does Mr. Ramos contact Ms. Rojas?
(A) To inform her of a mistake in a previous order
(B) To find out the exact shipping date of an order
(C) To change a meeting schedule with a client
(D) To check if a job can be done earlier

175. At 11:25, what does Ms. Porter most likely mean when she writes, "that will work"?
(A) She is happy that the equipment will be repaired in time.
(B) Her client will be pleased if a product is engraved in a day.
(C) She has a plan to interview a person for a position.
(D) She has chosen new items for a newly designed pamphlet.

Questions 176-180 refer to the following article and e-mail.

Daily Business News Report:
Invigorate Refurbishment Inc. (IRI)

Julius and Ivan Sheltons' two-year-old firm, Invigorate Refurbishment Inc. (IRI), is bringing a new sensation to the real estate market in central London. This mid-size company is working with current landlords in the area to renovate old residential buildings. These two consultants appraise houses and buildings to identify how to upgrade the properties to increase their value and more rental income.

From interior walls and floors to exterior surfaces including landscaping, IRI not only hires experienced workers but also trains them to be skilled in finishing project properly. Thus far, central London is the area most of their work has been focused on.

One of the landlords in the area, Everett Sims, made a few contracts with Sheltons' firm to renovate his residential building. "Since I started working with IRI, the revenue from my rental business has gone up to 10 percent due to cost-cutting in water and power as well as significant increases in tenant demand. Tenants called me and said that the new balconies are so nice that they are enjoying the beautiful views and fresh air. I will definitely use IRI for consultation again." said Mr. Sims.

More information on the Sheltons' business can be learned through its website, i-refurbish.com, where a detailed proposal for a project can be handed in.

E-MAIL

FROM	Devin Stevenson 〈dstevenson@placelife.net〉
TO	Julius Sheltons 〈jsheltons@i-refurbish.com〉
RE	propositions for renovation
DATE	August 11

Mr. Sheltons,

I am sending this e-mail as I have just acquired an office building in Southwark, a commercial district near London. I believed that you might be interested in the project. The sale price was very low because the actual state of the property is quite poor and not inhabitable at the moment. But it is located near a train station, which can be a huge advantage. I would like to convert the property into a great residential space with the ten flats in the building for rent within a few months.

Your help would be highly beneficial for my business since I don't have much experience in construction projects. In addition, is it possible to get some information about observance of new emission regulations and what impact this may bring on potential upgrading plans for the heating systems? Please notify me of your availability to talk about this with me.

Thank you,

Devin Stevenson

176. According to the article, what is NOT true about the Invigorate Refurbishment Inc. (IRI)?
(A) It has worked with clients in London.
(B) It employs workers to conduct its projects.
(C) It has been in business for over three years.
(D) It can make landlords more profits.

177. What change has been made to Mr. Sims' property?
(A) A few floors have been extended.
(B) Open areas were constructed to the exterior of the building.
(C) A cutting-edge elevator was installed.
(D) The furniture and appliances were upgraded.

178. According to the article, what are potential clients advised to do?
(A) E-mail a list of real estate agencies
(B) Provide the property price
(C) Access a website
(D) Request an estimate

179. What most likely is the reason Mr. Stevenson was able to buy the property at a low cost?
(A) It was used for commercial purposes.
(B) It needs to be renovated for rent.
(C) Overall real estate prices recently went down.
(D) Its location is far from the city.

180. How is Mr. Stevenson's proposition different from typical jobs for IRI?
(A) The project would be performed outside London.
(B) Mr. Stevenson has already consulted with other companies.
(C) The construction fee would be higher than expected.
(D) The constraint of time is not long enough to complete the work.

Questions 181-185 refer to the following e-mails.

E-MAIL

TO	t.salazar@sunny-field.net
FROM	simon@sheltonseatlife.com
DATE	October 11
SUBJECT	Shelton's Eat & Life

Dear Mr. Salazar,

For a given period of time, Shelton's Eat & Life is offering special rates on advertisements to businesses that have not yet placed theirs in our publication. Once you sign a contract with us for your advertisement, your business will be able to reach more than 40,000 potential clients in the agricultural sector in website and print alike. This is absolutely a great opportunity for you to expand your client base. Please be advised that this offer will last until November 10 and is only for first-time advertisers. The outlined details are below.

Monthly Price	Package	Type
$300	4" × 4" online ad plus one quarter-page print ad	A
$365	4" × 4" online ad plus one half-page print ad	B
$415	5" × 6" online ad plus one half-page print ad	C
$565	7" × 2" online ad plus one full-page print ad	D

To make a request for any of these advertisements in full color, consult one of our designers for your custom advertisement, or inquire about more information, please reply to this e-mail or call us at 892-1244-578. You can access further details for advertisements at www.sheltonseatlife.com/ads.

Sincerely,

Noel Simon
Head of Marketing
Shelton's Eat & Life

E-MAIL

TO	simon@sheltonseatlife.com
FROM	t.salazar@sunny-field.net
DATE	October 18
SUBJECT	Re: Shelton's Eat & Life

Hello Mr. Simon,

I have read the e-mail you sent and thought it would be good for our farm to place an advertisement in Shelton's Eat & Life. Yet, I need some specific information about the website ads. Although I have looked though the details on your website, the location of the advertisement is not clear. Where precisely would the 5" × 6" advertisement be placed on your website? Once I receive the specification, an electronic file of our advertisement with the payment details can be provided.

Thanks,

Todd Salazar
Owner, Sunny Field Farm

181. What is the main reason Mr. Simon sent an e-mail to Mr. Salazar?
(A) To give a discount on a subscription
(B) To announce a special promotional offer
(C) To inform him of the new release of a publication
(D) To promote some agricultural merchandise

182. What is indicated about Shelton's Eat & Life?
(A) A full-color magazine is available.
(B) Its readership has expanded recently.
(C) A special issue will be released soon.
(D) Its advertising rates have increased.

183. What is mentioned about Mr. Simon?
(A) He is a web designer for advertisements.
(B) He is capable of providing additional details.
(C) He will be away from the office in November.
(D) He has worked with Mr. Salazar before.

184. In the second e-mail, the word "place" in paragraph 1, line 1, is closest in meaning to
(A) put
(B) find
(C) employ
(D) consider

185. What type of advertisement is Mr. Salazar most likely going to use?
(A) Type A
(B) Type B
(C) Type C
(D) Type D

Questions 186-190 refer to following advertisement, e-mail, and website feedback.

Shawn's Healing Tours
★★★★★
Wellington, New Zealand

To celebrate Shawn's Healing Tours' 10th anniversary, all summer packages are being offered at 15 percent off the prices of last year's tours. Travel reservations made on or before 10th of August can benefit from this offer. Our summer tours are offered on a weekly basis, but you are advised to make your reservation as early as possible before they are booked up! The following are some of the lists of our tour packages.

- **Masterton and Palmerston:** This two-day tour starts with visiting one of the oldest harbors in New Zealand. Enjoy some of the best native arts and listen to modern live music. The tour will proceed to Palmerston, and explore not only ancient castles and ruins but also forests.
- **Napier:** Hike or climb Mt. Ruapehu and explore some parts of the mountain chains. Our four- and six-day tours take you to mountain cabins on Mt. Tongariro and Mt. Ngauruhoe.
- **Hastings and Wanganui:** The Town of Hastings boasts an aquafarm, fishing, and shipbuilding among its various industries. During this two-day tour, you will stop by art museums, take a walk in Hastings' gardens and parks, and visit many bookshops and cafes around Hastings College. Then move on to Wanganui, which has lots of small villages surrounded by peaceful natural landscapes.

The length and type of attractions in tours can be customized to your requests.

E-MAIL

FROM	horace@reservations.shawnshealingtour.com
TO	felix@venturetel.net
DATE	August 2
SUBJECT	Booking Confirmation

Dear Ms. Felix,

Thanks for making your trip reservation with Shawn's Healing Tours. This is to confirm your booking for one passenger:

Type of Tour: Hastings and Wanganui

Departure Date and Time from Wellington: Friday, 10 August, 10:30

Return to Wellingtony: Sunday, 13 August, 18:30

The total Rate: $175.00 (charged to your credit card)

Our experienced customer service representatives are always happy to take care of any concerns you may have prior to your travel. If you have a question, please e-mail plans@shawnshealingtour.com or call +51(0) 331 654 9266.

Feedback after taking part in a tour

As a professional photographer, on the tour I found the locations and views second to none. And also I felt that staff members were well trained to serve customers well. I will definitely be back for more adventures. Kenny Webb, our guide, was experienced and knowledgeable. Since he is a native of the area, he introduced a broad familiarity with the traditional culture and customs of the region. I became more interested in the area through his intriguing descriptions.

Posted by Pasty Felix

---

186. What is indicated about Shawn's Healing Tours?
(A) It has just opened a new branch in the region.
(B) It is about to release new tour packages.
(C) It schedules its tours more than one time in a month.
(D) It has expanded into a new market.

187. According to the advertisement, what can Shawn's Healing Tours provide to its clients?
(A) Free admission to traditional events
(B) Discounted rates for frequent customers
(C) A flexible duration of tours
(D) Various transportation options

188. What is indicated about Ms. Felix's tour?
(A) It took about six days.
(B) It provided free dinner every night.
(C) It was offered at a discounted price.
(D) It was organized only for photographers.

189. In the website feedback, the word "serve" in paragraph 1, line 2, is closest in meaning to
(A) give
(B) treat
(C) offer
(D) educate

190. What is suggested about Mr. Webb?
(A) He is from Hastings.
(B) He has been newly hired.
(C) He speaks more than one language.
(D) He graduated from Hastings college.

Questions 191-195 refer to the following information, e-mail and parking permit.

Newcastle Town
Lifelong Education Programs - July

All residents of Newcastle Town aged 19 and over are eligible for Lifelong Education Programs. Unless otherwise stated, the programs take place at the campus of Newcastle International University (NIU). Please refer to page 4 of this booklet for more information about tuition and registration fees.

Instructor: Bernice Patel, Patel Family Automotive Service
Owning and Caring for My Own Car
July 14 and 18, 1:00 P.M.~4:00 P.M.
Newcastle Technical High School, Automotive Division

Instructor: Johnny Perry, Small Business Development Institution
Making a Small Business Successful: What You Have To Do!
Mondays 6:00 P.M.~8:00 P.M.
Pedro Library, Room 105

Instructor: Janet Roberts, City and State Property Associates
How to Become the Right Person for Real Estate Industry
Tuesdays, 6:00 P.M.~9:30 P.M.
Bill Community Center, Room 203

Instructor: Lindsay Scott, professional photographer
A Happy and Joyful Life with Photography
Tuesdays 6:30 P.M.~9:30 P.M.
Bill Community Center, Room 204

E-MAIL

TO	Kari Mullins (and eleven others)
FROM	Ethel Marshall ⟨emarshall@newcastle.gov⟩
SUBJECT	Program called off
DATE	July 19

To all,

I'm sorry to inform you all that because of another event that she unexpectedly has to take care of, Ms. Roberts needs to call off her class. Yet, it will be rescheduled as soon as possible as the demand for her program is high. Once we set the exact date with her, we will let you all know by e-mail, and of course, a new parking ticket will be sent as well, since the current one you have received will no longer be valid any longer. Sorry for this last-minute change.

Sincerely,
Ethel Marshall
Program Organizer

Newcastle Town Parking Permit
TEMPORARY-ONLY GOOD FOR A DAY

Date of Validity: July 23
Time stamp: 5:50 P.M.
Section: Lot A2

* This ticket must be visible from outside of your vehicle, so please display it on the dashboard.

191. What is NOT suggested about participants in the Lifelong Education Programs?
(A) They need to pay a registration fee.
(B) They are at least 19 years old.
(C) They reside in Newcastle Town.
(D) They are graduates from NIU.

192. Who most likely is Bernice Patel?
(A) A high school teacher
(B) A local entrepreneur
(C) A town official
(D) A librarian

193. What is Mr. Mullins interested in?
(A) Repairing his own car
(B) Taking photographs
(C) Opening his own business
(D) Starting a career in real estate

194. In the e-mail, the word "take care of" in paragraph 1, line 2, is closest in meaning to
(A) be present at
(B) put off
(C) turn in
(D) arrange

195. On what date was the rescheduled program held?
(A) July 21
(B) July 22
(C) July 23
(D) July 24

Questions 196-200 refer to the following information, e-mail, and form.

Madeline University - Sudbury Town
Seeking a liaison coordinator for students

We are looking for a person who will serve as a liaison coordinator in the Department of Multicultural Education. The liaison coordinator will gather together every week with 15-25 students taking undergraduate courses. The students make up the Diversity Committee, which offers various supports to different racial, ethnic, and religious groups. In order to enhance community spirit for the diverse student population, the coordinator is also responsible for organizing events every other month in places throughout the campus.

Besides, consult with a similar group of students who plan to meet each month. If you would like to apply for this position, please contact the Personnel department at Madeline University at pd@madelineuni.edu.og.

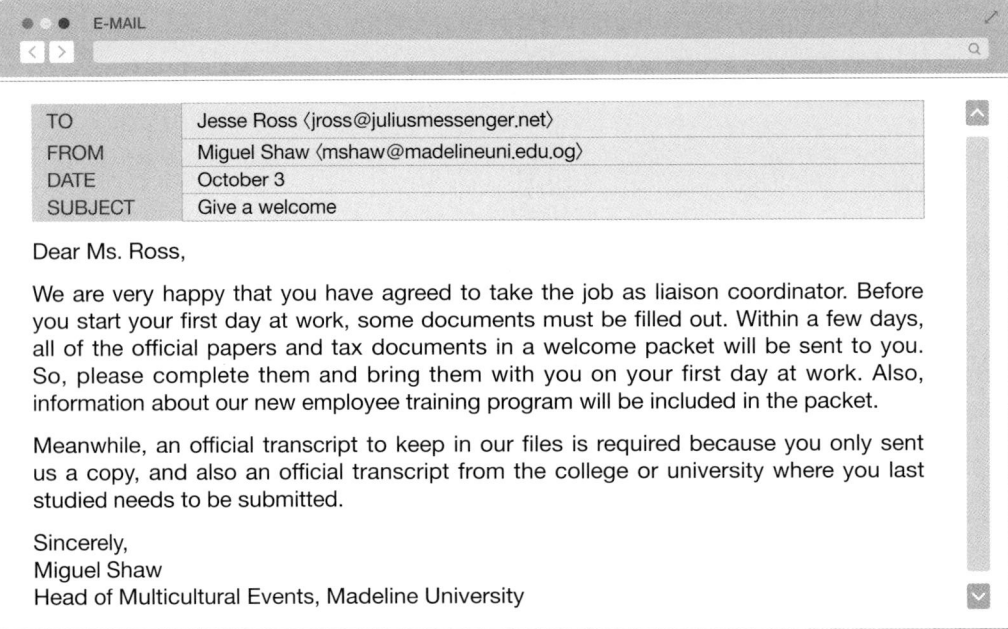

E-MAIL

TO	Jesse Ross ⟨jross@juliusmessenger.net⟩
FROM	Miguel Shaw ⟨mshaw@madelineuni.edu.og⟩
DATE	October 3
SUBJECT	Give a welcome

Dear Ms. Ross,

We are very happy that you have agreed to take the job as liaison coordinator. Before you start your first day at work, some documents must be filled out. Within a few days, all of the official papers and tax documents in a welcome packet will be sent to you. So, please complete them and bring them with you on your first day at work. Also, information about our new employee training program will be included in the packet.

Meanwhile, an official transcript to keep in our files is required because you only sent us a copy, and also an official transcript from the college or university where you last studied needs to be submitted.

Sincerely,
Miguel Shaw
Head of Multicultural Events, Madeline University

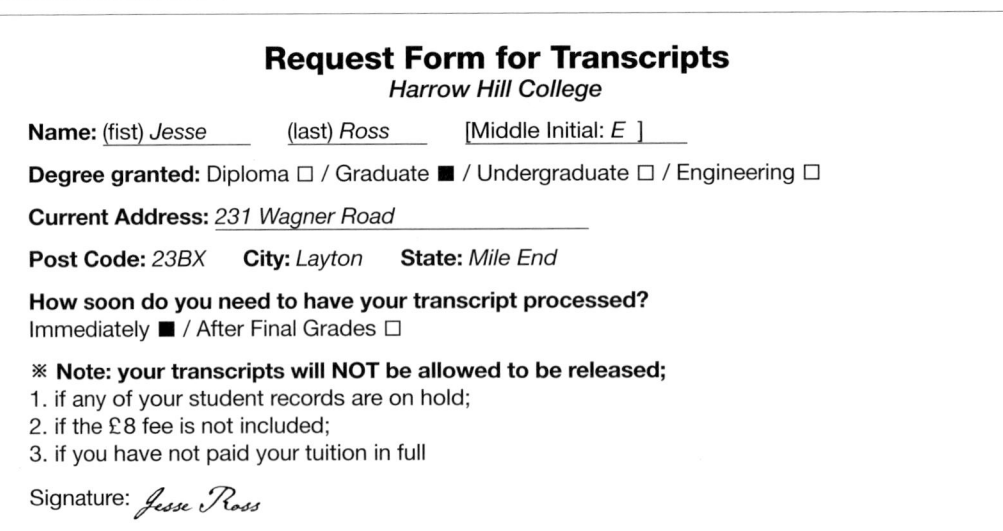

Request Form for Transcripts
Harrow Hill College

Name: (fist) *Jesse*   (last) *Ross*   [Middle Initial: *E*]

Degree granted: Diploma ☐ / Graduate ■ / Undergraduate ☐ / Engineering ☐

Current Address: *231 Wagner Road*

Post Code: *23BX*   **City:** *Layton*   **State:** *Mile End*

How soon do you need to have your transcript processed?
Immediately ■ / After Final Grades ☐

※ **Note: your transcripts will NOT be allowed to be released;**
1. if any of your student records are on hold;
2. if the £8 fee is not included;
3. if you have not paid your tuition in full

Signature: *Jesse Ross*

196. Why was the information written?
(A) To fill an open position
(B) To hire a new professor
(C) To promote a new department
(D) To recruit new committee members

197. How often will the Diversity Committee have a meeting with the liaison coordinator?
(A) Each month
(B) Once a week
(C) 7 days a week
(D) Once a month

198. What is Ms. Ross supposed to do at Madeline University?
(A) Assist students in choosing the right course
(B) Suggest changes to a student center
(C) Help various groups on campus
(D) Manage the multicultural education department

199. What will Ms. Ross receive within a few days?
(A) A school transcript
(B) An acceptance e-mail
(C) Some documents
(D) A copy of a receipt

200. What is indicated about Harrow Hill College?
(A) It is located near Madeline University.
(B) The majority of its students are from abroad
(C) It is the college Ms. Ross attended most recently.
(D) It does not have an engineering department.

해설

▶ 본문 해석/정답

PART 7 문제 풀이 기본 원칙

문제 147-148은 다음 공지를 참조하시오.

저희는 여러분 모두에게 Evelyn Nguyen 씨가 여기 Salvatore 법률 사무소에서 변호사직을 맡게 되었음을 알리게 되어 기쁩니다. Nguyen 씨는 Harold 국립 대학교에서 법을 공부했고 특허법과 저작권 분야가 전문 분야입니다. 그녀는 대학교 재학생 시절에도 이 분야에서 지속적으로 자신의 경력을 향상시켜왔습니다. 작년에 그녀는 투자가, 기술가, 기계 운전자를 포함하는 고객들에게 초점을 맞추는 Eduardo 법률 협회에서 인턴십을 마쳤습니다. 의심할 여지없이, Nguyen 씨는 그녀의 자리에 매우 적합한 사람이고, 저희 팀에 귀중한 팀원이 될 것입니다. 이번 주 금요일에 주 회의장에서 열리는 그녀를 위한 환영회에 참석해 주시기 바랍니다.

어휘 reception 환영 연회, 축하 연회   conference hall 회의장   patent 특허권   copyright 저작권   machinist 기계 운전자   Indubitably 의심할 여지없이, 틀림없이

---

147. 이 공지는 어디에서 보일 것 같은가?
(A) 인쇄소
(B) 채용 대행사
(C) 법률 사무소
(D) 기술 팀

정답 (C)

---

148. 직원들이 금요일에 하도록 요청 받은 일은 무엇인가?
(A) 법률 세미나에 참석하는 것
(B) 신입 직원을 만나는 것
(C) 국내 대학을 방문하는 것
(D) 공학 기술 회담에 참가하는 것

정답 (B)

CHAPTER 1. SINGLE PASSAGE

1-01. 답은 항상 keyword 옆에 있다.
1-02. 요구 사항은 답이 지문의 하단부에 있다.

문제 01-02는 다음 영수증을 참조하시오.

영수증 번호. 7484920

(조회를 위해 이 영수증 번호를 기억하고 계십시오. 고객 서비스 센터에 연락해야 할 때 필요할지도 모르기 때문입니다.)

6월 12일 토요일 오후 8시 Gerald Murray 재즈 콘서트 티켓

[신용카드 끝자리 7758-XXXX에 청구된 금액]
Justin Morris가 지불한 금액: Darrell Theater에 43달러

주의 사항: 사전 예약 주문된 티켓은 환불이 불가능합니다. 사전 예약 주문자 명단에서 당신의 이름을 확인하시려면, 공연이 시작되기 전 매표소로 와 주시기 바랍니다. 다른 양식의 영수증은 받지 않을 것이기 때문에, 꼭 이 영수증을 인쇄하셔서 공연장으로 갖고 와 주시기 바랍니다.

어휘 theater 극장, 공연장   pre-order 사전 예약 주문   ticket office 매표소   arena 경기장, 공연장

01. Morris 씨는 6월 12일에 무엇을 하기로 예정돼 있는가?
(A) 환불을 요청하는 것
(B) 매표소에 연락하는 것
(C) 음악 행사에 가는 것
(D) 카드 대금을 결제하는 것
정답 (C)

02. Morris가 가지고 와야만 하는 것은 무엇인가?
(A) 사전 예약 주문 명단
(B) 영수증 사본
(C) 조회 번호
(D) 인쇄된 티켓
정답 (B)

1-03. 목적은 처음 2줄에 90% 답이 있다.
1-04. 기간, 요일, 숫자 등은 keyword 옆에 있는 것이 답이다.

문제 03-04는 다음 편지를 참조하시오.

Colin 씨께,

고객님의 주문과 관련한 정보를 드리기 위해서 이렇게 편지를 씁니다. 고객님의 (주문) 확인 번호는 **DM-4382**입니다. 이 번호를 분실하지 마시기 바랍니다. 고객님의 주문에 대해 문의하기 위해서는 이 확인 번호가 필요합니다.

고객님께서 주문하신 책은 재고가 있어서 1주일 이내에 배송될 것입니다. 하지만 요청하신 오디오 테이프는 재고가 없어서 지금 주문이 들어갔습니다. 저희는 배송 도착일을 보증할 순 없지만, 7-8주 이내에 테이프를 받으시게 될 것입니다. 만일 10주 후에도 주문하신 물품을 모두 받지 못하셨다면 저희에게 연락해 주시기 바랍니다. 그래야 저희가 문제를 빠르게 처리해 드릴 수 있습니다.

이 절차를 좀 더 명확하게 하기 위해, 당사는 고객님이 배송품의 현재 위치를 확인할 수 있는 온라인 위치 추적도를 갖추고 있습니다. www.Fantasy4you.com에 로그인해 고객님의 (주문) 확인 번호를 이용하여 주문한 물건의 위치를 확인하실 수 있습니다.

저희에게 직접 연락하시려면 무료 전화 800-452-7245로 전화주세요. 월요일부터 금요일까지 동부 시간 오전 9시에서 오후 6시까지 언제든 고객 서비스 직원과 통화하실 수 있습니다.

어휘 provide sb with sth ~에게 …을 제공하다 regarding ~에 대하여 lose 잃어버리다 in order to + 동사원형 ~하기 위해 be in stock 재고가 있다 ship 배송하다 within a week 일주일 이내에 backorder 재고가 없어서 뒤로 미룬 주문, 이월 주문 at the moment 지금 estimate 예상하다, 추정[추산]하다 take care of ~을 처리하다 establish 만들다, 설립하다 directly 직접 representative 담당 직원

03. 이 편지의 목적은 무엇인가?
(A) 책과 오디오 테입에 대한 주문을 확인하기 위해
(B) 책이 재고가 없다는 것을 고객에게 알리기 위해
(C) 고객의 주문에 대한 정보를 제공하기 위해
(D) 주문 확인을 요청하기 위해

정답 (C)

04. 오디오 테입은 언제 고객에게 배송될 것인가?
(A) 1주일 이내에
(B) 9주 후에
(C) 7-8주 후에
(D) 10주 후에

정답 (C)

■ 1-05. 업종을 묻는 문제는 표의 구체적인 명목들이 답을 보여 준다.
1-06. 답은 항상 **paraphrasing**된다.
1-07. keyword 옆에 답이 없는 경우는 또 다른 keyword를 남긴다.

문제 05-07은 다음 송장을 참조하시오.

> 발송인: Eunice Loyal Services 사
> Levi Road, Rex Park, 웨일스 45T-3CH
>
> 송장:
> 배달 장소(7월 12일) 및 청구인
> Terry Nunez and Ortiz Oak 레스토랑
> 345번지 Ronnie, 웨스트우드
>
> | 물품 번호 | 물품 종류 | 수량 |
> |---|---|---|
> | 345Q | 다양한 야채 보관함 | 10 |
> | *96H | 여러 종류의 해산물 보관 자루 | 20 |
> | 42YN | 가정용품 세트 | 3 |
> | 68UT | 위생 모자 박스 | 10 |
>
> * 물품 번호 96H는 현재 일시 품절로 차후에 배달될 것입니다.

어휘 description 설명, 종류, 종목   crate 상자   utensil 가정용품   sanitary 위생의

05. Eunice Loyal Services는 무슨 회사인가?
(A) 출장 연회 서비스 회사
(B) 레스토랑 물품 공급 회사
(C) 배송 회사
(D) 레스토랑 체인점
정답 (B)

06. 7월 12일에 무슨 일이 발생할 것인가?
(A) 물품이 품절될 것이다.
(B) 돈이 지불될 것이다.
(C) 배달 물품이 도착할 것이다.
(D) 송장이 수정될 것이다.
정답 (C)

07. 해산물 보관 자루에 대해 언급된 것은 무엇인가?
(A) 현재 재고가 없다.
(B) 곧 판매가 시작될 것이다.
(C) 평상시보다 더 저렴하다.
(D) 곧 생산이 될 것이다.
정답 (A)

☐ 1-08. 목적은 처음 2-3줄에 답이 있을 확률이 90%이며 하단부 요구 사항에 답이 있을 확률은 10%이다.
1-09. I/You/제3자를 확인하고 각각의 직업을 파악하라.

문제 08-09는 다음 이메일을 참조하시오.

수신인: Johnny Perry 〈jperry@carlexpert.co.au〉
발신인: Holly Pierce 〈hpierce@carlexpert.co.au〉
날짜: 1월 21일
제목: 싱가포르

안녕하세요, Perry.

제가 감독하는 팀이 고속도로 건설 진행에 대한 보고서를 끝내는 데 예상했던 것보다 훨씬 많은 시간이 걸리고 있어요. 저는 여기 Singapore에 좀 더 머물러야 해서, New York에서 있을 목요일 회의를 취소해 주시길 바랍니다. 이렇게 되면, 제가 다음 주에 있을 Ramsey 고객과의 회의를 더 잘 준비할 수 있을 거예요.

또한 저는 당신이 가능한 한 빨리 현재의 계약서 세부 내역을 저에게 복사해 보내주시길 바랍니다. 제 캐비닛 혹은 TCY 문서를 보관하고 있는 제 책상에서 그것을 찾으실 수 있습니다. 제가 지금 복사본을 가지고 있지만 옛날 자료입니다.

당신은 다음 며칠 동안 전화 혹은 이메일로 제게 연락을 주실 수 있으므로, 만일 제 일정 변동과 관련해 고객에게서 전화가 온다면 주저하지 마시고 제 휴대폰으로 전화를 연결해 주시기 바랍니다.

당신의 도움에 미리 감사드립니다.

Carl Expert 사, 부사장, Holly Pierce

어휘 prolong 연장시키다, 연장하다 hesitate 망설이다

08. 이메일은 왜 쓰였을 것 같은가?
(A) 면접 일정을 정하기 위해
(B) 일정을 바꾸기 위한 도움을 요청하기 위해
(C) 건설 계획을 승인하기 위해
(D) 프로젝트 상태를 보고하기 위해
정답 (B)

09. Perry 씨는 누구인가?
(A) 건설 노동자
(B) 건축가
(C) 개인 비서
(D) 전화 교환원
정답 (C)

1-10. 문제점, 과거의 정보는 답이 앞에 있다.

문제 10-11은 다음 문자 메시지를 참조하시오.

발신인: **Arturo Powell**, 수요일, 9월 11일, 오후 1시 25분

Myron, 제가 **Sammy** 회담 센터에서 저희의 새로 나온 회의실 음향 시스템을 설치하는 중인데요. **Andy**가 **Patel** 호텔 업무로 바빠서, 제가 혼자서 이 작업을 하는 게 매우 힘드네요. 예상보다 시간이 더 걸리고 있어요. 그들은 한 개 이상의 행사가 같은 시간에 진행되어 회의실이 몇 개로 나눠질 경우를 대비해 시스템을 개별적으로 2개 설치해 주기를 원해요. 당신이 **Herman**에게 연락해서 저를 도울 수 있는 시간이 있는지 여쭤봐 주시겠어요? 그의 번호는 우리의 웹사이트에 회사 디렉토리에 있을 거예요.

어휘 time consuming 시간이 소모되는 get hold of ~와 연락하다

10. Powell 씨는 어떤 문제에 직면해 있는가?
(A) 그는 다른 업무를 할 예정이다.
(B) 그는 일을 끝내는 데 어려움이 있다.
(C) 그는 방을 나눌 수가 없다.
(D) 그는 회의에 늦을 것이다.
정답 (B)

11. Powell 씨는 왜 Myron에게 문자 메시지를 남겼는가?
(A) 그에게 동료에게 연락을 해 달라고 말하기 위해서
(B) 고객 미팅 일정을 조정하기 위해서
(C) 그에게 컨퍼런스 룸 예약을 부탁하기 위해서
(D) 작업 일정을 취소하기 위해서
정답 (A)

1-11. '사실'인 것을 찾는 문제는 보기의 Keyword를 먼저 정리한 후 본문을 검색한다.
1-12. 추후 연락처/연락 방법/지원 방법 등은 지문의 하단부에 답이 있다.

문제 12-13은 다음 공지를 참조하시오.

Canberra 도시 사업가 여러분 주목해 주세요.

Canberra 도시에 있는 사업체의 명부가 너무 빠르게 증가해서, 지역 신문에 그것들을 싣는 것은 신문 지면상에 너무 많은 공간을 차지합니다. 그러므로 종이에 인쇄된 명부는 더 이상 이용 가능하지 않고 대신에 온라인으로 제공될 것입니다.

명부는 아직 게시되지 않았지만, www.canberracitygo.com에 곧 게시될 것입니다. 이것이 이용 가능해지면, 여러분이 저희의 목록을 살펴보시고 정확한지 확인해 주시길 부탁드립니다. 만일 어떤 정보가 올바르지 않거나 어떤 링크가 적절하게 연결되지 않는다면, 오류를 고칠 수 있도록 저희에게 알려 주시기 바랍니다.

감사합니다.

Lothian Payne

Canberra 시의회
334-2241

어휘 directory 안내 책자, 명부

12. 사업체 명부에 대해 언급된 것은 무엇인가?
(A) 한 지역 이상에 있는 사업체가 다뤄질 것이다.
(B) 배분 날짜는 변경될 것이다.
(C) 온라인 버전만이 이용 가능해질 것이다.
(D) 명부의 목록이 줄어들 것이다.

정답 (C)

13. Payne 씨에게 왜 연락할 것인가?
(A) 접속 코드를 갱신하기 위해
(B) 마감일 연장을 요청하기 위해
(C) 정보를 수정하기 위해
(D) 신문에 기고하기 위해

정답 (C)

1-13. but, however, unfortunately 등 역접 뒤에 답이 있다.
1-14. 본문은 구체적이고 답은 항상 포괄적이다.

문제 14-15는 다음 상품 후기를 참조하시오.

http://www.julius.com			
메인 [홈]	야외/실내	옷/정장	운동화

현명한 구매자를 위한 줄리어스의 안내

운동화를 찾고 계십니까? 당신의 흥미를 돋우는 많은 선택들이 있습니다. **Air Pro Fit**과 같은 몇몇 브랜드들은 대대로 운영되어 왔습니다. **Wellious**와 같은 다른 브랜드들은 꽤 새롭고 가장 최신의 첨단 신소재를 자랑합니다. 다음은 우리의 가장 인기 있는 상품에 대한 평가입니다. 가격은 온라인 스토어에 따라 다소 다양할 수 있다는 것을 숙지하여 주십시오.

Hector Smith £ £ £*
이 신발은 출시된 이래로 프리미엄 시장에서 항상 우세했습니다. 그것들은 편안할 뿐만 아니라 가죽과 고무를 포함한 고품질 재료로 만들어져서 튼튼합니다. 신발은 몇 년 동안 유지될 수 있고, 운동을 자주하는 사람들에게는 최고의 선택입니다. 가격이 유일한 단점입니다.

Miguel RS £ £
이 방수화는 심지어 고르지 않은 날씨에 이루어지는 야외 운동에 대응하기 위해서 고급 가죽과 합성 물질이 사용됩니다. 그러나 밑창은 많이 사용하는 경우 예상보다는 오래 쓰지 못할 것으로 보입니다.

Wellious £
시장에서 새롭게 발명된 가장 가벼운 소재로 만든 이 신발은 더운 날씨에서 이상적이고, 어떠한 종류의 지역에서도 달리기에 적합합니다. 방수와 따뜻한 것을 찾는 사람들보다는 막 시작하는 사람들에게 최고의 선택일 것입니다.

Air Pro Fit 21X £
가격은 절대로 소비자들을 속이지 않을 것입니다. 이 신발은 최고의 값어치를 합니다. 합성 고무, 나일론, 가죽과 같은 소재는 물이 안으로 들어가는 것을 막기 위해 사용됩니다. 유연하지 않은 것은 유일한 단점이지만, 여러 번의 사용에도 여전히 형태를 유지하려는 경향이 있습니다.

* 가격 범위: £ = under £100 / £ £ = £100 to £150 / £ £ £ = £150 to £200

어휘 be capable of ~할 수 있다 cope with ~에 대처하다, ~에 대응하다 downside 불리한 면, 단점
in order for A to do A가 ~하기 위해서는 sole 밑창 be about to do 막 ~하려는 참이다
synthetic rubber 합성 고무 terrain 지형, 지역 be used to do ~하는 데 사용되다
enable A to do A가 ~을 할 수 있게 하다

14. Miguel RS 신발에 대한 문제로 언급된 것은?
(A) 신축성이 없다.
(B) 충분히 가볍지 않다.
(C) 내구성이 있지 않다.
(D) 다른 신발들보다 비싸다.
정답 (C)

15. 운동을 시작하는 사람들에게 가장 적합한 신발은 무엇일 것 같은가?
(A) Hector Smith
(B) Miguel RS
(C) Wellious
(D) Air Pro Fit 21X
정답 (C)

1-15. Not Question은 소거법을 이용한다.
1-16. 동의어 찾기 문제는 진짜 동의어를 찾는 것이 아니다.
1-17. 보기 문장 중에 한 단어 오류를 찾아라.

문제 16-19는 다음 기사를 참조하시오.

Books loved for good

3월 18일 – 15년간 Birchgrove City College에서 유럽 문학을 가르쳤던 Jennie Walsh는 아마도 West Randwick 시내의 가장 오래된 서점인 Lance Reading Place의 주인으로 더 잘 알려져 있을 것입니다. Lance Reading Place는 희귀한 서적들, 일요일에만 영업하는 것 같은 특이한 특징들로 또한 유명합니다. 직접 찾아온 사람들에게 판매한 금액이 Walsh 씨의 사업의 작은 부분을 차지하는 데 반해, 개인 수집가, 박물관, 대학교에서 오는 온라인이나 전화 주문은 분명히 이 서점에 큰 수입을 가져오는 주요한 원천입니다.

토요일에 Lance Reading Place는 15주년을 기념할 것입니다. "저희 아버지 Horace가 수년 전에 여기에서 몇 블록 떨어진 South Clovery Avenue에서 이 사업을 시작하셨을 때, 그는 50년 후에도 이 사업이 여전히 운영될 것이라고는 예상하지 못하셨을 겁니다." Walsh 씨는 말했습니다. 이것의 원래 간판은 여전히 출입구 너머로 보입니다.

외관은 현관 분위기를 그네, 흔들 의자, 벤치들이 있는 보통의 집처럼 보이게 유지하고 있습니다. 가게 구석에는 Walsh 가문의 끝없는 열정인 체스에 대한 책들로 가득 차 있습니다. 금요일 오후에, 가게는 가벼운 사교적인 클럽을 위한 장소가 됩니다. 분명히 회원들은 문학, 희귀한 책, 체스에 열광합니다.

다음 달에, Walsh 씨는 또 다른 중대 시점을 맞이할 것입니다. 즉, 그녀는 교수를 은퇴하려고 합니다. 그러나 그녀가 은퇴함에도 불구하고 Lance Reading Place는 시간을 연장하지 않고 일주일에 한 번 문을 열 것입니다. "교수직에서 은퇴하는 이유가 다른 곳에 더 많은 시간을 할애하기 위해서는 아닙니다." Walsh 씨는 덧붙였습니다. "대신에, 저는 수업이나 시험을 위한 준비에 시간을 소비할 필요가 없기 때문에 더 많은 시간을 제 아이들 그리고 친구들과 함께 보낼 수 있을 것입니다."

어휘 revenue 수익, 수입 walk-in 예약이 필요 없는, 사람이 출입할 수 있는 casual 가벼운, 격식을 차리지 않는 milestone 중대한 단계

16. 기사의 주요 목적은 무엇인가?
(A) 북클럽에 더 많은 사람들을 데리고 오기 위해
(B) 잘 알려진 사업체의 이전을 발표하기 위해
(C) 지역 사업가의 업적을 기념하기 위해
(D) 희귀한 물건을 판매하는 이점을 보고하기 위해
정답 (C)

17. Walsh 씨에 대해 언급되지 않은 것은 무엇인가?
(A) 그녀는 선생님으로서의 경력을 끝낼 계획이다.
(B) 그녀는 다른 사람들과 체스에 대해 말하는 것을 좋아한다.
(C) 그녀는 15년 간 Birchgrove City에서 거주했다.
(D) 그녀는 유럽 작가들이 쓴 책을 많이 읽었다.
정답 (C)

18. 세 번째 문단 첫 번째 줄의 "keeps"와 가장 의미가 가까운 것은 무엇인가?
(A) 예방하다
(B) 유지하다
(C) 보호하다
(D) ~와 연락하다
정답 (B)

19. Lance Reading Place에 대해 언급된 것은 무엇인가?
(A) 판매가 상당히 증가했을 것이다.
(B) 주중에 매일 문을 연다.
(C) 아이들의 책 코너가 확장될 것이다.
(D) 현재의 운영 시간에 변화가 없을 것이다.
정답 (D)

1-18. 답은 순서대로 배치된다.
1-19. 사람 이름은 항상 중요한 keyword이다.
1-20. '문맥' 추가 문제는 위치와 연결어가 관건이다.

문제 20-23은 다음 기사를 참조하시오.

5월 11일, 화요일

Devin Road에 있는 Sylvester 극장이 다음 달 초부터 문을 닫을 예정이지만, 이 아름다운 건물은 아주 오랫동안 사용할 수 없지는 않을 것입니다. 이 건물은 John Cooper가 소유한 Shawn Theater Group(STG)에 매각되었습니다.

STG 부회장인 Loretta Spencer에 따르면, 자사는 이 극장이 영업을 시작하기 전에 이 극장을 개조할 계획을 갖고 있다고 하였습니다. 그녀는 극장에 있는 화면, 음향 시스템, 그리고 의자와 같은 모든 기구가 교체될 것이라 말했습니다. — [1] — "그럼에도 불구하고," Spencer 씨는 말했습니다. "Sylvester 극장의 오래된 영사기들 중 한 대는 원본 형식으로 고전 영화를 대중에게 계속 보여 주기 위해 유지될 것입니다."

이전에는, Sylvester 극장은 예술적이고, 비상업적이고, 국제적인 영화를 보여 주는 것에 초점을 맞춰 왔습니다. — [2] — 이전 소유주이자 최근에 은퇴한 J.Terry 씨는 Sylvester 극장을 예술 영화들을 위한 최고의 장소로 만들고 싶어 했습니다. 10년에 걸쳐 성공적인 것처럼 보였지만, 관객 수가 지난 몇 년간 급격히 떨어졌고 소유주는 극장을 팔기로 결정했습니다. — [3] —

"제가 그러한 결정을 내리는 것은 쉽지 않았습니다." J.Terry 씨는 말했습니다. "저는 극장뿐만 아니라 저와 함께 일해 온 모든 사람들이 벌써 그립습니다. 그러나, STG 사가 오래된 극장을 분명히 소생시킬 것이란 사실은 좋은 일입니다."

새 경영진 하에서, 극장은 더 많은 사람들을 불러 모으기 위해 주류 영화뿐만 아니라 이따금씩 예술 영화를 계속해서 상영할 것입니다.

극장은 8월 5일에 대중에게 재개장될 것으로 예정돼 있습니다. 게다가, 고전 영화에 초점을 맞추는 연례 영화 축제가 9월 11일에 시작해 2주 동안 극장에서 계속 주최될 것입니다. 이 행사에 대해 한 가지만 제외하고 변경되는 사항은 없을 것입니다. 행사는 Sylvester Film Festival로 불리지 않고 Shawn Theater Group Movie Festival로 불릴 것입니다. — [4] —

어휘 cinema 영화관, 극장 structure 구조물, 건물 projector 영사기 piece 그림, 작품 definitely 분명히 revitalize 새로운 활력을 주다, 소생시키다 mainstream 주류, 대세

20. Sylvester 극장에 대해 언급된 것은 무엇인가?
(A) 다음 달에 재개관할 것이다.
(B) 고객들이 J.Terry 씨의 공연을 그리워 할 것이다.
(C) 기구들이 곧 교체될 것이다.
(D) 예술 영화만 상영할 것이다.

정답 (C)

21. 기사에 따르면, J.Terry 씨에게 힘든 일은 무엇이었는가?
(A) 가장 적합한 기구를 찾는 것
(B) 그의 극장에서 상영할 예술 영화를 선별하는 것
(C) 극장을 판매하기로 결정하는 것
(D) 그의 퇴임 기념 파티를 위한 장소를 찾는 것

정답 (C)

22. Spencer 씨는 누구인가?
(A) 건설사   (B) 사업주   (C) 임원   (D) 엔지니어

정답 (C)

23. [1], [2], [3] 그리고 [4]로 표시된 자리 중에서 다음 문장이 들어가기에 가장 알맞은 위치는 어디인가?
  "1층에 있는 로비가 없어질 것이다."
(A) [1]   (B) [2]   (C) [3]   (D) [4]

정답 (A)

☐ 1-21. 동의어는 문맥상 대체할 수 있는 단어를 찾는 것이다.
☐ 1-22. '문맥' 추가 문제는 지시형용사, 지시대명사, 부사들이 답을 연결한다.

문제 24-26은 다음의 기사를 참조하시오.

Stuart 공원 재정비 사업
Forrest Paul 작성

Camden (8월 21일) — 10년 된 Stuart 공원을 재정비하자는 결의안이 만장일치로 Camden 시의회에서 승인되었습니다. 이러한 계획은 원래 제안된 4년 전부터 고려되었습니다. 그러나 Rick Shalib가 시장으로 공식적으로 임명되기 전까지는 이러한 변화는 승인되지 못했습니다. "이 계획을 실행에 옮기는 것을 가장 우선시할 것이라고 약속드립니다. 그리고 제가 한 약속을 지키기 위해서 노력할 것입니다."라고 인터뷰에서 말했습니다. — [1] —.

일단 공원이 완성되었을 때, 개울가를 따라 나무가 늘어선 4킬로미터의 산책로는 Camden 시민들이 산책하는 장소로서 역할을 하는 것처럼 보였습니다. 그러나 사람들이 이 장소가 아이들을 위한 최고의 선택이 아니라는 것을 알아차렸기 때문에 오랫동안 지속되지 않았습니다. — [2] —.

"우리는 종종 산책하러 오지만, 아이들은 공을 갖고 놀고 싶어 합니다."라고 마을 시민인, Alvin Rice가 말했습니다. "아이들이 뛰어다니고 자유롭게 놀 수 있는 장소가 충분하지 않아요. 그리고 충분한 의자와 테이블이 없기 때문에 공원은 소풍을 계획하는 데에 적합하지 않습니다." — [3] —.

다양한 야외 활동을 할 수 있는 드넓은 푸른 공간이 확보되기 위해서는 일련의 작업이 필요합니다. 피크닉 테이블, 의자, 그리고 축구 경기장과 농구 코트를 갖춘 운동장은 좋은 추가 사항이 될 것입니다. — [4] —. 이것들은 언제나 운동을 하고 싶어 하는 사람들을 위해 마을의 스포츠 단체 중 한 곳이 요청했습니다. 전반적인 정리 과정은 겨울 동안 진행될 것이고, 그 장소는 내년 봄에 대중들에게 선보일 것입니다.

어휘 refurbish 재단장하다 resolution 결의안 unanimously 만장일치로 initiative 계획 appoint 임명하다 priority 우선 사항 last 지속하다 appropriate 적절한 clear 개간하다

24. 공원의 재정비에 대하여 언급된 것은 무엇인가?
(A) 내년 봄에 시작할 것으로 일정이 잡혀 있다.
(B) 시의회 멤버 중 누구도 반대하지 않았다.
(C) 완료되기까지 1년 이상의 기간이 필요하다.
(D) Shalib 시장은 오래 전에 이 계획을 제안했다.
정답 (B)

25. 첫 번째 문단 네 번째 줄의 "initiative"와 의미가 가장 가까운 것은?
(A) 시작
(B) 장점
(C) 행동
(D) 계획
정답 (D)

26. [1], [2], [3], [4]로 표시된 자리 중에서 다음 문장이 들어가기에 가장 알맞은 위치는 어디인가?
"그리고 저녁에 이용하는 사람들을 위해 가로등이 산책로를 따라서 설치될 예정이다."
(A) [1]   (B) [2]   (C) [3]   (D) [4]
정답 (D)

1-23. 문맥 추가 문제는 위아래 문맥을 연결해 주는 논리의 근거를 확보해야 한다.

문제 27-29는 다음 기사를 참조하시오.

> **High Street Business에 대한 개요**
>
> Keith 서점은 Victoria East의 223 Bond Street에 있는 현재 이 가게의 최근 공간 옆에 있는 소매 공간을 인수하는 계약을 체결했습니다. 잘 알려진 시내 중심가 건축물은 필요한 확장을 위해 이 새 공간을 이용할 예정입니다. — [1] —. "저희 서점이 4년 전에 개장된 이래로, 저희 사업은 항상 성공적이었습니다." 공동 창립자이자 소유주인 Todd Sanders는 말했습니다. "저희에게 사람들은 저희 서점과 같은 작은 서점들은 한 때 그랬던 것처럼 더 이상 성공적이지 않다고 말했습니다." — [2] —. Sanders는 덧붙였습니다. "보수된 Keith 서점은 원래보다 더 공간이 넓어질 것입니다."
>
> "재개장 축하 행사는 6월 25일에 열릴 것입니다." Sanders는 말했습니다. — [3] —. 추가 공간은 저희뿐만 아니라 저희 고객들을 매우 기쁘게 만들어 줄 것입니다. — [4] —. 이 공간은 저희가 출판 기념회, 책 사인회, 그리고 작가와의 만남과 같은 흥미진진한 행사들을 개최하도록 해 줄 것입니다.

어휘 High Street 시내 중심가   bookstore 서점   close a deal 계약을 체결하다   premises 토지, 건물
hit the ground running 성공적으로 잘 되어 나가다

---

27. 기사는 무엇을 다루고 있는가?
(A) 책 사인 행사
(B) 출간
(C) 지역 업체에서의 몇 가지 변화들
(D) 유명 작가의 약력
정답 (C)

---

28. Sanders 씨는 누구인가?
(A) 건물 조사관
(B) 유명한 작가
(C) 기업가
(D) 신문 기자
정답 (C)

---

29. 표시된 자리인 [1], [2], [3] 그리고 [4] 중에서 다음 문장이 들어가기에 가장 알맞은 위치는 어디인가?

"우리는 반대 사례가 존재한다는 것을 증명했습니다."

(A) [1]
(B) [2]
(C) [3]
(D) [4]
정답 (B)

> 1-24. 온라인 채팅 '의도' 문제는 위아래 연결어가 있거나 전체적인 상황을 포괄적으로 묘사하는 것이 답이다.
> 1-25. online chat은 등장인물들의 관계도를 먼저 이해한다.

문제 30-31은 다음 문자 메시지 대화를 참조하시오.

Lettie Arron   [오전 12시 14분]
Wolfe 씨, 제가 이메일로 수정된 계약서를 보내 드렸는데요. 받으셨나요?

Neal Wolfe   [오전 12시 16분]
네, 제가 지금 보는 중이예요. 수정해 주셔서 감사합니다.

Lettie Arron   [오전 12시 17분]
괜찮습니다. 제게 그 문제에 관해 말씀해 주셔서 감사합니다. 지금 계약서에는 수락된 기사에 대해 100달러 대신에 150달러가 지불될 것이라고 명확히 적혀 있습니다.

Neal Wolfe   [오전 12시 18분]
훌륭하네요. 제가 가능한 한 빨리 그것을 당신에게 보내 드리기 위해 다시 한 번 세부 내용을 검토해서 서명하도록 할게요.

Lettie Arron   [오전 12시 20분]
감사합니다. 그리고 만약 다른 것이 필요하다면 저에게 알려 주세요. 아시다시피, 저희는 다양한 임대 공간과 부동산을 가지고 있어요.

어휘 accepted 수락된, 용인된   a range of 다양한

30. 오전 12시 17분에, Arron 씨가 "No problem"이라고 적을 때 의미하는 것은 무엇인가?
(A) 그녀는 요청 사항을 기꺼이 이행했다.
(B) 그녀는 여전히 계약서에 서명하는 것을 고려 중이다.
(C) 그녀는 계약서 세부 내용에 대해 확실히 알고 있다.
(D) 그녀는 이메일이 이미 발송되었다는 것을 알았다.
정답 (A)

31. Arron 씨는 어디에서 일할 것 같은가?
(A) 컨설팅 회사
(B) 법률 회사
(C) 은행
(D) 부동산 중개소
정답 (D)

1-26. online chat은 등장인물들의 담당 업무와 진행되는 일의 상황을 파악해야 한다.

문제 32-33은 다음 문자 메시지 대화를 참조하시오.

Julia Ross [오전 10:36]
당신이 도착하기 전에 발표를 시작해도 괜찮을까요? 고객님이 이미 도착하셔서요.

Jesus Ruiz [오전 10:38]
네, 시작해 주세요. 저는 제시간에 도착하지 못할 것 같아요.

Julia Ross [오전 10:40]
알겠어요 그러면, 제가 개요 부분으로 시작해서 저희 상품에 대한 새 특징들에 대한 토론으로 옮겨 갈게요. 당신은 늦어도 11시 이전에 이곳에 도착하셔야 해요.

Jesus Ruiz [오전 10:41]
물론이죠, 당신은 잘하실 거예요.

Julia Ross [오전 10:42]
네, 하지만 비용 절감에 대한 발표는 당신이 해 주시는 게 나을 것 같아요. 그건 정말 제 분야가 아니거든요.

Jesus Ruiz [오전 10:44]
알겠습니다. 가능한 한 빨리 도착하도록 할게요.

어휘 overview 개관, 개요   no later than 늦어도, ~까지는

32. 오전 10시 38분에, Ruiz 씨가 "Yes, go ahead"라고 적었을 때 의미하는 것은 무엇인가?
(A) 몇 가지 수치들을 그녀에게 보내길 원한다.
(B) Ross 씨가 일정표를 따르길 원한다.
(C) 짧은 휴식이 추가되어야 한다고 생각한다.
(D) 스케줄상의 충돌에 불만스럽다.

정답 (B)

33. Ross 씨에 따르면, Ruiz 씨가 가장 잘 알고 있는 분야는 무엇인가?
(A) 판매
(B) 디자인
(C) 재무
(D) 선적

정답 (C)

1-27. 3인 이상이 등장하는 online chat
1-28. 미래의 계획은 상대방 대사에서 권유/제안으로 답이 제시되기도 한다.

문제 34-37은 다음 온라인 채팅 대화를 참조하시오.

> **Deanna Schultz** [오후 2:32]
> 다음 주 지점장 매니저의 회의를 준비하기 위해서, 저는 공항에서부터의 차편을 마련해야 합니다. 그러니 모두들 항공편 정보를 저한테 알려주세요. 이렇게 회의를 주관하는 것이 처음이기에, 모든 것이 제대로 조직되어야 합니다.
>
> **Lynn Santos** [오후 2:33]
> 믿을 수 없어요. 만약 제가 차량을 이용하면, 여행 경비는 환급 받을 수 있나요? 저는 New York에서 출발하는 비행기를 예약하려고 했지만, 모든 좌석이 전부 매진되었어요.
>
> **Celia Sharp** [오후 2:34]
> 저는 아침 7시 10분에 San Francisco에서 출발해 Washington DC에 도착하는 Leroy 항공사 31편의 좌석을 예매했습니다.
>
> **Deanna Schultz** [오후 2:35]
> 이런, 안타깝네요. 당신을 위해서 다시 확인해 보겠습니다.
>
> **Seth Stanley** [오후 2:35]
> Detroit에서 출발하는 모든 비행편도 벌써 예약이 끝났습니다. 그래서 저는 New Jersey까지 버스를 타고 가서 그곳에서 비행기를 탑승해 아침 7시 5분에 도착할 예정입니다. 저는 워싱턴 DC로 가는 마지막 좌석을 간신히 예약했습니다.
>
> **Deanna Schultz** [오후 2:37]
> 60마일 이상 떨어져 있는 행사까지 운전해 오는 것은 환급에 해당하지 않는다는 정책을 확인했습니다. 그리고 그날 근처 도시의 어느 공항도 지금 탈 수 있는 항공편은 없습니다. 기차를 타고 오는 것은 어떤가요? 가능한 빨리 예약을 해서 저에게 여행편을 알려 주세요.
>
> **Lynn Santos** [오후 2:38]
> 가능성이 있겠어요. 해 볼게요.
>
> **Deanna Schultz** [오후 2:40]
> Sharp 씨와 Stanley 씨, 정보에 대해서 고마워요. 당신의 도착에 맞춰서 택시가 마련되어 있을 것입니다.

어휘 transportation 교통 수단; 차편 reimburse 배상[변제]하다 manage to V 간신히 ~하다 qualified 자격이 있는 grateful 고마워하는

---

34. 오후 2시 33분에 Santos 씨가 "믿을 수 없어요"라고 적었을 때 의미하는 것은 무엇인가?
(A) 회의가 다음 주로 미루어졌다고 생각했다.
(B) 그녀는 항공권을 예매할 수 없었다.
(C) Schultz 씨가 여행 목적지에 대해서 물어볼 거라고 예상치 못했다.
(D) 공항에서 출발하는 무료 교통편에 대해서 안내 받지 못했다.

정답 (B)

---

35. 오후 2시 35분에 Schultz 씨는 무엇을 확인할 것인가?
(A) 공항에서부터 이용 가능한 교통 수단
(B) Sharp 씨의 여행편에 대한 정보
(C) 환급에 대한 회사 정책
(D) 뉴욕에서 출발하는 할인된 항공권

정답 (C)

36. 지점장들에 대해서 언급된 것은 무엇인가?
(A) 그들은 같은 도시에서 올 것이다.
(B) 그들은 공항에서 자신들의 택시를 마련해 놓을 것이다.
(C) 그들은 올해 회의에서 발표를 해야 한다.
(D) 그들은 Washington DC에서 회의를 할 것이다.

정답 (D)

37. Santos 씨는 어떻게 지점장 매니저 회의에 도착할 것인가?
(A) 그녀는 버스를 탈것이다.
(B) 그녀는 기차를 탈 것이다.
(C) 그녀는 항공편을 이용할 것이다.
(D) 그녀는 자신의 차를 탈 것이다.

정답 (B)

CHAPTER 2. DOUBLE PASSAGE

☐ 2-01. 본문 중에 구체적인 단서들을 모아서 포괄적인 답을 찾는다.
2-02. 4가지 항목이 있는 문서는 공통 정보를 찾는 문제가 출제된다.
2-03. 5문제 중 반드시 한 문제 이상은 두 문서를 동시에 이용해야 답이 나온다.

문제 01-05는 다음 공지와 책자의 페이지를 참조하시오.

Joel 서점
가을 선정 책자

고객용 정보:

저희의 새로 나온 책자를 살펴봐 주십시오. 4쪽부터 시작해서, 식음료 부문에서는 업무용 주방과 개인용 주방에 관심을 갖고 있는 전문 요리사와 음식 애호가들을 위한 표제를 찾을 수 있습니다. 6쪽의 여행과 관광업 부문에서는 올 가을에 어디를 방문하든 당신을 도와줄 여행 안내 자료와 일상 회화 사전을 포함하고 있습니다. 상업 건축과 주택 건축에 관한 최신 소식들은, 디자인과 건축 표제(8쪽)를 확인하세요. 10쪽을 시작으로 유명한 전문가들은 올해의 베스트셀러로 인정받은 영업 마케팅 백과사전을 갖고 관리와 사업 부문에서 최근 보도 내용을 강조합니다.

저희가 보유하고 있는 최신 잡지의 일부만이 이 책자에 반영되어 있습니다. 전체 표제에 대한 더 많은 정보는, www.joelbookstore.com을 방문하세요. Paddington 지역에 거주하시는 분들은 웹사이트에서 이용할 수 없는 많은 읽을거리를 위해 저희 가게에 들러 주십시오.

Joel 서점 올림

신세대 경영 관리
Frederick Wells와 Lance Williamson 지음

상태: 모서리와 가장자리가 약간 닳았고 상태 꽤 좋음. 26.85파운드

사업가와 학생들에게 유용합니다. 작가는 실용적인 사례 분석으로 이론적인 원리와 실생활의 예시를 잘 결합해 놓았습니다. 높은 평가를 받는 이 책은 건실한 경영 관리론뿐만 아니라 효과적인 적용법도 강조합니다.

영업 마케팅 백과사전
Leroy Snyder 지음

상태: 표지에 약간의 마모의 흔적이 있고 괜찮음. 33.75파운드

이 책은 확실히 사업 세계에 입문하는 모든 초보자들에게 필수품이고 영업과 마케팅에서 3,100개 이상의 필수 용어에 대한 정의를 담고 있습니다.

소규모 자영업자들을 위한 회계 기본서
Clarence Russell 지음

상태: 거의 새 것. 35.50파운드

소기업을 운영하고 회계와 세금 문제를 처리해야 하는 분들께 필수 도서입니다.

재정 분석 교본
Neal Cowden 지음

상태: 사용 흔적이 거의 없고 상급. 34.85파운드

핵심을 설명하는 재미있는 만화를 통해 자금 분석과 관리 방법에 대한 읽기 쉽고 명확한 내용을 소개하고 추천 학습 활동들이 가득 포함되어 있습니다. 교사들은 수업 활동으로 사용할 원고를 복사해서 사용하셔도 됩니다.

Joel 서점

어휘 commercial 상업적인 phrase book 일상 회화 사전 latest 최신 소식 residential 주택의 renowned 유명한 highlight 강조하다 cyclopedia 백과사전 acquisition 구입품 wear 닳음 combine 결합하다 theoretical 이론적인 principle 원리 instance 사례 practical 실제적인 sound 건실한 application 적용법 fair 온전한, 괜찮은 sign 흔적 must-have 필수품, 꼭 필요한 novice 초보자 nuts and bolts 기본, 요점 run 운영하다 handle 다루다 illustrate 분명히 보여 주다 readable 읽기 쉬운

01. 공지에 따르면, Joel 서점에서 어떤 책을 이용할 수 있는가?
(A) 아마추어 요리사를 위한 훈련 매뉴얼
(B) 아시아의 최고 관광 명소에 대한 가이드
(C) 시간 여행 소설
(D) 잘 알려진 삽화가의 자서전

정답 (B)

02. 공지에서, 두 번째 단락, 세 번째 줄에서 "deal"과 의미가 가장 가까운 것은?
(A) 처리하다
(B) 양
(C) 계약
(D) 거래

정답 (B)

03. Joel 서점에 대해 사실인 것은 무엇인가?
(A) 한 달에 한 번 책자를 출판한다.
(B) 온라인 할인을 제공한다.
(C) 많은 지점을 보유하고 있다.
(D) 중고 도서를 갖고 있다.

정답 (D)

04. 책자 페이지에서 책에 대한 설명으로 언급되지 않은 무엇인가?
(A) 핵심을 설명하는 그림들
(B) 실제 사업 세계에서 얻은 사례들
(C) 개업하는 데 필요한 정보
(D) 복사 가능한 자료들

정답 (C)

05. 누가 상을 받았는가?
(A) Cowden 씨
(B) Snyder 씨
(C) Wells 씨
(D) Russell 씨

정답 (B)

□ 2-04. 표나 시각 자료 등에는 직접적인 답이 많지 않다.
2-05. 두 문서를 동시에 이용하는 연계 문제 유형 1
2-06. 두 문서를 동시에 이용하는 연계 문제 유형 2

문제 06-10은 다음 광고와 이메일을 참조하시오.

Winnipeg Transport Solutions

Winnipeg Transport Solutions는 Winnipeg의 가장 평판이 좋은 개인 소유의 임대 대리점입니다. 다양한 유형의 차량이 가능한 한 가장 합리적인 가격에 제공됩니다. 만일 당신이 더 저렴한 비용을 제공하는 다른 임대 회사를 발견하신다면, 저희는 기꺼이 가격을 비교해 당신에게 다음 번 임차 시 쓰실 수 있는 할인 쿠폰을 제공해 드리겠습니다.

아래는 임대 가능한 차량입니다.

일별 가격	세부 사항	유형
48달러	5명 탑승 시 적절합니다. (4도어 자동차) 3개의 대형 여행 가방과 2개의 작은 가방을 실을 수 있습니다.	프리미엄
32달러	6명 탑승 시 적절합니다. (4도어 자동차) 2개의 대형 여행 가방과 1개의 작은 가방을 실을 수 있습니다.	표준
24달러	4명 탑승 시 적절합니다. (2도어 자동차) 1개의 대형 여행 가방과 2개의 작은 가방을 실을 수 있습니다.	콤팩트
19달러	5명 탑승 시 적절합니다. (2도어 자동차) 1개의 대형 여행 가방과 1개의 작은 가방을 실을 수 있습니다.	이코노미

만일 당신이 직접 저희의 계산대에 방문하시어 결제하신다면, 위에 명시된 가격이 적용될 것입니다. 당신은 각 유형의 차량에 대한 특징에 관해 더 자세한 내용과 할인된 가격을 저희 웹사이트인 www.winnipegtransportsolution.com에서 찾으실 수 있습니다. 만일 당신이 돈을 더 많이 아끼고 싶으시다면, 3월과 4월에 추가로 15퍼센트가 할인된 가격이 제공될 것이기 때문에 이때가 가장 좋은 시기가 될 것입니다.

발신인: alfonsosteele@stewart.net
수신인: vehiclereservation@winnipegtransportsolution.com
날짜: 2월 23일
주제: 임대 문의

안녕하세요,

제가 다음 달 초에 출장을 갈 계획이어서 귀사의 웹사이트에서 방금 차량을 예약하려고 했습니다. 저는 저와 함께 출장을 가는 5명의 동료들과 이 출장을 안전한 출장이 되도록 만들고 싶고, 이러한 마음으로 4도어 차량을 빌리기로 결정했습니다. 그리고 저희 예산에 다소 제한이 있기 때문에 비용이 40달러 이상이 되면 안 됩니다. 그런데, 저는 차량을 픽업하고 반납할 장소, 제가 필요한 몇 가지 기구에 관한 정보가 웹사이트에 분명히 설명되어 있지 않거나 제가 찾을 수 없어서 예약 절차를 완벽히 마치지 못하고 있습니다. 제가 차를 픽업할 Dugald 지점으로 차량을 반납하지 않고 Rosser이나 Carlin 지점으로 차를 반납하면 추가 요금이 있을까요? 또, 저는 Winnipeg에 처음 출장을 가기 때문에 네비게이션을 차에 달 생각입니다.
이 일들이 가능하다면, 임차비로 얼마가 들지 알려주시겠어요?

미리 감사드립니다.

Glen Tran

어휘 rental agency 임대 기관   register counter 계산대   drop off at ~에 갖다 놓다

06. 광고에 언급되지 않은 것은 무엇인가?
(A) 차량별 임차 비용이 얼마인지
(B) 각 차량에 사람들이 얼마나 탈수 있는지
(C) 각 차량을 이용하려면 얼마나 많은 연료가 필요한지
(D) 각 차량에 짐을 실을 공간이 얼마나 큰지

정답 (C)

---

07. Tran 씨는 어떤 유형의 차량을 임차하겠는가?
(A) 이코노미
(B) 콤팩트
(C) 표준
(D) 프리미엄

정답 (C)

---

08. Winnipeg Transport Solutions에 대해 언급된 것은 무엇인가?
(A) 현금 보증금이 온라인 예약 시 요구된다.
(B) 최근에 Dugald에서 새 지점이 오픈했다.
(C) 한 개 이상의 지점이 다양한 장소에서 운영된다.
(D) 사업가들이 주요 고객이다.

정답 (C)

---

09. Tran 씨에 대해 언급된 것은 무엇인가?
(A) 그는 네비게이션 시스템이 구비된 본인 소유의 차량을 가질 것이다.
(B) 그는 절감된 비용으로 차량을 빌릴 수 있을 것이다.
(C) 그는 종종 그의 동료들과 출장을 간다.
(D) 그는 전에 Winnipeg으로 출장을 간 적이 있다.

정답 (B)

---

10. 이메일에 따르면, Tran 씨가 찾을 수 없는 정보는 무엇인가?
(A) 회사가 제공하는 차량의 유형
(B) 특정 장비의 이용 가능성
(C) 회사의 지점 위치
(D) 회사의 운영 시간

정답 (B)

2-07. 수동태형 문제는 상대방이 작성한 문서에 답이 있다.
2-08. 키워드를 이용하는 문제
2-09. 두 문서를 동시에 이용하는 연계 문제 유형 3

문제 11-15는 다음 이메일을 참조하시오.

수신인: b.vargas@leopt.net
발신인: l.vasquez@angieelectronicmarketing.com
날짜: 화요일, 8월 7일
제목: Angie Electronic Marketing 기술 지원부

Bessie 씨께

Angie Electronic Marketing에 지원해 주신 데 다시 한번 감사의 말씀을 드립니다. 저희는 지난주 금요일 당신과의 인터뷰가 매우 인상 깊었고, 당신께 저희 기술 지원부에 합류해 주실 것을 요청드리게 되어 매우 기쁩니다. 당신도 아시다시피, 당신이 맡으실 업무는 소프트웨어 시스템뿐만 아니라 하드웨어상의 문제를 돕기 위해 저희 고객에게 방문하는 것을 포함합니다. 당신이 저희가 제조하는 상품에 대한 기술상의 세부적인 내용을 명확하게 이해하고 계시고 저희 고객을 지원하기 위해 이 정보를 효율적으로 이용하실 수 있으심이 분명하기 때문에, 컴퓨터 기술에 대한 당신의 폭넓은 지식은 귀중한 자산이 될 것입니다.

업무 첫 날은 9월 12일로 저희 본사가 있는 London의 TotteNahum에서 직접 훈련을 받는 것과 함께 시작될 것입니다. 정확한 시간은 아직 결정되지 않았지만, London에 살지 않는 사람들을 위해 저희는 가능한 한 많은 사람들에게 적절한 시간을 찾아야만 합니다. 저희에게 그 날짜에 몇 시가 좋으신지 알려주시기 바랍니다.

이 자리는 파트타임 직이고, 저희가 제공하는 훈련 프로그램을 제외하고는, 당신이 선택하는 시간대에 멀리 떨어진 지역에서 업무가 수행될 것입니다. 언급했듯이, 업무별 복잡성의 정도에 따라 임금은 다양합니다. 저희 인사부장인 Alicia Wagner가 당신이 작성해야 할 모든 문서 작업을 위해 며칠 내에 당신께 연락드릴 것입니다.
저희는 당신과 곧 함께 일하는 것을 기대하고 있습니다!

Leslie Vasquez
Angie Electronic Marketing

수신인: 기술 지원 부서의 모든 신규 직원들
발신인: l.vasquez@angieelectronicmarketing.com
날짜: 수요일, 8월 8일
주제: AEM 훈련

신입 기술 지원 부서 직원들께
저희는 여러분들의 응답에 기초해 그 날짜의 오후에 훈련 일정을 잡았습니다. 훈련은 오후 1시부터 오후 6시까지 열릴 것입니다. London에서 떨어져 사시는 분들이라도 훈련이 시작하기 한 시간 전에 도착해야만 하고 여러분들이 원하신다면 저희와 현재 일하고 있는 몇몇 기술자분들과 함께 하는 점심식사를 준비할 것입니다. 당신의 이동과 관련된 모든 비용은 저희가 지불할 것입니다. 이 부분에 대한 더 많은 정보들은 추후에 제공될 것입니다. 우선, 저는 당신이 달력에 이 일정을 반드시 기입해 주시길 부탁드립니다.

Leslie Vasquez
Angie Electronic Marketing

어휘 hands-on training (말만 하지 않고) 직접 해 보는   paperwork 문서 업무

11. Vasquez 씨의 이메일이 Bessie 씨에게 보내진 목적은 무엇인가?
(A) 임금 협상을 위해
(B) 기술 지원을 위해
(C) 그에게 일자리를 제공하기 위해
(D) 훈련 행사를 홍보하기 위해

정답 (C)

12. Bessie 씨는 무엇을 제공하도록 요청 받았는가?
(A) 그의 현재 고용주로부터 받은 추천서
(B) 몇몇 기술 문제에 관한 세부 사항
(C) 그의 행사 참석 가능 시간
(D) 그의 이전 경험

정답 (C)

13. 기술 지원부 직원에 대해 언급된 것은 무엇인가?
(A) 함께 일하곤 했다.
(B) 임금이 서로 같지 않다.
(C) 한 건물 안에서 일할 것이다.
(D) 여행 경비는 상환되지 않는다.

정답 (B)

14. Wagner 씨가 왜 Bessie 씨에게 연락하는가?
(A) 운송을 준비하기 위해
(B) 입사 서류를 요청하기 위해
(C) 몇 가지 필수 요건을 분명하게 하기 위해
(D) 직원 정책을 설명하기 위해

정답 (B)

15. Bessie 씨는 9월 12일 오후 12시에 무엇을 할 것인가?
(A) 과제를 제출하는 것
(B) Tottenham에 도착하는 것
(C) 훈련에 참석하는 것
(D) Wagner 씨와 만나는 것

정답 (B)

2-10. 두 문서를 동시에 이용하는 연계 문제 유형 4
2-11. 요구와 제안은 하단부에 답이 있다.

문제 16-20은 다음 웹사이트와 공지를 참조하시오.

---

http:www.Albertastate.com

| Home | Dining | Hiking | Shopping | Featured Areas |

Alberta 주의 명소들

The Lake Area
다양한 음악가와 예술가 단체들이 이 지역에서 활발하게 예술 작품들을 만들어내고 있습니다. 매년 특별 전시회를 주최하는 방문할 만한 많은 갤러리와 박물관이 있습니다. Edson Square에 있는 Trevor Arena에서는 다양한 음악회가 제공됩니다. 이곳은 좌석이 많고, 공연은 무료입니다.

The South End
이 지역은 Leduc Avenue를 따라 이곳의 품질 좋고 맛있는 음식점뿐만 아니라 다채로운 저녁 풍경으로 유명합니다. 이 지역의 많은 곳들이 매우 다양한 이국적인 요리를 제공하는 것으로 유명합니다.

The Historic Zone
이곳은 주에서 가장 오래된 지역일 뿐만 아니라 옛날 주 열차역과 Wade's Monument Tower 등의 매우 매혹적인 구조물과 장소들을 자랑합니다. 도시 중심가에 있는 관광 사무국은 가이드 투어를 마련해 줄 수 있습니다. Min 거리에서 말이 끄는 마차 투어도 당신의 방문을 최고로 기억할 만한 추억으로 만들어 줄 수 있습니다.

Drayton Valley
이곳은 Alberta 주의 자연 환경을 대표합니다. The Alberta State National Glass House는 한 해의 언제든지 4계절을 강조할 수 있습니다. 케이블카를 이용하여, 방문객들은 매우 아름다운 계곡의 광경을 즐길 수 있습니다.

공지: Alberta 주 퍼레이드

Wade's Monument Tower에서 다음 주 금요일 오후 4시부터, 가장 유명한 연례 행사 중 하나인, Alberta 주 퍼레이드가 시작될 것입니다.
지난해와 같이, 모든 퍼레이드 팀은 모여서 Jose Road의 아래에서부터 위로 행진해 나가다가 Sherri Street에서 방향을 바꿀 것입니다. 이 퍼레이드 길은 Edson Square로 향해 있고, 지역 팀이지만 유명한 음악 팀인 Gayle Rock Band가 퍼레이드가 끝난 뒤 Trevor Arena에서 오후 8시에 공연을 시작할 것입니다. 퍼레이드에서 최고의 참가자를 인정하는 시상식도 있을 것입니다. 퍼레이드 때문에 일시적으로 도로가 폐쇄되므로, 도로 주차는 불가능하며 시민들은 퍼레이드 코스에 근접해 있는 도로들로 우회해 주시기 바랍니다. 시 공무원들은 대중교통 이용을 매우 추천하고 있으며, 버스와 트램의 운영 시간은 오전 1시까지 연장될 것입니다.

어휘 vibrantly 진동하여, 원기왕성하게 eatery 음식점, 식당 premises 부지, 지역 exquisite 매우 아름다운

16. 누가 웹사이트에 방문하겠는가?
(A) 부동산 개발업자들
(B) Alberta 주 관광객들
(C) 퍼레이드 주최자들
(D) 시 공무원들

정답 (B)

17. 웹사이트에 따르면, South End에서 발견될 수 있는 것은 무엇인가?
(A) 말이 끄는 마차 투어
(B) 훌륭한 자연 경관
(C) 유명한 건축 현장
(D) 다양한 식사 장소

정답 (D)

18. Alberta 주에 대해 언급되지 않은 것은 무엇인가?
(A) 자연의 아름다움으로 유명하다.
(B) 활발한 역사가들의 고향이다.
(C) 퍼레이드가 매년 열린다.
(D) 마차 투어를 할 수 있다.

정답 (B)

19. 퍼레이드가 끝난 뒤 열리는 음악 공연에 대해 언급된 것은 무엇인가?
(A) 전문적인 음악가들만 참가한다.
(B) 입장료는 대중에게 무료이다.
(C) Drayton Valley가 음악 공연이 열릴 본래의 장소였다.
(D) 한 개 이상의 밴드가 참여한다.

정답 (B)

20. 공지에서 어떤 제안이 언급되었는가?
(A) 록 공연 티켓을 예약하는 것
(B) 행사의 멋진 광경을 보기 위해 Jose Road를 이용하는 것
(C) 완공된 Wade's Monument Tower를 방문하는 것
(D) 혼잡을 줄이기 위해 대중교통을 이용하는 것

정답 (D)

CHAPTER 3. TRIPLE PASSAGE

> 3-01. 표나 그래프 등 시각 자료는 다른 문서와 연결하여 답을 찾는 문제가 주로 나온다.
> 3-02. 가격/비용/날짜 등을 묻는 문제는 본문에서 모든 정보를 찾아서 순서대로 배열한 후에 최종 답을 찾는다.
> 3-03. 마지막 문제의 답은 주로 세 번째 문서에 등장한다.

문제 01-05는 다음 신용카드와 이메일을 참조하시오.

Cameron Terry 2페이지

계좌 번호: 7878-98575-04-352134-23432   5월 3일-6월 2일

구매 내역

금액	장소	날짜
35.45	Randal Bistro	5월 4일
37.15	Terrance Women's Store	5월 5일
27.20	Inez Fresh Restaurant	5월 7일
25.35	Swanson Café	5월 13일
41.50	Leslie Souvenir	5월 16일
52.70	Angie Eatery	5월 29일
100.55	Tucker Office Stationery	6월 1일

수신인: cusomtercare@lesliesouvenir.com
발신인: cameronterry@skynet.com
날짜: 6월 6일
주제: 잘못 청구된 금액

관계자 분께,
저는 **Leslie Souvenir**가 청구한 제 신용카드 금액에 관해 문의 드리고 싶어 이메일을 보냅니다. 저는 전화로 장갑 한 켤레를 주문했는데, 온라인상의 안내 책자에는 장갑 한 켤레의 금액이 35.50파운드라고 나와 있음에도 불구하고, 41.50파운드가 부과되었습니다. 표준 배달료는 6파운드입니다. 그런데, 제 주문품은 30파운드가 넘는 금액이었고, 이 것은 귀사의 웹사이트에서 보여 주듯이, 배달비가 부과되지 않아야 하는 것을 말합니다. 당신이 이 실수를 조사하시고 부당하게 청구된 금액인 6파운드를 제게 환불해 주신다면 좋겠습니다.

감사합니다,
Cameron Terry

수신인: cameronterry@skynet.com
발신인: rickywebb@lesliesouvenir.com
날짜: 6월 7일
주제: 당신이 문의하신 부당하게 청구된 금액

Terry 씨께
6월 6일에, 신용카드에 부당하게 청구된 금액에 대해 문의하신 당신의 이메일 내용이 확인되었습니다. 우선, 불편을 끼쳐드려 진심으로 죄송합니다. 그 비용은 당신이 요청하신 물품을 선물 포장하는 비용이었는데 착오가 있었던 것 같습니다. 즉, 선물 포장 서비스에 해당하는 추가 비용이 추가된 것입니다. 당신이 완성한 첨부된 주문 양식에서 해당 내용을 보실 수 있습니다. 서비스에 대한 분명한 공지가 목록에 나와 있어야만 했는데, 그러지 못했습니다. 다시 한 번 사과드립니다. 그런데, 저희는 당신에게 이번 구매에 5.50파운드 포인트를 제공해 드리거나 다음 번에 35파운드 이상 주문 시 12파운드 할인을 제공해 드리고 싶습니다. 저희는 당신이 어떤 제안을 선택하실지 알려주시는 대로 처리하겠습니다. 저희는 항상 저희와의 거래에 감사드리고 앞으로도 도와드리고 싶습니다.

감사합니다.

Ricky Webb
판매부장

어휘 overcharge 부당한 값, 바가지요금 waive 포기하다, 철회하다

01. Terry 씨는 5월에 무엇을 위해 가장 자주 신용카드를 사용했는가?
(A) 문구류
(B) 식사
(C) 기념품
(D) 의류
정답 (B)

02. Terry 씨가 전화로 주문한 날이 언제인가?
(A) 5월 13일
(B) 5월 16일
(C) 6월 1일
(D) 6월 6일
정답 (B)

03. 첫 번째 이메일, 둘째 줄에서, 'indicated'와 의미가 가장 가까운 것은?
(A) 강조된
(B) 조사된
(C) ~에 실려 있는
(D) 그려진
정답 (C)

04. 선물 포장 비용은 얼마인가?
(A) 6파운드
(B) 5.50파운드
(C) 10파운드
(D) 12파운드
정답 (A)

05. Webb 씨는 Terry 씨에게 무엇을 묻고 싶어 했는가?
(A) 그녀가 서비스를 다시 이용할지
(B) 어디로 그녀에게 선물을 보내야 할지
(C) 어떤 유형의 보상을 그녀가 원하는지
(D) 그녀에게 언제 연락을 취해야 할지
정답 (C)

3-04. 목적이 앞부분에 없을 때는 하단부에 나오는 요구 사항에 답이 있다.
3-05. 보기가 모두 장소이거나 시간, 사람 이름 등이면 모두 본문에서 검색해 두어야 한다.
3-06. Paraphrasing된 표현을 주의하라.
3-07. 문제가 주는 힌트나 지문 내에 답에 영향을 주는 모든 요소들을 이용한다.
3-08. 한 단어로만 답을 찾으려 하지 말고 구체적인 정보들을 모아서 포괄적인 답을 찾는다.

문제 06-10은 다음 이메일, 공지, 주문 양식을 참조하시오.

수신인: **Edwin Mendoza**
발신인: **Clifford Mason**
주제: 배송 회사
날짜: 4월 1일

안녕하세요, Mendoza 씨.
시설 재배를 전문으로 하는 이곳 저희 소유의 농장에서 저희가 재배하는 다양한 신선한 과일과 야채들의 위탁 판매를 신청해 주셔서 감사합니다. 저는 당신뿐만 아니라 당신의 단골 고객들이 저희 농장에서 제공하는 농산물에 만족할 것임을 확신합니다.

당신의 가게가 위치한 지역이 저희에게는 꽤 새로운 곳이어서, 저희들 사이에서는 저희의 품질 좋은 농산물을 가지고 새 시장에 진입하는 것에 대해 기대감이 높습니다. 그런데, 저희가 현재 이용하고 있는 **Chichester**에 기반을 두고 있는 배송 서비스가 **Eastbourne**로 배송 서비스를 제공하지 않기 때문에 문제가 있습니다. 만일 당신이 선호를 갖고 있는 특정 회사가 있어서 그곳을 알려주신다면, 저희는 가능한 한 빨리 저희의 농산물을 제공할 수 있도록 그들과 함께 기쁘게 일하겠습니다. 당신이 주실 제안에 미리 감사드립니다.

감사합니다.
Clifford Mason

Green Life 식료품 마트
이번 주 신상품!

Dereck Family Farm에서 온 농산물   4월 27일

고객 분들께
여러분들께 신선 농산물 코너에서 가장 새로운 농산물을 선보이게 되었음을 알리게 되어 기쁩니다. 저희 고객들 사이에서는 방금 막 신선하게 추수된 지역 농산물에 대한 높은 수요가 있었습니다. 여기에서 한두 시간 정도 떨어진 곳에 있는 **Brighton**에 위치한 **Dereck Family Farm**은 충분히 저희 고객들의 수요를 충족시켜줄 것입니다.

√ 무 (묶음)
√ 당근
√ 상추와 양배추
√ 베리 (라즈베리, 블루베리)
√ 호박

여름에, **Portsmouth**에 있는 **Sunny Field Orchard**에서 오는 더 다양한 과일들이 판매될 것입니다. 만일 궁금하신 질문이 있으시다면, 주저하지 마세요.

주문서
Dereck Family Farm

이름	Green Life 식료품 마트
주문 날짜	4월 30일
도착 날짜	5월 4일

주문 세부 사항:
아래의 변경 사항을 포함하여, 지난주에 했던 주문과 같은 주문입니다.
– 상추와 양배추는 이번 주에(만) 필요했었어요.
– 무 한 묶음을 한 봉투 안에 넣고 이것들을 상자 안에 넣어 배송해 주세요. (당신의 책자에 있는 것과 같아야 합니다.)

추신. 새 배송 회사와 관련해, Cecil Shipping 사는 상당히 좋습니다. 물품들 상태가 좋았고, 배달원들은 예의바르고 매우 친절했으며, 저희가 주문한 농산물을 실은 트럭은 말할 것도 없이 제 시간에 도착했습니다.

이름: Edwin Mendoza, 구매부장
서명: *Edwin Mendoza*

어휘 consignment sale 위탁 판매   greenhouse cultivation 시설 재배   crate 상자

06. Mason 씨가 이메일을 보낸 주된 이유는 무엇인가?
(A) 새 물품을 홍보하기 위해
(B) 추천을 얻기 위해
(C) 배송 견적을 알리기 위해
(D) 절차 변경 사항을 공지하기 위해
정답 (B)

07. Green Life 식료품은 어디에 위치해 있는가?
(A) Chichester에
(B) Brighton에
(C) Portsmouth에
(D) Eastbourne에
정답 (D)

08. 공지에 따르면, Dereck Family Farm 농산물에 대해 언급된 것은 무엇인가?
(A) 여름부터 이용 가능할 것으로 예정돼 있다.
(B) 절감된 비용으로 팔릴 것이다.
(C) 상대적으로 식료품 마트와 가까운 곳에서 경작된다.
(D) 다른 농장의 농작물보다 더 저렴하다.
정답 (C)

09. Green Life 식료품 마트가 5월 4일에 아마 받을 수 있는 것은 무엇인가?
(A) 오이
(B) 상추
(C) 양배추
(D) 당근
정답 (D)

10. Mendoza 씨가 주문 양식에서 언급한 것은 무엇인가?
(A) 그가 주문한 약간의 농작물이 제시간에 도착하지 않았다.
(B) 베리가 고객들 사이에서 인기가 있다.
(C) 그는 포장 방법에 신경을 쓰는 경향이 있다.
(D) Cecil Shipping 사의 신입 배달원이 예의바르지 않았다.
정답 (C)

3-09. 문제 중에 키워드가 있으면 해당지문에서 검색된 키워드 위주로 정보를 연결한다.
3-10. 특정 명사가 지칭하는 대상을 확인하라.
3-11. 차액/변경 사항들은 original과 new로 정보를 구분해 두어야 한다.
3-12. 할인의 조건/자격은 빈출 연계 문제이다. 문제의 키워드 옆에 답이 없다면 또 다른 키워드를 남긴다.
3-13. 특정인과 관련한 사실 확인 문제는 해당 지문과 연계 지문을 동시에 봐야 한다.

문제 11-15는 다음 쿠폰, 메모와 이메일을 참조하시오.

할인권
단 하루뿐

연말 세일
6월 19일 토요일만 유효

- 할인된 재고 상품: 50%까지 세일
- 정상 가격 상품: 30%까지 세일

재킷, 티셔츠, 코트, 바지, 액세서리, 신발 등을 포함하여 그 이상의 **Antton Lilia Co**의 모든 제품들을 구매하실 수 있습니다. 영업시간은 행사 기간 동안 오전 9시 30분부터 오후 10시까지 연장됩니다.

다른 판촉 할인에 이 쿠폰은 적용되지 않습니다. **Althea, Estela**, 또는 **Alyce** 브랜드는 이 특별 할인 대상이 아닙니다. 손님 한 분당 한 장의 쿠폰만을 사용할 수 있습니다. 환불, 교환, 적립금은 재고 상품에 적용되지 않습니다.

Antton Lilia

수신: **Antton Lilia** 전 직원
발신: **Mary Smith**, 판매 매니저
날짜: 6월 18일
답장: 다가오는 할인 행사

우리는 즉각적인 주의를 요하는 긴급한 문제가 있습니다. **The Noreen's Daily**에서 인쇄한 쿠폰에 **Yesenia** 브랜드 제품이 정상 가격 제품 할인에 포함되지 않는다는 것이 언급되지 않았습니다. 그러므로 이 특정 브랜드의 제품을 구매하려는 고객님들에게 문제를 설명하고 사과의 말씀을 드리세요. 그럼에도 불구하고 할인을 받을 수 있음을 예의상 고객님들에게 잊지 말고 알려주세요.

게다가 모든 언론 매체에서 광고를 보고 올 쇼핑객들이 평상시보다 더 많을 거라고 예상하기 때문에 오후 2시부터 오후 8시까지 근무할 판매원이 세 명 더 필요합니다. 그러니 그날 오후와 저녁에 추가로 근무를 하고 싶다면 가능한 빨리 저에게 알려주세요.

감사합니다.

발신: 〈cusomercare@anttonlilia.co.us〉
수신: Jerome Warren 〈troynave@supermail.co.us〉
날짜: 6월 19일, 오후 4:43
제목: 구매 영수증

Warren 씨께,
귀하의 요청에 따라 다음은 Antton Lilia Co의 전자 영수증입니다.

물건	가격	수량
Marvin 가죽 재킷 판촉 할인 50% **물건 가격**	350.00달러 −175.00달러 **175.00달러**	1
Yesenia 겨울 부츠 판촉 할인 30% **물건 가격**	120.00달러 −36.00달러 **84.00달러**	1
Lance 모피 스카프	28.00달러	1
총합 총 절약 금액	287.00달러 211.00달러	

JeelBR 신용카드 XXXX XXXX XXXX 4032에 청구된 금액
Antton Lilia에서 구매해 주셔서 감사합니다.

어휘 good 유효한 valid 유효한 promotional 홍보의 be subject to ~의 대상이다 store credit 적립금 applicable 해당되는 neglect 잊어버리다 as a courtesy 예의상 honor 지키다; 이행하다 representative 직원; 판매원 shift 교대 근무

---

11. 쿠폰에서, 6월 19일의 행사에 대해 무엇이라고 하는가?
(A) 가게는 더 오랜 시간 동안 열려 있을 것이다.
(B) 고객들은 계산대에서 추가로 쿠폰을 받을 수 있다.
(C) 반품 제품은 전액 환불 받을 수 있다.
(D) 새로운 물건이 가게로 배송될 것이다.
정답 (A)

---

12. 메모에 따르면, 판매원들은 무엇을 요청 받고 있는가?
(A) 고객들에게 멤버십 가입 요청하기
(B) 고객들에게 설문지 작성 권장하기
(C) 추가 근무 의사 공지하기
(D) 평상시보다 일찍 근무 시작하기
정답 (C)

---

13. 원래 Warren 씨의 신용카드에 청구된 금액은 얼마인가?
(A) 323.00달러   (B) 287.00달러   (C) 175.00달러   (D) 295.00달러
정답 (A)

---

14. Warren 씨는 겨울 부츠를 구매했을 때 무엇을 받지 못했겠는가?
(A) 설명   (B) 사과   (C) 상품권   (D) 할인
정답 (C)

---

15. Warren 씨에 대해서 언급된 것은 무엇인가?
(A) 물건 값을 현금으로 지불했다.   (B) Antton Lilia의 단골 손님이다.
(C) 정상 가격 제품을 구매했다.   (D) 최근에 새로운 일을 시작했다.
정답 (C)

해설

▸ 실전 모의고사 FINAL TEST

FINAL TEST 정답

147 (B)	148 (C)	149 (C)	150 (C)	151 (A)	152 (C)	153 (D)	154 (B)	155 (D)
156 (D)	157 (A)	158 (C)	159 (B)	160 (B)	161 (B)	162 (D)	163 (D)	164 (B)
165 (C)	166 (C)	167 (D)	168 (C)	169 (B)	170 (B)	171 (D)	172 (B)	173 (B)
174 (D)	175 (B)	176 (C)	177 (B)	178 (C)	179 (B)	180 (A)	181 (B)	182 (A)
183 (B)	184 (A)	185 (C)	186 (C)	187 (C)	188 (C)	189 (B)	190 (A)	191 (D)
192 (B)	193 (D)	194 (A)	195 (C)	196 (A)	197 (B)	198 (C)	199 (C)	200 (C)

147번 문제 풀이 순서

STEP 1 지문에서 무엇을 홍보하는지 묻는 문제이다. 업종을 묻는 문제는 문장의 구체적인 명목들이 답을 보여 준다.

STEP 2 지문의 More than 30 exciting outdoor rides에서 놀이기구가 있는 곳을 홍보하고 있음을 알 수 있으므로 정답은 (B) 놀이공원이다.

148번 문제 풀이 순서

STEP 1 할인을 받을 수 있는 사람이 누구인지 묻는 문제이다. 문제의 키워드인 discount를 검색한다.

STEP 2 discount라는 단어가 검색되지 않을 때에는 유사 단어를 검색한다.
지문의 Prices for groups can be applicable to parties of 10 or more.에서 '단체 가격'은 10명 이상의 단체에 해당됨을 언급하고 있다. 따라서 정답은 (C)이다.

Drop By and Enjoy

Genevieve Field

147. 업종을 묻는 문제는 문장의 구체적인 명목들이 답을 보여 준다.
(B) An amusement park

- More than 30 exciting **outdoor rides**
- More than 40 enjoyable games and activities with prizes
- A special indoor area only for children under 7
- The province's most extensive outdoor food and drink stands
- Fantastic music events including parades all year around

Genevieve Field is running throughout the year, Tuesday through Saturday. Admission passes are available online or at the main gate. **Prices for groups** can be applicable to parties of 10 or more.

148. discount라는 단어가 검색되지 않을 때에는 유사 단어를 검색한다. '단체 가격'은 10명 이상의 단체에 해당됨을 언급하고 있다.

모의고사 해석
문제 147-148은 다음 광고를 참조하시오.

잠깐 들러 즐기세요.

Genevieve Field

- 30대 이상의 흥미진진한 실외 놀이기구
- 40개 이상의 즐거운 게임과 경품이 있는 활동들
- 7세 이하의 아이들만 이용할 수 있는 특별한 실내 공간
- 이 지역의 가장 광범위한 야외에 있는 식음료 가게들
- 일 년 내내 퍼레이드를 포함하는 환상적인 음악 행사

Genevieve Field는 화요일부터 토요일까지 일 년 내내 열립니다. 입장권은 온라인이나 정문에서 구매하실 수 있습니다. 단체 가격은 10명 이상의 단체에 해당됩니다.

147. 무엇이 홍보되고 있는가?
(A) 식음료 박람회
(B) 놀이공원
(C) 자선 행사
(D) 음악 공연

148. 할인은 누가 받을 수 있는가?
(A) 온라인에서 입장권을 구매하는 사람들
(B) 7세 이하의 아이들을 동반하는 사람들
(C) 단체로 티켓을 구매하는 사람들
(D) 일 년에 세 번 이상 방문하는 사람들

149번 문제 풀이 순서

STEP 1 처음 2줄을 skimming하여 주요 정보와 대략의 상황을 파악한다.
we can provide / software programs / on-site hardware

STEP 2 Business Answers가 제공하는 서비스가 무엇인지 묻는 문제이다. 문제의 키워드인 services를 먼저 검색한다.

STEP 3 services라는 단어가 검색되지 않을 때에는 유사 단어 we can provide를 검색한다.

STEP 4 지문의 Regular management of applications and databases including upgrades에서 확인한다.
업그레이드를 포함하여 애플리케이션과 데이터베이스를 정기적으로 관리해 주는 서비스를 제공함을 언급하고 있다. 따라서 소프트웨어 개선이라는 (C)가 정답이다.

150번 문제 풀이 순서

STEP 1 컴퓨터에 대한 지속적인 관리에 대해 언급된 것이 무엇인지 찾는 문제이다.
문제의 키워드인 ongoing maintenance를 먼저 검색한다.

STEP 2 지문의 상단부인 Personalized software programs and on-site hardware including periodic care service (six-month contract required)에서 지속적인 관리 서비스를 포함하는 출장 장비 서비스는 6개월 계약을 필수로 한다고 언급하고 있다.

STEP 3 ongoing maintenance = periodic care service이기 때문에 정답은 (C)이다.

Business Answers

This is **what we can provide**

> 149. services라는 단어가 검색되지 않을 때에는 유사 단어 we can provide를 검색한다.

- Personalized **software programs** and **on-site hardware** including **periodic care service (six-month contract required)**
- Regular management of applications and databases including **upgrades**
- Data backup and recovery service as well as data

> 149. (C) Software improvement

- A 24-hour customer service center for offering resolution of any issues without delay
- Our exclusive Business Remote Overseeing (BRO) system (access rights)

For our corporate clients like you
- Access to state of the art technology
- The less use, the less pay; thus cutting hardware and software expenses
- An ongoing streamlined billing procedure that can be paid up-front

> 150. (C) contracted / at least six months

모의고사 해석
문제 149-150은 다음 웹페이지를 참조하시오.

Business Answers

이것들은 저희가 제공해 드릴 수 있는 것입니다.

- 개인 맞춤형 소프트웨어 프로그램과 주기적인 관리 서비스를 포함하는 출장 장비 서비스 (6개월간의 계약이 필수임)
- 업그레이드를 포함하는 정기적인 애플리케이션과 데이터베이스 관리
- 데이터 저장뿐만 아니라 데이터 백업과 복구 서비스
- 지체 없이 모든 문제에 대한 해결책을 제공해 드리기 위한 24시간 고객 서비스 센터
- 저희의 독점적인 **BRO** 시스템 (접근권)

당신과 같은 기업 고객을 위해

- 최첨단 기술로의 접근 권한 제공
- 적게 사용할수록 적은 비용이 듭니다. 따라서 하드웨어와 소프트웨어 비용이 줄어들 것입니다.
- 진행 중인 선불로 지불될 수 있는 간결한 대금 청구 절차

149. Business Answers가 제공하는 서비스 중 하나는 무엇인가?
(A) 법적 문제에 대한 의견
(B) 회계 서비스
(C) 소프트웨어 개선
(D) 건물 수리 작업

150. 컴퓨터에 대한 지속적인 관리에 대해 언급된 것은 무엇인가?
(A) 외부 전문가에 의해 실행된다.
(B) 오래된 컴퓨터 시스템을 위해 필요하다.
(C) 최소 6개월 동안 계약되어야 한다.
(D) 새 고객들만 이용할 수 있다.

151번 문제 풀이 순서

STEP 1 편지를 쓴 목적은 본문의 앞부분을 먼저 skimming한다.

STEP 2 본문의 앞부분에서 힌트를 찾는다.
I would like to express my sincere gratitude to you for writing a professional reference letter for me.에서 Moreno 씨는 O'Brien 씨에게 추천서를 써 줘서 감사하다고 언급하고 있다. 따라서 정답은 (A)이다.

152번 문제 풀이 순서

STEP 1 Moreno 씨가 무슨 업종에서 일하는지 묻는 문제이다. 해당하는 사람이 I / You / 제3자인지를 확인한다.

STEP 2 Moreno는 편지를 쓴 I이다.

STEP 3 두 번째 문장의 The reference letter supporting my application surely helped me a lot to be offered the job as business news analyst at TTM Station.에서 Moreno 씨는 TTM 방송국에서 경제 뉴스 분석가로 일할 수 있는 일자리를 얻게 되었음을 언급하고 있다. 따라서 정답은 (C)이다.

Tim Moreno
4944 Westminster Avenue
Goreno Town, WC 99812

July 18

Neil O'Brien
223 Candice West Road
Estelle, RO 11212

Dear Mr. O'Brien

151. 목적 (A) To say how grateful he is

I would like to express my sincere gratitude to you for writing a professional reference letter for me. The reference letter supporting my application surely helped me a lot to be offered the job as business news analyst at TTM Station. The experience acquired while I worked with you, particularly through analyzing [...] de me well prepared for this position. It would be [...] **152. (C) A broadcasting company** re involves not only analyzing but also reporting business data in the new program. Again, I really appreciate your help.

Yours sincerely,
Tim **Moreno**

Tim Moreno

모의고사 해석
문제 151-152는 다음 편지를 참조하시오.

Tim Moreno
4944 Westminster Avenue
Goreno Town, WC 99812

7월 18일

Neil O'Brien
223 Candice West Road
Estelle, RO 11212

O'Brien 씨께

당신이 저를 위해 전문가 추천서를 써 주신 데 대해 진심으로 감사한 마음을 표현하고 싶습니다. 제 지원을 지지해 주는 그 추천서는 확실히 제가 **TTM** 방송국에서 경제 뉴스 분석가 일자리를 제공받을 수 있도록 많이 도와주었습니다. 제가 당신과 일하는 동안 얻은 경험, 특히 국가와 국제 경제 트렌드를 분석하는 것을 통한 경험은 제가 이 자리에 더 준비된 사람이 되도록 만들어 주었습니다. 이곳에서의 제 업무는 경제 데이터를 분석하는 것뿐만 아니라 새 프로그램에서 그것을 보고하는 업무도 있음을 알리게 되어 매우 기쁩니다. 다시 한 번, 당신의 도움에 정말 감사드립니다.

감사합니다.
Tim Moreno

151. Moreno 씨가 편지를 쓴 목적은 무엇인가?
(A) 그가 얼마나 감사해 하는지를 말하기 위해
(B) 고용 기회를 주기 위해
(C) 경제 분석을 요청하기 위해
(D) 약간의 정보를 분명하게 하기 위해

152. Moreno 씨는 무슨 업종에서 일하는가?
(A) 경영 대학원
(B) 고용 대행사
(C) 방송국
(D) 비즈니스 컨설팅 기관

153번 문제 풀이 순서

STEP 1 해당하는 사람이 I / You / 제3자인지를 확인한다.
질문의 키워드인 Peters는 제3자이다.

STEP 2 Peters와 관련된 내용을 지문에서 찾아 보기와 대조한다. 지문의 Mr. Peters' well-attended session last year on staying in shape through simple exercises indicated that.에서 Peters 씨가 작년에 협회에서 staying in shape에 대해 발표했었음을 알 수 있으므로 정답은 (D)이다.

154번 문제 풀이 순서

STEP 1 처음 2줄을 skimming하여 주요 정보와 대략의 상황을 파악한다.
From: Forrest Paul / To: Ralph Morgan / presenters / Convention / on 1st of July

STEP 2 문제를 분석한다. [위치 / 키워드 / 유형별 풀이 전략]
상단부에 목적이 없을 경우 하단부에 요구/요청 사항을 확인한다.

STEP 3 지문의 하단부에서 be advised/please/명령문을 찾는다.

STEP 4 두 번째 문단 마지막 줄에서 간단한 약력 프로필을 보내 줄 것을 요청하고 있다.

STEP 5 your brief biographical profile이 personal information으로 paraphrasing되었다. 따라서 정답은 (B)이다.

155번 문제 풀이 순서

STEP 1 주어진 문장(sentence)에서 키워드를 정한다.
"If you need it, there is visual equipment available to use such as a projector"에서 키워드는 visual equipment이다.

STEP 2 문단별로 주제를 파악하고 equipment가 언급되거나 유사한 정보들이 있는 문단을 찾는다.

STEP 3 [4]의 앞 문장의 의미를 파악한다.
Also, please make sure to inform me if any additional equipment is required for your presentation.에서 추가적인 기구가 필요하다면 자신에게 알려달라고 언급하고 있다. 추가적인 기구의 예로 시청각 장비가 뒤이어 나오는 것이 문맥상 적절하므로 정답은 [4]이다.

Dear **Mr. Morgan**, 〔받는 이: You〕

I'm so happy that you are willing to be one of the presenters at our third annual Bristol Healthy Life Convention on 1st of July. Even though our invitation was rather last minute, I appreciate that you have agreed to step in for Shane Peters. – [1] –. Your valued expertise as a personal trainer will be useful to our attendees. Mr. Peters' well-attended session last year on staying in shape through simple exercises indicated that. – [2] –. 〔**155. spoke / convention / last year**〕 will certainly draw much attention at this year's event.

If you would like to sell video copies of your exercise lectures, please send them a few days ahead to give us enough time to display them. – [3] –. Also, please make sure to inform me if any additional equipment is required for your presentation. – [4] –. Lastly, for inclusion in our convention program, please e-mail me your brief biographical profile as soon as possible.

〔**154. (B) request / personal information**〕

Regards,

Forrest Paul 〔보낸 이: I〕

모의고사 해석
문제 153-155는 다음 이메일을 참조하시오.

수신인	Ralph Morgan 〈bodyinshape@healthlifeschem.uk〉
발신인	Forrest Paul 〈fpaul@ptfintnessservice.uk〉
날짜	6월 4일
주제	브리스틀 건강한 생활 협회

Morgan 씨께

저는 당신이 7월 1일 저희의 제 3회 연례 브리스틀 건강한 생활 협회의 발표자가 되어 주셔서 매우 기쁩니다. 저희의 초대가 다소 늦은 감이 있었음에도, 당신이 Shane Peters를 대신해 일을 해 주시겠다고 해 주셔서 정말 감사합니다. -[1]- 개인 트레이너로서의 당신의 귀중한 전문지식은 저희 참석자들에게 매우 유용할 것입니다. 작년에 간단한 운동을 통한 건강 유지를 주제로 한 Peters 씨의 참석률이 높았던 모임이 말해 주고 있습니다. -[2]- 당신의 건강에 대한 독특한 접근 방법은 분명히 올해의 행사에 더 많은 관심을 끌어 모을 것입니다.

만일 당신의 운동 강의를 담고 있는 비디오를 판매하고 싶으시다면, 저희에게 진열할 충분한 시간을 줄 수 있도록 그것들을 며칠 전에 보내 주시기 바랍니다. -[3]- 또한, 추가적인 기구가 당신의 발표를 위해 필요하다면, 저에게 반드시 알려주시기 바랍니다. -[4]- 마지막으로, 저희의 협회 프로그램에 포함하기 위해, 가능한 한 빨리 저에게 당신의 간단한 약력 프로필을 이메일로 보내 주시기 바랍니다.

감사합니다.

Forrest Paul

153. Peters 씨에 대해 언급된 것은 무엇인가?
(A) 그는 개인 트레이너가 되기 위해 공부 중이다.
(B) 그는 운동 비디오를 출시했다.
(C) 그는 Morgan 씨의 동료이다.
(D) 그는 작년에 협회에서 발표했다.

154. Paul 씨가 이메일을 보낸 주된 이유는 무엇인가?
(A) Morgan 씨에게 행사에 올 것을 요청하기 위해
(B) 개인 정보를 요구하기 위해
(C) Morgan 씨의 추천을 요청하기 위해
(D) 시간대를 수정할 것을 요청하기 위해

155. [1], [2], [3], 그리고 [4]로 표시된 자리 중에서 다음 문장이 들어가기에 가장 알맞은 위치는 어디인가?

"당신이 필요하시다면, 영사기와 같은 사용 가능한 시청각 장비가 있습니다."

(A) [1]
(B) [2]
(C) [3]
(D) [4]

156번 문제 풀이 순서

STEP 1 세미나가 의도한 대상이 누구인지 묻는 I / You / 제3자 중 You에 대한 질문이다. 본문 중에 You가 언급된 부분을 찾는다.

STEP 2 10:00 A.M.: Getting Started 부분에서 your business를 찾을 수 있다.
해당 문장 Deal with vital topics small businesses inevitably encounter. Not only set long and short term goals for your business, but also identify areas that need to be improved.에서 your business는 소규모 기업의 소유주를 가리키고 있음을 알 수 있다. 따라서 정답은 (D)이다.

157번 문제 풀이 순서

STEP 1 문제의 키워드인 identifying objectives를 찾는다.

STEP 2 10:00 A.M.: Getting Started 부분을 살펴본다.
Not only set long and short term goals for your business, but also identify areas that need to be improved. 문장을 통해 장단기 목표를 설정하고 개선할 부분을 확인하는 작업은 Getting Started 즉, 시작하기 시간에 이뤄짐을 알 수 있다. 따라서 정답은 (A)이다.

158번 문제 풀이 순서

STEP 1 Not Question의 키워드 participants in the seminar를 확인한다.

STEP 2 보기의 키워드를 정리한다.
(A) work / team
(B) free lunch
(C) learn / software
(D) pay a fee

STEP 3 보기의 키워드를 본문 중에서 검색한다.

STEP 4 본문에서 검색한 내용과 보기의 내용을 비교하여 오류를 찾는다.
본문의 $35 per person에서 (D)가 언급되고 있고, There are two options of complimentary entrees for participants에서 (B)가 언급되고 있다. 또한 세미나의 주제가 팀워크와 관련된 내용이므로 (A)를 유추할 수 있다. 그러나 지문의 마지막 문장인 Learn how common office software programs can be used to manage progress in your business.에서는 새로운 소프트웨어를 배운다는 내용이 아니라 새로운 소프트웨어의 역할에 대해 배운다는 것이다. 따라서 정답은 (C)이다.

Seminar: Team Work `158. (A)`
May 21
10:00 A.M. to 5:00 P.M.
$35 per person `158. (D)`

10:00 A.M.: Getting Started `156. (D) Owners of small companies`
Deal with vital topics **small businesses** inevitably encounter. Not only set long and short term goals for **your business**, but also identify areas that need to be improved. `157. identifying objectives`

10:30 A.M.: Creating Fellowship
Get advice on ways to help foster an ambiance of staff members working together rather than competing with each other at all levels in your company.

12:10 P.M.: Break for Lunch `158. (B) free lunch`
There are two options of **complimentary** entrees for participants: shrimp sandwiches with potato chips or corned-beef salad with mashed potatoes.

1:20 P.M.: Group Activities
Exercises for building good relationships, and cooperating with each other in both small and large teams. Work as a group with your teammates in order to create an ideal plan that can be used for your businesses.

> **3:30 P.M.: Assessment Techniques**
> Learn about methods for determining whether exercises for building a good relationship, and cooperating with each other result in the intended effect by setting clear criteria. Learn how common office software programs can be used to manage progress in your business.

158. (C) learn은 등장하지만 software를 배우는 것은 아니다.

모의고사 해석
문제 156-158은 다음 의제를 참조하시오.

세미나: 팀워크
5월 21일
오전 10시부터 오후 5시까지
1인당 35달러

오전 10시: 시작하기
소규모의 기업들이 불가피하게 마주칠 중요한 주제들을 다룹니다. 당신의 사업의 장단기 목표를 설정하는 것뿐만 아니라, 개선시킬 필요가 있는 부분들을 확인하세요.

오전 10시 30분: 동료애 쌓기
귀사의 전 직원들 간에 경쟁보다 협동하는 환경을 만드는 데 도움이 되는 방법에 관해 조언을 얻으세요.

오후 12시 10분: 점심시간 동안의 휴식
참가자들을 위해 감자칩과 새우 샌드위치 혹은 으깬 감자와 콘비프 샐러드라는 두 가지 옵션의 무료 요리가 있습니다.

오후 1시 20분: 그룹 활동
좋은 관계를 쌓고, 작고 큰 팀 사이에서 서로 간 협동하기 위해 훈련을 하세요. 귀사에서 이용할 수 있는 이상적인 계획을 만들기 위해 팀원들과 그룹으로 일을 하세요.

오후 3시 30분: 평가 기법
좋은 관계를 쌓고 서로 협동하기 위한 활동이 분명한 기준을 설정함으로써 의도된 결과를 가져오는지를 결정하는 방법을 배우세요. 일반적인 사무실 소프트웨어 프로그램이 귀사에서 진행 상황을 관장하기 위해 어떻게 사용될 수 있는지 배우세요.

156. 세미나가 의도한 대상은 누구인가?
(A) 인사 전문가
(B) 경제 기자
(C) 소규모 기업의 신규 직원
(D) 소규모 기업의 소유주

157. 목표를 확인하는 것은 어떤 시간에 이뤄지는가?
(A) 시작하기
(B) 동료애 쌓기
(C) 그룹 활동
(D) 평가 기법

158. 세미나 참석자에 대해 언급되지 않은 것은 무엇인가?
(A) 팀으로 일할 것이다.
(B) 무료 점심식사를 제공받을 것이다.
(C) 새 소프트웨어를 배울 것이다.
(D) 참석 비용을 지불해야 한다.

159번 문제 풀이 순서

STEP 1 의도 문제는 주어진 표현과 같은 뜻을 찾는 것이 아니라 위아래 문맥을 포괄적으로 설명하는 것이 답이 된다.

STEP 2 따라서 위아래 문맥을 보면
Walter 씨가 접속 비밀번호를 입력했는데 비밀번호가 맞지 않다고 나오자, Woods는 I'd better check that for you. 즉, 자신이 직접 확인해 보겠다고 언급하였다. 그리고 나서 Walter 씨가 초대 이메일에 문제가 좀 있는 것 같다고 말하자 Woods 씨 "No, problem"이라고 말한 뒤 새로운 접속 비밀번호를 알려주었다. 따라서 Woods는 Walter가 받은 초대장이 큰 문제는 없는 것으로 확인한 뒤, 새로운 접속 비밀번호를 알려준 것으로 볼 수 있으므로, 문제의 원인을 확인했다는 (B)가 정답으로 적절하다.

160번 문제 풀이 순서

STEP 1 등장인물은 총 2명이다.
참가자 Jordan Walters / 온라인 교육 훈련 관리자 Joel Woods

STEP 2 대화의 주제 파악과 업무의 진행 상황을 정리한다.

STEP 3 마지막 문제의 답은 하단부에 위치한다.
지문 하단부의 Before you start, please make sure to click the mute button at the bottom of the screen on the first page of our training site to prevent any background noise from your side 에서 Walter 씨 쪽에서 소음이 나오는 것을 막기 위해 음소거 버튼이 체크되어 있어야만 한다고 언급했으므로, Walter 씨가 훈련 중에 말을 하도록 요구 받지 않는다는 사실을 알 수 있다. 따라서 정답은 (B)이다. 보기 (A), (C), (D)는 지문에 언급되지 않은 내용이다.

Jordan Walters 10:15 A.M.
There might be a problem with the e-mail invitation I got.

Joel Woods 10:15 A.M.
No problem. I can give you a new access code. Please can you try 393910?

159. (B)

Jordan Walters 10:16 A.M.
Yeah, it does work.

Joel Woods 10:16 A.M.
That's good. Before you start, please make sure to click the mute button at the bottom of the screen on the first page of our training site to prevent any background noise from your side, but your computer speaker needs to be on so that you can hear the trainer.

160. (B) not / speak / during the training

모의고사 해석
문제 159-160은 다음 온라인 채팅 대화를 참조하시오.

Jordan Walters 오전 10:11
제가 온라인 교육 훈련에는 참가해 본 적이 없어서요. 제가 받은 초대 이메일을 보면 Join Button을 클릭해야만 한다고 적혀 있는데요. 맞나요?

Joel Woods 오전 10:12
맞습니다! 접근 비밀번호 2352525를 입력하라고 적혀 있을 거예요.

Jordan Walters 오전 10:13
어머. 제가 잘못한 게 있는 것 같아요. "비밀번호가 정확하지 않습니다. 다시 한 번 기입해 주세요."라고 나오네요. 다른 번호를 입력해야 할까요?

Joel Woods 오전 10:14
제가 대신 확인해 볼게요.

Jordan Walters 오전 10:15
제가 받은 초대장에 문제가 좀 있는 것 같아요.

Joel Woods 오전 10:15
괜찮아요. 제가 새로운 접근 비밀번호를 보내 드릴게요. 393910으로 입력해 보시겠어요?

Jordan Walters 오전 10:16
네, 되네요.

Joel Woods 오전 10:16
잘됐네요. 교육 훈련을 시작하기 전에, 당신 쪽에서 발생하는 잡음을 방지하기 위해 훈련 사이트의 첫 페이지 화면 하단에 있는 음소거 버튼이 체크되어야만 하는데, 트레이너의 소리는 들려야 하니 당신의 컴퓨터 스피커는 켜져 있어야 해요.

159. 오전 10시 15분에, Woods 씨가 "No problem"이라고 말할 때 의미한 것은 무엇인가?
(A) 그는 Walter 씨의 지식에 좋은 인상을 받았다.
(B) 그는 문제의 원인을 확인했다.
(C) 그는 새로운 시스템을 막 시작하려던 참이다.
(D) 그는 Walter 씨가 주최한 행사에 초대받았다.

160. Walter 씨에 대해 언급된 것은 무엇인가?
(A) 그는 새 컴퓨터를 최근에 구매했다.
(B) 그는 교육 훈련 중에 말을 하도록 요구 받지 않는다.
(C) 그는 적절한 컴퓨터 스피커를 가지고 있지 않다.
(D) 그는 틀린 웹사이트에 접속했다.

161번 문제 풀이 순서

STEP 1 처음 2줄을 skimming하여 주요 정보와 대략의 상황을 파악한다.
Cotswolds / interest / more shopping places

STEP 2 첫 번째 문제를 분석한다. [위치 / 키워드 / 유형별 풀이 전략]

161. How many shopping malls are currently in Cotswolds?
첫 번째 문제 - 지문 상단부 / 키워드 shopping mall / 유형 - 키워드 옆에 답이 있다.

STEP 3 지문의 상단부에서 키워드를 찾는다. 키워드 근처에 있는 보기가 답이 된다.
Some have suggested constructing a third shopping mall in the next few years.
현재 Cotswolds에 있는 쇼핑몰의 개수를 묻는 문제이다. 지문의 Some have suggested constructing a third shopping mall in the next few years.에서 몇몇 사람들이 제3의 쇼핑몰을 건설할 것을 제안했다는 내용으로 보아, 현재 2개의 쇼핑몰이 있음을 알 수 있다. 따라서 정답은 (B)이다.

> **(B)** 세 번째 쇼핑몰을 짓는 것을 제안한다는 내용이므로 현재는 2개의 쇼핑몰이 있다.

An increasing number of Cotswolds residents' as well as many visitors' have expressed interest to town officials that there should be more shopping places. – [1] – Some have suggested constructing **a third shopping mall** in the next few years.

In order for town officials to learn the extent of the interest in an additional shopping place, a data-collection project has been scheduled to start on Tuesday, conducted by Anita Publicity Association, through the weekend when the current shopping areas in the town are normally overcrowded.

– [2] – Once the study is done, an updated receptive capacity of the current influx of visitors to the area will be provided so as to determine the feasibility of a new shopping mall construction project. – [3] –

"With the office and residential complex projects people in the area have seen over the past three years, the demand can be understood." the Planning Director anecdotally added. – [4] –

162번 문제 풀이 순서

STEP 1 처음 2줄을 skimming하여 주요 정보와 대략의 상황을 파악한다.
Cotswolds / interest / more shopping places
suggested constructing / third

STEP 2 두 번째 문제를 분석한다. [위치 / 키워드 / 유형별 풀이 전략]
두 번째 문제 - 지문 상단부 / 사실인 것을 묻는 문제는 보기를 먼저 정리한다.

162. What is implied about **the survey** in the article?

(A) search / locations / a shopping mall
(B) led by / Cotswolds' planning director
(C) filled out / by Anita Publicity Association
(D) identify / extent of the need / shopping mall

STEP 3 보기의 키워드를 본문에서 검색하여 나머지 문장 중에 오류 요소를 제거한다.
질문의 키워드인 survey와 관련된 내용을 지문에서 찾아 보기와 대조하는 문제이다. 지문의 In order for town officials to learn the extent of the interest in an additional shopping place, a data-collection project has been scheduled to start on Tuesday에서 추가적인 쇼핑 장소에 대한 관심의 정도를 알기 위해, 자료를 수집하는 프로젝트 즉, 설문조사가 시행될 것임을 언급하고 있다. 따라서 정답은 (D)이다.

> **(A)** shopping mall은 있지만 적합한 위치를 찾는다는 내용은 없다.

An increasing number of Cotswolds residents' as well as many visitors' have expressed interest to town officials that there should be more shopping places. – [1] – Some have suggested constructing a third shopping mall in the next few years.

> **(D)** It will identify the extent of the need of a shopping mall.

In order for town officials to learn the extent of the interest in an additional shopping place, a data-collection project has been scheduled to start on Tuesday, **conducted by** Anita Publicity Association, through the weekend when the current shopping areas in the town are normally overcrowded.

> **(B)** Cotswold의 기획자에 의해 지휘되는 것은 아니다.

– [2] – Once the study is done, an updated receptive capacity of the current influx of visitors to the area will be provided so as to determine the feasibility of a new shopping mall construction project. – [3] –

> **(C)** 주체는 맞았지만 동사가 다르다.

"With the office and residential complex projects people in the area have seen over the past three years, the demand can be understood. "the Planning Director anecdotally added. – [4] –

162. What is implied about the survey in the article?

(A) It will search for appropriate locations for a shopping mall.
(B) It will be led by Cotswolds' planning director.
(C) It will be filled out by Anita Publicity Association.
(D) It will **identify** the **extent** of the **need** for a **shopping** mall.

163번 문제 풀이 순서

STEP 1 해당 문장의 키워드를 확보한다.
"However, hard data is needed to consider constructing another shopping mall."
하지만, 또 다른 쇼핑몰 건설을 고려하기 위해서는 확실한 정보가 필요하다.

STEP 2 빈칸의 앞뒤에서 반대의 내용이나 부정적인 내용이 연결되는 곳을 찾는다.
- 더 많은 쇼핑 장소가 있어야만 한다는 의견을 밝혔다. –[1]– 몇몇 사람들은 앞으로 ~ [긍정 + 긍정]
- 프로젝트가 화요일에 착수될 예정이다. –[2]– 조사가 시작되면 ~ [긍정 + 긍정]
- 방문객에 대한 수용력이 업데이트되어 제공될 것이다. –[3]– "이 지역 주민들이 ~ [긍정 + 긍정]
- "이 지역 주민들이 지난 3년 간 봐 온 사무실과 거주 단지 프로젝트를 보면, 이 수요가 이해될 수 있다."고 기획부장은 일화처럼 말했다. –[4]– [긍정 + 부정] 정답

STEP 3 단순히 수요 문제가 아니라, 쇼핑 장소를 또 건설할지 여부를 판단할 때는, 사무실과 주거 단지 프로젝트 외에 확실한 정보가 필요하다는 내용이 위 문장 뒤에 나오는 것이 적절하므로 정답은 (D)이다.

모의고사 해석
문제 161-163은 다음 기사를 참조하시오.

여러분의 예리한 통찰력을 기다리며: 추가 쇼핑 단지에 대한 조사

많은 방문객뿐만 아니라 많은 **Cotswolds** 거주민들이 시 공무원에게 더 많은 쇼핑 장소가 있어야만 한다는 의견을 밝혔다. -[1]- 몇몇 사람들은 앞으로 몇 년 안에 제3의 쇼핑몰을 건설할 것을 제안했다.

시 공무원이 추가적인 쇼핑 장소에 대한 관심의 정도를 알기 위해, 현재의 쇼핑 지역이 보통 혼잡해지는 주말 내내 **Anita Publicity Association**가 실행하는, 자료를 수집하는 프로젝트가 화요일에 착수될 예정이다.

-[2]- 조사가 시작되면, 새 쇼핑몰 건설 프로젝트의 실행 가능성을 결정하기 위해, 이 지역으로 현재 유입되는 방문객에 대한 수용력이 업데이트되어 제공될 것이다. -[3]-

"이 지역 주민들이 지난 3년 간 봐 온 사무실과 거주 단지 프로젝트를 보면, 이 수요가 이해될 수 있다."고 기획부장은 일화처럼 말했다. -[4]-

161. 현재 얼마나 많은 쇼핑몰이 Cotswolds에 있는가?
(A) 1개
(B) 2개
(C) 3개
(D) 4개

162. 기사에서 설문조사에 대해 언급된 것은 무엇인가?
(A) 쇼핑몰을 위한 적절한 장소를 찾을 것이다.
(B) Cotswold의 기획 이사가 이끌 것이다.
(C) Anita Publicity Association이 설문조사 양식을 기입할 것이다.
(D) 쇼핑몰에 대한 수요의 범위를 확인할 것이다.

163. [1], [2], [3], [4]로 표시된 자리 중에서 다음 문장이 들어가기에 가장 알맞은 위치는 어디인가?
  "하지만, 또 다른 쇼핑몰 건설을 고려하기 위해서는 확실한 정보가 필요하다."
(A) [1]
(B) [2]
(C) [3]
(D) [4]

164번 문제 풀이 순서

STEP 1 영어 단어들은 한 단어가 여러 뜻을 가지며 여러 개의 동의어를 갖는다.
따라서 contemporary는 '같은 시대의, 현대의, 동시의, 같은 나이의' 등의 동의어가 있다.

STEP 2 'contemporary'가 해당 위치에서 어떤 의미로 쓰였는지를 먼저 확인한다.
Please visit the Result of the New Polls page to see what people's general view is on contemporary issues in the world.
전 세계의 '동시대적인' 이슈에 관해 사람들의 일반적인 견해를 보려면 페이지를 방문하라고 언급하고 있다. '동시대적인, 현대의'의 의미로 contemporary가 사용되었으므로 보기 중 (B)가 정답이다.

165번 문제 풀이 순서

STEP 1 처음 2줄을 skimming하여 주요 정보와 대략의 상황을 파악한다.
Craig Moore Institution / collecting / public opinions / various issues / through polls telephone / aged 18 years or older / subject to all our polls

STEP 2 두 번째 문제를 분석한다. [위치 / 키워드 / 유형별 풀이 전략]
두 번째 문제 - 지문 상단부 / 사실인 것을 묻는 문제는 보기를 먼저 정리한다.

165. What is indicated about **poll respondents**?

(A) intentionally / selected
(B) interviewed / regularly
(C) not interviewed / in person
(D) up to 18 years old

STEP 3 보기의 키워드를 본문에서 검색하여 나머지 문장 중에 오류 요소를 제거한다.
질문의 키워드인 poll respondents와 관련된 내용을 지문에서 찾아 보기와 대조하는 문제이다. 지문의 Based on telephone interviews, those living in specific polling areas, aged 18 years or older, are subject to all our polls.에서 전화 인터뷰에 기반을 두고 여론 조사를 진행한다고 언급하고 있으므로 직접 만나서 인터뷰가 진행되지 않는다는 (C)가 정답이다.

> (C) 직접 인터뷰(in person)를 하는 것이 아니라 전화로 인터뷰를 했기 때문에 정답이다.

> (D) 18세까지(up to)가 아니라 이상(older)이라고 언급되어 있다.

Craig Moore
As Your View Matte...

...'s, the Craig Moore Institution has been dedicated to collecting public opinions on various issues **through polls. Based on telephone interviews**, those living in specific polling areas, **aged 18 years or older**, are subject to all our polls. In order to give an equal opportunity of being contacted to everyone in the age group within a polling area, our own computer system chooses potential interviewees by **randomly** selecting contact information.

> (A) randomly는 '무작위로'라는 뜻이므로 답지와 일치하지 않는다. (≒ intentionally)

... see what people's general view is on ...ts are released every week, and posted online to allow the public to access them. If you would like to look up the results of polls on a specific subject, see the Subject Direction page. If you intend to reproduce any graphics such as tables and charts designed by Craig Moore, go to the Permissions...

> (B) 여론조사는 규칙적으로(regularly) 실행되지 않는다.

...nline form to fill in with information on where and ...ually, you will receive a response within a couple of days of submission.

166번 문제 풀이 순서

STEP 1 세 번째 질문은 대부분 지문의 중간 부분에 답이 있다.
STEP 2 문제의 키워드인 Craig Moore 협회와 보기에 키워드들을 먼저 정리한다.
STEP 3 보기의 키워드는 모두 본문 중에 있다.
본문의 키워드 부분을 보기와 검색하여 맞는 내용과 오류 내용을 꼼꼼하게 대조한다. 포괄적인 내용일 경우 구체적인 복수의 정보를 함께 고려해야 한다.

Craig Moore
As Your View Matters

Over the past twenty five years, the Craig Moore Institution has been dedicated to collecting public opinions on various issues through polls. Based on telephone interviews, those living in s_____ or older, are subject to all our polls. In order to give a_____ **(B) own computer software** ted to everyone in the age group within a polling area, **our own computer system chooses potential interviewees by randomly selecting contact information.**

Please visit the Result of the New Polls page to see what p**(A) update / regularly** contemporary issues in the world. **Gathered results are released every week**, and posted online to allow the public to access them. If you would like to look up the results of polls on a specific subject, see the Subject Direction page. **If you intend to reproduce any graphics such as tables and charts designed by Craig Moore, go to the Permissions page which will provide you with an online form to fill in with information on where and how you are planning to use them.** Usually, you will receive a response within a couple of days of submission. **(D) permits / people / use / data**

(C) It is ~~looking for~~ a new web ~~designer~~.
[사람들의 견해를 보려면 웹사이트를 방문하라고 했지 디자이너를 모집한다는 이야기는 아니다.]

167번 문제 풀이 순서

STEP 1 네 문제 중 마지막 문제이기 때문에 마지막 문단을 확인한다.
STEP 2 문제를 분석한다. [위치 / 키워드 / 유형별 풀이 전략]
수단의 방법 – 지문 하단부 / 키워드 – graphic information
STEP 3 지문의 하단부에서 해당 정보를 살펴보자.
If you intend to reproduce any graphics such as tables and charts designed by Craig Moore, go to the Permissions page which will provide you with an online form to fill in with information on where and how you are planning to use them.에서 Permission page에 가서 온라인 양식을 작성해 제출할 것을 제안하고 있다. 따라서 온라인상에 정보를 남기면 된다는 내용의 (D)가 정답이다.

Please visit the Result of the New Polls page to see what people's general view is on contemporary issues in the world. Gathered results are released every week, and posted online to allow the public to access them. If you would like to look up the results of polls on a specific subject, see the Subject Direction page. If you intend to reproduce **any graphics such as tables and charts** designed by Craig Moore, go to the Permissions page which will provide you with **an online form to fill in** with information on where and how you are planning to use them. Usually, you will receive a response within a couple of days of submission.

> 키워드인 graphic information을 중심으로 앞뒤 문장에서 정답을 확인할 수 있다.

모의고사 해석
문제 164-167은 다음 웹사이트를 참조하시오.

Craig Moore
당신의 견해에 관한 사안으로

지난 25년 동안, Craig Moore 협회는 다양한 이슈에 대한 여론을 여론 조사를 통해 수집하는 데 헌신해 왔습니다. 전화 인터뷰에 기반을 두고 있으며, 특정 투표 지역에 살고 있는 18세 이상의 성인들이 저희의 모든 여론 조사의 대상입니다. 투표를 할 수 있는 나이 대의 모든 사람들에게 연락 받을 기회를 동등하게 주기 위해, 저희 소유의 컴퓨터 시스템은 무작위로 연락처를 만들어 냄으로써 잠재적인 인터뷰 대상자들을 선택합니다.

전 세계의 동시대적인 이슈에 관해 사람들의 일반적인 견해가 무엇인지 보시려면 **Result of New Polls** 페이지를 방문하시기 바랍니다. 수집된 결과는 매주 발표되고, 대중들이 그것에 접근할 수 있도록 온라인에 게시됩니다. 만일 특정 주제의 여론 조사 결과를 찾고 싶으시다면, **Subject Direction** 페이지를 보십시오. 만일 당신이 Craig Moore가 만든 제표와 도표와 같은 시각 자료를 복사하고자 하신다면, 당신이 그것을 어디서 어떻게 이용할 계획인지에 대한 정보를 기입할 온라인 양식을 제공해 주는 **Permission page**로 가 보세요. 보통, 당신은 제출하고 2~3일 내에 답변을 받으실 것입니다.

164. 두 번째 문단 두 번째 줄의 "contemporary"와 의미가 가장 가까운 것은?
(A) 최신 유행의
(B) 현재의
(C) 습관적인
(D) 심각한

165. 여론조사 대상자에 대해 언급된 것은 무엇인가?
(A) 의도적으로 선별된다.
(B) 정기적으로 인터뷰에 응한다.
(C) 직접 만나서 인터뷰가 진행되지 않는다.
(D) 18세까지가 대상이다.

166. Craig Moore 협회에 대해 언급되지 않은 것은 무엇인가?
(A) 정기적으로 사이트를 최신 정보로 업데이트한다.
(B) 협회 소유의 컴퓨터 소프트웨어를 가지고 있다.
(C) 새 웹 디자이너를 찾고 있다.
(D) 사람들이 협회의 정보를 이용하는 것을 허락한다.

167. 대중이 시각 자료를 이용할 수 있는 방법은 무엇인가?
(A) 팩스를 보냄으로써
(B) 전화를 함으로써
(C) 서면으로 상세한 내용을 적어 제출함으로써
(D) 온라인상에 정보를 남김으로써

168번 문제 풀이 순서

STEP 1 목적은 대부분 본문의 상단부에 답이 있다.

STEP 2 보기의 키워드들을 먼저 정리한다.
(A) way / start / small business
(B) discuss / strategies / attract
(C) announce / entrepreneur's visit / home town
(D) advantages / small business

STEP 3 보기 중에 지문의 상단부에서 언급한 내용을 포괄적으로 묘사한 것이 답이다.
기사는 Franklin Willis, regarded as the "small business expert" by *Dawson City Chronicle*, has been invited as the keynote speaker at the fourth annual Dawson City Small Business Fair (DCSBF).에서 Willis 씨가 Dawson 시에 방문하도록 초청받았는데, Willis 씨는 지문에서 Mr. Willis has been running his successful business in New York, in which he has lived with his family for the last 15 years. 즉, 뉴욕에서 사업을 운영하는 사업가이며, "I was born and raised in Dawson City." 라고 말한 것에서 알 수 있듯이 그의 고향이 Dawson 시임을 알 수 있다. 따라서 사업가인 Willis 씨가 그의 고향에 방문할 것을 알리기 위함이라는 (C)가 정답이다.

Dawson City Welcomes Small-Business Expert

Dawson City (June 11) – **Franklin Willis, regarded as the "small business expert" by** *Dawson City Chronicle*, **has been invited as the keynote** speaker **at the fourth annual Dawson City Small Business Fair (DCSBF)**. The fair is scheduled to be held at the Dawson City Conference Center from July 1 through July 4. About 1,500 small business owners are expected to attend seminars and run their booths which can allow visitors to ask questions as well as collect information.

A DCSBF press release indicated that Mr. Willis will emphasize some of the tips covered in his popular book "Success Is Equal to Efforts" published a few months ago. Mr. Willis is confident that any new business scheme requires several key decisions to turn into a successful one. "Just creating goods you will sell won't make your business successful." Mr. Willis reflects his strong view in his book. "Creating goods people want to purchase is the key element. It is also a basic policy, and must be kept to succeed in business." Mr. Willis has been running **his successful business in New York**, in which he has lived with his family for the last 15 years.

"I was **born and raised** in Dawson City." Mr. Willis added. "I would like to help people in my home town live a successful life, so it is a good chance to do it by participating in the fair. Small business owners can find many outstanding opportunities to make their businesses prosper if they follow the important and clear directions I suggest, and these will definitely make many other small businesses successful."

Admission to the fair is $120. Tickets can be purchased through the fair's website at www.dawsoncityfair.com/gr.

> Willis의 고향이 언급되었다.

(A) To report ~~a way~~ to start a new **small business**
(B) To discuss ~~new strategies~~ to attract customers
[방문객들이 질문을 한다고 그랬지 고객들을 유입할 전략에 대해 논의할 거라는 내용은 언급되지 않았다.]
(C) To announce an **entrepreneur's visit** to **his home town**
(D) To ~~talk about the advantages~~ of starting a **small business**

169번 문제 풀이 순서

STEP 1 문제의 키워드인 Willis 씨와 관련된 내용을 지문에서 찾아 보기와 대조하는 문제이다.
STEP 2 Willis 씨 근처에는 보기 중에 해당하는 내용이 없다.
STEP 3 Willis 씨 근처에 또 다른 키워드는 his popular book "Success Is Equal to Efforts"이다.
STEP 4 또 다른 keyword인 "Success Is Equal to Efforts"를 찾아보자.
지문 상단부의 A DCSBF press release indicated that Mr. Willis will emphasize some of the tips covered in his popular book "Success Is Equal to Efforts" published a few months ago.에서 Willis 씨는 몇 달 전에 "Success Is Equal to Efforts"라는 책을 출판했음을 알 수 있다. 따라서 정답은 (B)이다.

170번 문제 풀이 순서

STEP 1 구체적인 내용을 묻는 문제이다.
What, Mr. Willis, key를 키워드로 잡고 본문에서 스키밍(skimming)과 스캐닝(scanning)을 하여 찾아낸다.
STEP 2 두 번째 단락 Creating goods people want to purchase is the key element.에서 사람들이 구매하고 싶어 하는 상품을 만드는 것이 중요하다고 언급하고 있다. 따라서 소비자들의 관심을 끄는 물품을 확보하는 것이라는 (B)가 정답이다.

Dawson City Welcomes Small-Business Expert

Dawson City (June 11) – Franklin Willis, regarded as the "small business expert" by *Dawson City Chronicle*, has been invited as the keynote speaker at the fourth annual Dawson City Small Business Fair (DCSBF). The fair is scheduled to be held at the Dawson City Conference Center from July 1 through July 4. About 1,500 small business owners are expected to attend seminars and run their booths which can allow visitors to ask questions as well as collect information.

169. (B) He has published a book.

A DCSBF press release indicated that Mr. Willis will emphasize some of the tips covered in his popular book "Success Is Equal to Efforts" published a few months ago. Mr. Willis is confident that any new business scheme requires several key decisions to turn into a successful one. "Just creating goods you will sell won't make your business successful." Mr. Willis reflects his strong view in his book. "Creating goods people want to purchase is the key element. It is also a basic policy, and must be kept to is successful business in New York, ears.

170. (B) merchandise / appeals / customers

171번 문제 풀이 순서

STEP 1 170번을 해결한 후에는 중반부 이후의 나머지 지문을 읽지 않고 바로 171번 문제 분석을 먼저 한 후에 나머지 지문을 읽어야 한다.

STEP 2 문제를 분석한다. [위치 / 키워드 / 유형별 풀이 전략]
Why does Mr. Willis wants to participate in the fair? 마지막 문제 - 지문의 하단부 / wants 요구

STEP 3 지문의 하단부에서 I would like to라는 문장을 찾는다.
그 중에 live a successful life라는 키워드와 유사 어휘가 있는 부분이 답이다.

STEP 4 본문은 구체적 live a successful life이지만 답은 유사 어휘인 help가 있는 부분이 답이 된다.
Willis 씨가 박람회에 참석하려는 이유를 묻는 문제이다. 지문의 "I would like to help people in my home town live a successful life, so it is a good chance to do it by participating in the fair."에서 Willis 씨는 자신의 고향 사람들이 성공적인 삶을 살 수 있도록 만들어 주고 싶었는데, 박람회에 참석하는 것이 이 일을 할 수 있는 좋은 기회임을 언급하고 있다. 따라서 영세 기업 전문가인 Willis 씨가 자신의 고향의 기업가들을 돕기 위해 박람회에 참석하려고 함을 알 수 있으므로 정답은 (D)이다.

"I was born and raised in Dawson City." Mr. Willis added. "I would like to help people in my home town live a successful life, so it is a good chance to do it by participating in the fair. Small business owners can find many outstanding opportunities to make their businesses prosper if they follow the important and clear directions I suggest, and these will definitely make many other small businesses successful."

Admission to the fair is $120. Tickets can be purchased through the fair's website at www.dawsoncityfair.com/gr.

모의고사 해석
문제 168-171은 다음 기사를 참조하시오.

Dawson 시는 영세 기업 전문가를 환영합니다.

Dawson 시(7월 11일) – Dawson City Chronicle에서 영세 기업 전문가로 간주되는 Franklin Willis가 제4회 연례 Dawson 시 영세 기업 박람회(DCSBF)에 기조 연설자로 초청받았다. 박람회는 Dawson 시 회담 센터에서 7월 1일부터 7월 4일까지 열릴 예정이다. 약 1500명의 영세 기업 소유주들이 세미나에 참석하고, 정보를 수집할 수 있을 뿐만 아니라 방문객들이 질문을 할 수 있는 부스를 운영할 것으로 기대된다.

DCSBF 보도 자료에 따르면 Willis 씨는 몇 달 전에 출판된 그의 인기 있는 책인 "Success Is Equal to Efforts"에서 다룬 몇 개의 조언들을 강조할 것이다. Willis 씨는 모든 새로운 사업 계획은 몇 개의 주요 의사결정들을 성공적인 결정으로 바꿀 것을 요구한다고 확신한다. "당신이 팔려고 상품을 만드는 것은 당신의 사업을 성공적으로 만들지 못할 것이다." Willis는 그의 책에 그의 강한 견해를 반영한다. "사람들이 구매하고 싶어 하는 상품을 만드는 것은 중요한 요소이다. 그것은 또한 기본적인 정책이고, 사업에서 성공하기 위해서는 유지돼야 한다." Willis 씨는 지난 15년 간 그의 가족들과 함께 살아 왔던 뉴욕에서 성공적인 사업을 운영해 오고 있다.

"저는 Dawsin 시에서 태어나고 자랐습니다." Willis 씨는 덧붙였다. "저는 제 고향 주민들이 성공적인 삶을 살도록 해 주고 싶었기 때문에, 박람회에 참석하여 일을 해 보는 것은 좋은 기회입니다. 영세 기업 소유주들이 만일 제가 제안한 중요하고 분명한 지침을 따른다면, 그들은 그들의 사업을 번영하게 만들 많은 훌륭한 기회들을 발견할 수 있고, 이러한 지침들은 분명히 많은 다른 영세기업들이 성공하도록 만들 것입니다."

박람회 입장료는 120달러이다. 입장 티켓은 박람회 웹사이트인 www.dawsoncityfair.com/gr.를 통해 지불할 수 있다.

168. 기사의 목적은 무엇인가?
(A) 영세 기업을 새로 시작하는 방법을 보고하기 위해
(B) 고객의 관심을 끌어당길 새로운 전략을 논의하기 위해
(C) 한 사업가가 그의 고향을 방문하는 것을 알리기 위해
(D) 영세 기업 개장의 장점에 대해 말하기 위해

169. Willis 씨에 대해 언급된 것은 무엇인가?
(A) 많은 세미나를 이끌었다.
(B) 책을 발간했다.
(C) 상을 탔다.
(D) Dawson 시를 방문한 적이 없다.

170. Willis 씨는 성공적인 기업가에게 중요한 점이 무엇이라고 언급하는가?
(A) 공격적인 마케팅 전략을 개발하는 것
(B) 소비자들의 관심을 끄는 물품을 확보하는 것
(C) 상품을 효율적인 비용으로 만드는 방법을 고안해 내는 것
(D) 뛰어난 제조 시설을 갖는 것

171. 왜 Willis 씨는 박람회에 참가하려고 하는가?
(A) 보고서를 위한 약간의 정보를 얻기 위해
(B) 매우 자질 있는 직원을 고용하기 위해
(C) 그의 현재 사업을 향상시키기 위해
(D) 그의 고향에 있는 사업가들을 돕기 위해

172번 문제 풀이 순서

STEP 1 등장하는 사람들이 어떤 직종에서 근무하는지를 묻는 문제이다.
What, kind, product를 키워드로 잡고 본문에서 스키밍(skimming)과 스캐닝(scanning)을 하여 찾아낸다.

STEP 2 지문에서 That's a customized gold bracelet, right? The process for engraving a client's personalized message on an item normally needs at least 2 days.에서 순금 팔찌를 취급하는 회사임을 알 수 있다. 따라서 정답은 (B)이다.

173번 문제 풀이 순서

STEP 1 172번을 해결한 후에는 상단부 이후의 나머지 지문을 읽지 않고 바로 173번 문제 분석을 먼저 한 후에 나머지 지문을 읽어야 한다.

STEP 2 문제를 분석한다. [위치 / 키워드 / 유형별 풀이 전략]
What does the client ask to do? 두 번째 문제 - 지문 상단부 / ask 요구

SETP 3 지문의 상단부에서 the client wanted라는 문장을 찾는다.
그 중에 add라는 키워드와 유사 어휘가 있는 부분이 답이다.

STEP 4 본문은 구체적 add이지만 답은 유사 어휘인 update가 있는 부분이 답이 된다.
고객이 요청하는 사항이 무엇인지 묻는 문제이다. 지문의 If you haven't, the client wanted us to add item #882-S1.에서 고객은 새로운 제품을 주문 내역에 추가하고 싶다고 언급했음을 알 수 있다. 따라서 정답은 (B)이다.

Eleanor Porter - 4 May, 11:15
Curtis, have you sent **order** #0022-B5 yet?
If you haven't, the client wanted us to **add item** #882-S1.

173. (B) Update an order

Curtis Ramos - 4 May, 11:18
That's a customized **gold bracelet**, right? The process for engraving a client's personalized message on an item normally needs

172. (B) Jewelry

174번 문제 풀이 순서

STEP 1 등장인물은 총 3명이다.
Eleanor Porter : 보석 가게에서 일하는 사람
Curtis Ramos: 보석 가게에서 일하는 사람
Francies Rojas: 글자를 새기는 세공가

STEP 2 대화의 주제 파악과 업무의 진행 상황을 정리한다.
Eleanor Porter 고객의 수정 사항을 알림 → Curtis Ramos 상황 파악 후 세공사(Francies Rojas)에게 이를 알림 → 세공가 Francies Rojas 고객의 주문을 더 빨리 처리 가능

STEP 3 세 번째 문제의 답은 중반부에 위치한다.

STEP 4 사람 이름은 가장 중요한 키워드이다.
Ramos가 Rojas에게 연락한 이유는 Porter 씨가 고객의 주문이 더 빨리 처리될 수 있는지 묻자 Ramos는 I'd better talk with a person from the engraving division. 즉, 글자를 새기는 부서에 연락해 보겠다고 말하며 Francies에게 연락해 묻고 있다. 따라서 정답은 (D)이다.

175번 문제 풀이 순서

STEP 1 의도 문제는 주어진 표현과 같은 뜻을 찾는 것이 아니라 위아래 문맥을 포괄적으로 설명하는 것이 답이 된다. 따라서 문맥을 보면
How soon does it need to be completed? Would a day be okay?
얼마나 빨리 완성되어야만 하나요? 하루면 괜찮나요?

STEP 2 보기에서 오류 내용을 제거한다.
(A) She is happy that ~~the equipment will be repaired in time~~.
(B) Her client will be pleased if a product will be engraved in a day.
(C) She has a ~~plan to interview a person~~ for a position.
(D) She has ~~chosen new items~~ for a newly designed pamphlet.

Eleanor Porter - 4 May, 11:19
Is it possible to get it done more quickly? The client wants it sooner than that.

Curtis Ramos - 4 May, 11:21
I'd better talk with a person from the engraving division.

Curtis Ramos - 4 May, 11:23
Francies, could you do an urgent work on a bracelet? The model number is #882-S1, which is for order #0022-B5.

174. (D) check if / done earlier

Francies Rojas - 4 May, 11:24
How soon does it need to be completed? Would a day be okay?

Eleanor Porter - 4 May, 11:25
Great, that will work. Thanks both of you for help!

175. (B) client / pleased / in a day

모의고사 해석
문제 172-175는 다음 문자 메시지를 참조하시오.

Eleanor Porter – 5월 4일, 11시 15분
Curtis, 주문 번호 0022-B5 발송했나요?
아직 안했다면, 고객 분이 제품 번호 883-S1를 추가해 주길 원하셨어요.

Curtis Ramos – 5월 4일, 11시 18분
주문 제작형 순금 팔찌 말씀하시는 거 맞으시죠? 고객 분의 개인적인 메시지를 새기는 과정은 보통 최소 이틀이 필요해요.

Eleanor Porter – 5월 4일, 11시 19분
더 빨리 끝낼 수 있을까요? 고객 분이 더 빨리 완성되길 원하시거든요.

Curtis Ramos – 5월 4일, 11시 21분
글자를 새기는 부서의 사람과 대화하는 게 낫겠어요.

Curtis Ramos – 5월 4일, 11시 23분
Francies, 팔찌 업무가 급한데 이것부터 해 주시겠어요? 모델 번호는 883-S1이고, 주문 번호는 0022-B5입니다.

Francies Rojas – 5월 4일, 11시 24분
얼마나 빨리 완성되어야만 하나요? 하루면 괜찮나요?

Eleanor Porter – 5월 4일, 11시 25분
네, 좋습니다. 두 분 다 도와주셔서 감사합니다!

172. 이 회사는 어떤 상품을 취급하는가?
(A) 포장재
(B) 보석류
(C) 의류
(D) 묘비

173. 고객이 요청하는 사항은 무엇인가?
(A) 환불 받는 것
(B) 주문 내역을 업데이트하는 것
(C) 배송지의 주소를 변경하는 것
(D) 다른 포장 방법을 시도하는 것

174. Ramos 씨는 왜 Rojas 씨에게 연락했는가?
(A) 그녀에게 이전의 주문품에 실수가 있었음을 알려주기 위해
(B) 정확한 주문품의 배송 일자를 알기 위해
(C) 고객과의 만남 일정을 변경하기 위해
(D) 업무가 더 일찍 처리될 수 있는지 확인하기 위해

175. 11시 25분에, Porter 씨가 "that will work"라고 적을 때 의미한 것은 무엇인가?
(A) 그녀는 장비가 제시간 안에 수리되어서 기쁘다.
(B) 상품이 하루 안에 새겨진다면 그녀의 고객은 기뻐할 것이다.
(C) 그녀는 이 자리에 적합한 사람을 인터뷰할 계획을 가지고 있다.
(D) 그녀는 새롭게 제작되는 팸플릿을 위해 새 물건을 선택했다.

176번 문제 풀이 순서

STEP 1 문제에 article이 언급되었기 때문에 답은 첫 번째 문서에서 찾아야 하며 Not Question은 보기의 키워드를 본문에서 하나씩 소거해야 한다.

(A) It has worked with clients in London.
(B) It employs workers to conduct its projects.
(C) It has been in business for over three years.
(D) It can make landlords more profits.

**Daily Business News Report:
Invigorate Refurbishment Inc. (IRI)**

176. (C) 개업 2년

Julius and Ivan Sheltons' two-year-old firm, Invigorate Refurbishment Inc. (IRI), is bringing a new sensation to the real estate market in central London. This mid-size company is working with current landlords in the area to renovate [176. (A)] ntial buildings. These two consultants appraise houses and buildings to identify how to upgrade the properties to increase their value and more rental income.

176. (D)

From interior walls and floors to exterior surfaces including landscaping, IRI not only hires experienced workers but also trains them to be skilled in finishing project properly. Thus far, central London is the area most of their work has been focused on.

One of the landlords in the area, Everett Sims, made a few contracts with Sheltons' firm to renovate his residential building. "Since I started working with IRI, the revenue from my rental business has gone up to 10 percent due to cost-cutting in water and power as well as significant increases in tenant demand. Tenants called me and said that the new balconies are so nice that they are enjoying the beautiful views and fresh air. I will definitely use IRI for consultation again." said Mr. Sims.

More information on the Sheltons' business can be learned through its website, i-refurbish.com, where a detailed proposal for a project can be handed in.

176. (B)

STEP 2 Not Question은 보기의 키워드가 본문에서 검색되지 않는 것이 답이 된다. 따라서 개업한 지 2년 된 회사라고 언급했으므로 정답은 (C)이다.

177번 문제 풀이 순서

STEP 1 본문의 내용은 구체적이지만 답은 포괄적이다.

STEP 2 Sims change라는 키워드가 답을 결정한다. 세번째 문단에서 Mr. Sims가 언급되고 있다.
cost-cutting / increases in tenant demand / new balconies 등을 종합해 보면 건물을 개조하면서 많은 변화가 일어났음을 알 수 있다.

STEP 3 Tenants called me and said that the new balconies are so nice that they are enjoying the beautiful views and fresh air.에서 임대인들이 새로 만들어진 발코니에 대해서 칭찬을 했기에 정답은 (B)이다.

178번 문제 풀이 순서

STEP 1 본문을 읽기 전에 반드시 문제를 먼저 분석해야 한다. 문제는 다음의 세 가지를 알려준다.
① 답의 위치 ② 문제 풀이 전략 ③ 키워드

178. According to the article, what are **potential clients advised** to do?
- According to the article, 첫 번째 문서에 답이 있다.
- 요청/제안의 내용은 문서 하단부에 있다.

STEP 2 보기의 키워드들을 검색하고 오류가 있는 보기를 소거한다.

**Daily Business News Report:
Invigorate Refurbishment Inc. (IRI)**

Julius and Ivan Sheltons' two-year-old firm, Invigorate Refurbishment Inc. (IRI), is bringing a new sensation to the <u>real estate market</u> in central London. This mid-size company is working with current landlords in the area to renovate old residential buildings. <u>These two consultants appraise houses and buildings to identify how to upgrade the properties to increase their value and more rental income.</u>

From interior walls and floors to exterior surfaces including landscaping, IRI not only hires experienced workers but also trains them to be skilled in finishing project properly. Thus far, central London is the area most of their work has been focused on.

One of the landlords in the area, Everett Sims, made a few contracts with Sheltons' firm to renovate his residential building. "Since I started working with IRI, the revenue from my rental business has gone up to 10 percent due to cost-cutting in water and power as well as significant increases in tenant demand. Tenants called me and said that the new balconies are so nice that they are enjoying the beautiful views and fresh air. I will definitely use IRI for consultation again." said Mr. Sims.

<u>More information on the Sheltons' business can be learned through its website, i-refurbish.com, where a detailed proposal for a project can be handed in.</u>

(C) Access a website

STEP 3 본문의 내용은 항상 paraphrasing된다.
can be learned through its website, i-refurbish. com, where a detailed proposal for a project can be handed in.에서 건물을 보수하기를 원하는 고객들이 사이트에 접속해서 신청서를 올려야 하므로 정답은 (C)이다.

179번 문제 풀이 순서

STEP 1 문제에서 제시되는 사람은 두 번째 문서에 있다.
이 경우에는 특정 사람이 언급된 문서에서 조건을 정리하여 두 번째 문서에서 답을 선택해야 한다.

STEP 2 두 번째 문서에서 Mr. Stevenson이 건물을 싸게(at a low cost) 살 수 있었던 이유를 먼저 정리한다.
The sale price was very low because the actual state of the property is quite poor and not inhabitable at the moment.
실제 매물 상태가 꽤 오래 되었고 그 당시에는 살기에 적합하지 않아 매매 가격은 낮았습니다.

STEP 3 본문의 내용은 구체적이지만 답은 포괄적이다.
주거용으로 부적합했기에 가격이 낮았다는 점에서 정답은 (B)이다.

180번 문제 풀이 순서

STEP 1 문제에서 제시되는 사람은 두 번째 문서에 있다.
이 경우에는 특정인이 언급된 문서에서 조건을 정리하여 두 번째 문서에서 답을 선택해야 한다.

STEP 2 두 번째 문서에서 Mr. Stevenson의 요구 사항에 대하여 먼저 정리한다.

> 런던 근처에서 사무실 건물을 사서 residential space로 바꾸고자 한다.

STEP 3 첫 번째 문서에서 Thus far, central London is the area most of their work has been focused on.에서 지금까지 주요 업무는 런던 중심에 집중되어 있음을 알 수 있고 Stevenson의 건물은 런던 중심부가 아닌 곳에서 위치해 있다는 내용의 (A)가 정답이다.

180. How is Mr. Stevenson's proposition different from typical jobs for IRI?

❶ 문제 키워드 확인

FROM	Devin **Stevenson** <dstevenson@placelife.net>
TO	Julius Sheltons <jsheltons@i-refurbish.com>
RE	propositions for renovation
DATE	August 11

Mr. Sheltons,

❷ 요구 사항을 확인

I am sending this e-mail as I have just acquired an office building in **Southwark**, a commercial district **near London**. I believed that you might be interested in the project. The sale price was very low because the actual state of the property is quite poor and not inhabitable at the moment. But it is located near a train station, which can be a huge advantage. I would like **to convert** the property into **a great residential space** with the ten flats in the building for rent within a few months.

Daily Business News Report: Invigorate Refurbishment Inc. (IRI)

Julius and Ivan Sheltons' two-year-old firm, Invigorate Refurbishment Inc. (IRI), is bringing a new sensation to the real estate market in central London. This mid-size company is working with current landlords in the area to renovate old residential buildings. These two consultants appraise houses and buildings to identify how to upgrade the properties to increase their value and more rental income.

From interior walls and floors to exterior surfaces including landscaping, IRI not only hires experienced workers but also trains them to be skilled in finishing project properly. Thus far, central London is the area most of their work has been focused on.

❸ 차이점을 확인

모의고사 해석
문제 176–180은 다음 기사와 이메일을 참조하시오.

일일 비즈니스 뉴스:
Invigorate Refurbishment 주식회사. (IRI)

Julis와 Ivan Shelton의 2년 된 회사인, Invigorate Refurbishment 주식회사(IRI)는 런던 중심부에 있는 부동산시장에 새로운 열풍을 가져오고 있습니다. 이 중소기업은 그 지역에 있는 임대주들과 오래된 주택을 개조하기 위해서 일을 하고 있습니다. 두 명의 상담가는 더 높은 가치와 더 많은 임대 수입을 위해 부동산을 개선할 방법을 찾기 위해 집과 건물들을 감정합니다.

내부 벽과 바닥부터 조경을 포함한 외부 표면까지, IRI는 경험이 풍부한 직원을 고용할 뿐만 아니라 그들이 제대로 공사를 끝낼 수 있도록 훈련시키고 있습니다. 지금까지, 런던 중심부는 대부분의 작업이 집중되어 있던 지역입니다.

그 지역 집주인 중 한 명인, Everett Sims는 그가 가진 주택을 개조하려고 Sheltons의 회사와 여러 번 계약을 맺었습니다. "제가 IRI와 일을 시작한 이후부터, 수도와 전력에서의 비용 절감과 입주 수요의 상당한 증가 때문에 임대 사업의 수익은 10%까지 올라갔습니다. 세입자들은 저게 전화를 해서 새로운 발코니가 너무 멋져서 아름다운 풍경과 맑은 공기를 즐길 수 있다고 말했습니다. 저는 틀림없이 IRI에게 상담을 또 요청할 것입니다."라고 Sims 씨가 말했습니다.

Sheltons의 사업에 대한 더 많은 정보는 웹 사이트, i-refurbish.com.og,에서 알 수 있고 여기서 프로젝트에 대한 상세한 제안서를 제출할 수 있습니다.

발신 : Devin Stevenson 〈dstevenson@placelife.net〉
수신: Julius Sheltons 〈jnichols@i-refurbish.com.og〉
제목: 수리 제안서
날짜: 8월 11일

Sheltons 씨께.

저는 런던 근처에 있는 상업 지구인, Southwark에 사무실 건물을 막 구입해서, 이 이메일을 보냅니다. 당신이 이 프로젝트에 관심이 있을 거라고 믿습니다. 실제 매물 상태가 꽤 오래되었고 그 당시에는 살기에 적합하지 않아 매매 가격은 낮았습니다. 그러나 기차역 근처에 위치해 있고, 이는 엄청난 이점이 될 수 있습니다. 저는 몇 달 이내에 이 건물을 임대가 가능한 10가구를 갖춘 멋진 거주 공간으로 바꾸고 싶습니다.

저는 건설 사업에 있어서 경험이 많지 않기에 당신의 도움은 사업에 있어서 대단히 유익할 것입니다. 게다가 새로운 배출 가스 규제 준수에 대한 정보와 난방에 대한 잠재적인 보수 계획이 어떤 영향을 가져올지에 대한 정보를 알 수 있을까요? 저와 이런 사항에 대해서 이야기를 나눌 수 있는지 알려주세요.

감사해요.

Devin Stevenson

176. 기사에 따르면, Invigorate Refurbishment Inc. (IRI)에 대해서 사실이 아닌 것은 무엇인가?
(A) 런던에서 고객과 일해 왔다.
(B) 프로젝트를 수행할 직원들을 고용한다.
(C) 3년 넘게 영업해 오고 있다.
(D) 임대주에게 더 많은 이익을 가져다줄 수 있다.

177. Sims의 부동산에 어떤 변화가 일어났는가?
(A) 몇 군데의 바닥은 확장되고 있다.
(B) 개방된 공간이 건물 외벽에 건축되어 있다.
(C) 최첨단의 승강기가 설치되어 있다.
(D) 가구와 전자기기는 업그레이드되어 있다.

178. 기사에 따르면, 잠재적인 고객들이 무엇을 하도록 조언 받고 있는가?
(A) 부동산 중개업소의 목록을 이메일로 보내기
(B) 부동산 가격을 알려주기
(C) 웹 사이트에 접속하기
(D) 견적을 요청하기

179. Stevenson 씨가 낮은 가격에 부동산을 살 수 있었던 이유는 무엇인가?
(A) 상업적인 목표로 사용되었다.
(B) 임대용으로 바뀌어야 한다.
(C) 전반적인 매물 가격은 최근에 하락했다.
(D) 위치는 시내를 벗어나 있다.

180. Stevenson의 제의는 **IRI**에 대한 기존의 일과 다른 점은 무엇인가?
(A) 프로젝트는 런던 밖에서 진행될 것이다.
(B) **Stevenson** 씨는 이미 다른 회사들과 상담했다.
(C) 건설비는 예상한 것보다 비싸다.
(D) 시간 제약은 일을 끝내기에 충분히 길지 않다.

181번 문제 풀이 순서

STEP 1 기본적인 정보인 이메일의 목적을 묻는 문제이다.
목적은 본문의 상단부에서 언급된다. 본문의 첫 문장에서 For a given period time, Shelton's Eat & Life is offering special rates ~로 보아 이 이메일의 주제나 목적을 말하고 있음을 알 수 있다.

STEP 2 특별 광고 할인 혜택을 홍보하기 위해 Salazar 씨에게 이메일을 보냈음을 알 수 있으므로 (B)가 정답이다.
(A)는 할인(discount)은 맞지만 구독료 할인(discount on a subscription)을 해 주는 것이 아니다.
(C)는 어떤 정보를 알려주는 것은 맞지만 책(publication)의 신간에 대한 것을 알려주는 것은 아니므로 오답이다.
(D)는 홍보를 하고 있는 것은 맞지만 농업 관련 상품에 대한 것은 아니므로 오답이다.

TO	t.salazar@sunny-field.net
FROM	simon@sheltonseatlife.com
DATE	October 11
SUBJECT	Shelton's Eat & Life

Dear Mr. Salazar,

For a given period of time, Shelton's Eat & Life is **offering special rates on advertisements** to businesses that have not yet placed theirs in our publication.

182번 문제 풀이 순서

STEP 1 처음 2줄을 skimming하여 주요 정보와 대략의 상황을 파악한다.
Shelton's Eat & Life / special rates / advertisements to business
sign a contract / more than 40,000 potential clients / agricultural sector

STEP 2 두 번째 문제를 분석한다. [위치 / 키워드 / 유형별 풀이 전략]
두 번째 문제 - 지문의 상단부 / 사실인 것을 묻는 문제는 보기를 먼저 정리한다.

182. What is indicated about **Shelton's Eat & Life**?
(A) full-color magazine / available
(B) readership / expanded / recently
(C) special issue / released / soon
(D) advertising rates / increased

SETP 3 보기의 키워드를 본문에서 검색하여 나머지 문장 중에 오류 요소를 제거한다.
질문의 키워드인 Shelton's Eat & Life와 관련된 내용을 지문에서 찾아 보기와 대조하는 문제이다. 지문의 To make a request for any of these advertisements in full color, consult one of our designers for your custom advertisement, or inquire about more information, please reply to this e-mail or call us at 892-1244-578.에서 광고 전면을 컬러로 요청할 수 있음을 언급하고 있으므로 정답은 (A)이다.

TO	t.salazar@sunny-field.net
FROM	simon@sheltonseatlife.com
DATE	October 11
SUBJECT	Shelton's Eat & Life

Dear Mr. Salazar,

(C) 특별호(special issue)가 아닌 특별 할인(special rate)이다
(D) 광고료는 언급되었으나 할인해 준다는 내용만 언급(increase x)

For a given period of time, Shelton's Eat & Life is offering **special rates** on advertisements to businesses that have not yet placed theirs in our publication. Once you sign a contract with us for your advertisement, your business will be able to reach more than 40,000 potential clients in the agricultural sector in website and print alike. This is absolutely a great **opportunity** for you to **expand** your **client base**. Please be advised that this offer will last until November 10 and is **(B) 고객의 고객층을 확장한다고 언급 (주체가 다름)** The outlined details are below.

Monthly Price	Package	Type
$300	4" × 4" online ad plus one quarter-page print ad	A
$365	4" × 4" online ad plus one half-page print ad	B
$415	5" × 6" online ad plus one half-page print ad	C
$565	7" × 2" online ad plus one full-page print ad	D

To make a request for any of these advertisements **in full color**, consult one of our designers for your custom advertisement, or inquire about more information, please reply to this e-mail or call us at 892-1244-578. You can access further details for advertisements at www.sheltonseatlife.com/ads.

Sincerely,

Noel Simon
Head of Marketing
Shelton's Eat & Life

183번 문제 풀이 순서

STEP 1 문제의 키워드인 Mr. Simon은 첫 번째 지문과 두 번째 지문 모두 나온다. 이 경우에는 두 문서를 동시에 이용해야 한다.

TO	t.salazar@sunny-field.net
FROM	simon@sheltonseatlife.com
DATE	October 11
SUBJECT	Shelton's Eat & Life

– 중략 –

<u>To make a request for any of these advertisements in full color, consult one of our designers for your custom advertisement, or inquire about more information, please reply to this e-mail or call us at 893-1244-578.</u> You can access further details for advertisements at www.sheltonseatlife.com/ads.

> Simon 씨는 Salazar 씨에게 질문할 사항이 있다면 발신인인 자신에게 메일을 보내줄 것을 요청하였다.

STEP 2 두 번째 문서에서 요구 사항을 확인해야 한다.

TO	simon@sheltonseatlife.com
FROM	t.salazar@sunny-field.net
DATE	October 18
SUBJECT	Re: Shelton's Eat & Life

> Salazar 씨는 위의 주소로 웹사이트 광고에 관해 구체적인 정보를 줄 것을 요청하였다.

Hello Mr. Simon,

I have read the e-mail you sent and thought it would be good for our farm to place an advertisement in Shelton's Eat & Life. <u>Yet, I need some specific information about the website ads.</u>

STEP 3 Simon 씨는 Salazar 씨에게 추가적인 세부 정보를 줄 수 있는 사람임을 알 수 있으므로 정답은 (B)이다.

184번 문제 풀이 순서

STEP 1 보기의 단어들은 모두 place와 동의어이다.
  (A) put = place 놓다, 두다
  (B) find = place (적절한 직업이나, 집을) 찾다
  (C) employ = place (사람을) 고용하다
  (D) consider = place (장점을) 고려하다, 생각하다

TO	simon@sheltonseatlife.com
FROM	t.salazar@sunny-field.net
DATE	October 18
SUBJECT	Re: Shelton's Eat & Life

Hello Mr. Simon,

I have read the e-mail you sent and thought it would be good for our farm to place an advertisement in Shelton's Eat & Life. ~

STEP 2	동의어 찾기 문제는 단순히 같은 뜻을 찾는 것이 아니다. 본문에서 문맥상 대체할 수 있는 단어를 보기 중에서 선택한다.

I have read the e-mail you sent and thought it would be good for our farm to place an advertisement in Shelton's Eat & Life.에서 Shelton's Eat & Life에 광고를 '내는' 것이 농장에 도움이 된다고 언급을 하고 있다. '(광고를) 내다, 게시하다'의 뜻으로 place가 사용되었으므로 보기 중 '놓다, 두다'의 뜻인 (A) put이 정답이다.

185번 문제 풀이 순서

STEP 1	문제에서 제시되는 사람은 두 문서에 모두 언급되고 있다.

첫 번째 문서는 광고성 이메일로 일반적인 내용만을 언급하고 있다. 이 경우에는 특정 사람이 보낸 문서에서 조건을 정리하여 첫 번째 문서에서 답을 선택해야 한다.

STEP 2	두 번째 문서에서 Salazar 씨가 원하는 조건을 먼저 정리한다.

Where precisely would the 5" × 6" advertisement be placed on your website?에서 Salazar 씨는 5" × 6" 광고를 이용하려고 함을 알 수 있다

STEP 3	첫 번째 지문의 표에서 5" × 6" 크라인 광고는 (C)에 해당됨을 알 수 있으므로 정답은 (C)이다.

모의고사 해석
문제 181-185는 다음 이메일들을 참조하시오.

수신인	t.salazar@sunny-field.net
발신인	simon@sheltonseatlife.com
날짜	10월 11일
주제	Shelton's Eat & Life

Salazar 씨께

주어진 기간 동안, **Shelton's Eat & Life**는 저희 출판물에 광고를 게시한 적이 없는 사업체에 광고에 대한 특별 할인을 제공해 드리고 있습니다. 당신의 광고를 위해 저희와의 계약에 서명하신다면, 당신의 기업은 웹사이트와 인쇄물 상의 농업 분야에서 40,000명 이상의 잠재적인 고객들에게 접근하실 수 있으십니다. 이것은 당신의 고객 기반을 확장시키기 위해 당신이 이용하셔야만 하는 좋은 기회임이 틀림없습니다. 이 제안은 11월 10일까지 지속될 것이고, 처음 이용하시는 광고주에게만 해당되는 사항임을 기억하시기 바랍니다. 대략적인 세부 사항은 아래와 같습니다.

월별 가격	패키지	유형
300달러	4" × 4" 온라인 광고와 1/4 페이지 인쇄물 광고	A
365달러	4" × 4" 온라인 광고와 1/2 페이지 인쇄물 광고	B
415달러	5" × 6" 온라인 광고와 1/2 페이지 인쇄물 광고	C
565달러	7" × 2" 온라인 광고와 한 페이지 전면 인쇄물 광고	D

이 광고들 전면을 컬러로 요청하시거나, 당신이 주문한 광고를 위해 저희 디자이너와 상담하시거나, 더 많은 정보에 관해 질문하시려면, 위의 주소로 이메일을 보내 주시거나 892-1244-578로 저희에게 전화주시기 바랍니다. 당신은 www.sheltonseatlife.com/ads에서 광고에 관한 더 자세한 세부 사항을 보실 수 있으십니다.

감사합니다.

Noel Simon
마케팅 담당자
Shelton's Eat & Life

수신인	t.salazar@sunny-field.net
발신인	simon@sheltonseatlife.com
날짜	10월 18일
주제	Shelton's Eat & Life

안녕하세요, Simon 씨.

저는 당신이 보내신 이메일을 읽었는데, **Shelton's Eat & Life**에 광고를 내는 것이 저희 농장에 수익을 가져다 줄 것이라 생각했어요. 그런데, 저는 웹사이트 광고에 대한 구체적인 정보가 좀 필요해요. 제가 귀사의 웹사이트 상에서 세부 사항들을 살펴봤는데, 광고의 위치가 명확하지 않더군요. 5" × 6" 광고는 귀사의 웹사이트에서 정확히 어디에 게시되나요? 제가 자세한 설명 내용을 받으면, 지불 내역과 함께 저희 광고의 전자 파일을 보내 드리겠습니다.

감사합니다.

Todd Salazar
Sunny Field Farm 소유주

181. Simon 씨가 Salazar 씨에게 이메일을 보낸 주된 이유는 무엇인가?
(A) 그녀에게 구독료 할인을 주기 위해
(B) 특별 프로모션 행사를 발표하기 위해
(C) 그에게 출판물의 새로운 출시를 알려주기 위해
(D) 농업 상품을 홍보하기 위해

182. Shelton's Eat & Life에 대해 언급된 것은 무엇인가?
(A) 전면을 컬러로 하는 잡지가 구매 가능하다.
(B) 구독률이 최근에 늘었다.
(C) 특별호가 곧 출시될 것이다.
(D) 광고비가 증가됐다.

183. Simon 씨에 대해 언급된 것은 무엇인가?
(A) 광고 웹디자이너이다.
(B) 추가적인 세부 정보를 제공할 수 있다.
(C) 11월에 사무실을 떠날 것이다.
(D) 전에 Salazar 씨와 일했었다.

184. 두 번째 이메일에서, 첫 번째 문단 첫 번째 줄의 "place"와 가장 의미상 가까운 것은 무엇인가?
(A) 놓다
(B) 찾다
(C) 고용하다
(D) 고려하다

185. Salazar 씨가 이용하려는 광고의 유형은 무엇인가?
(A) A 유형
(B) B 유형
(C) C 유형
(D) D 유형

186번 문제 풀이 순서

STEP 1 처음 2줄을 skimming하여 주요 정보와 대략의 상황을 파악한다.
celebrate / Shawn's Healing Tours / 10th anniversary
summer packages / 15 percent off / Travel reservations / before 10th of August / benefit from this offer

STEP 2 첫 번째 문제를 분석한다. [위치 / 키워드 / 유형별 풀이 전략]
첫 번째 문제 - 지문 상단부 / 사실인 것을 묻는 문제는 보기를 먼저 정리한다.

186. What is indicated about Shawn's Healing Tours?

(A) ~~opened / new branch~~ / in the region
(B) release / ~~new tour packages~~
(C) schedules / **more than one time in a month**
(D) ~~expanded~~ / into a new market. [사업 확장에 관해 언급하지 않음]

STEP 3 보기의 키워드를 본문에서 검색하여 나머지 문장 중에 오류 요소를 제거한다.
질문의 키워드인 Shawn's Healing Tours와 관련된 내용을 지문에서 찾아 보기와 대조하는 문제이다. 첫 번째 지문의 Our summer tours are offered on a weekly basis, but you are advised to make your reservation as early as possible before they are booked up!에서 여름 투어가 매주 있을 것이라 언급하고 있으므로 한 달에 한 번 이상 투어가 예정되어 있다는 내용의 (C)가 정답이다.

Shawn's Healing Tours
★★★★★
Wellington, New Zealand

186. (A) 새 지점 개업이 아닌 10주년 축하

To celebrate Shawn's Healing Tours' **10th anniversary**, **all summer packages** are being offered at 15 percent off the **prices of last year's tours**. Travel reservations made on or before 10th of A[...] Our summer tours are **offered on a weekly basis**, but [...] servation as early as [...] they are booked up! The following are some of the lists of our tour packa[...]

186. (B) 작년과 올해의 동일 상품

186. (C) 매주 여행 상품 존재

▶ *Masterton and Palmerston*: This two-day tour starts with visiting one of the oldest harbor in New Zealand. Enjoy some of the best native arts and listen to modern live music. The tour will proceed to Palmerston, and explore not only ancient castles and ruins but also forests.

187번 문제 풀이 순서

STEP 1 본문의 내용은 구체적이지만 답은 포괄적이다.

STEP 2 provide라는 키워드가 답을 결정한다.
여성 패키지 목록인 Masterton and Palmerston / Napier / Hastings and Wanganui를 종합해 보면 고객들에게 여행 상품을 제공한다는 것을 알 수 있다.

STEP 3 clients 또한 중요한 키워드이다.
하단부의 The length and type in attractions in tours can be customized to your requests.를 통해 투어의 길이를 고객의 요청에 따라 조정할 수 있음을 언급하고 있다. 따라서 유연한 투어 시간이라는 내용의 (C)가 정답이다.

188번 문제 풀이 순서

STEP 1 문제 중의 키워드는 Ms. Felix's tour이다. Ms. Felix는 두 번째 문서에 등장한다.

STEP 2 두 번째 지문에서 Felix 씨에게 8월 2일에 여행 예약 확인 메일이 보내졌음을 알 수 있다.

STEP 3 첫 번째 지문에서 두 번째 키워드를 확인한다.
To celebrate Shawn's Healing Tours' 10th anniversary, all summer packages are being offered at 15 percent off the prices of last year's tours. Travel reservations made on or before 10th of August can benefit from this offer.에서 8월 10일 이전에 여행 예약이 이뤄지면 할인된 가격을 적용 받을 수 있다고 언급되었다.

STEP 4 Felix 씨는 할인된 가격으로 여행을 다녀왔음을 알 수 있으므로 정답은 (C)이다.

189번 문제 풀이 순서

STEP 1 영어 단어들은 한 단어가 여러 뜻을 가지며 여러 개의 동의어를 갖는다.
따라서 serve의 동의어는 여러 단어가 있다. '같은 시대의, 현대의, 동시의, 같은 나이의' 등의 동의어가 있다.

STEP 2 'serve'이 해당 위치에서 어떤 의미로 쓰였는지를 먼저 확인한다.
And also I felt that staff members were well trained to serve customers well.
직원들이 고객들을 잘 '응대하도록' 잘 훈련 받았음을 느꼈다고 언급하고 있다. '(고객을) 응대하다, 시중 들다'의 뜻으로 serve가 사용되었으므로 보기 중 '(사람을) 다루다, 대하다'의 뜻인 (B) treat이 정답이다.

190번 문제 풀이 순서

STEP 1 문제의 키워드인 Mr. Webb은 세 번째 지문에 있다.

Feedback after taking part in a tour

As a professional photographer, on the t[...]nd to none. And also I felt that staff members w[...] I will definitely be back for more adventures. **Kenny Webb, our guide**, was experienced and knowledgeable. Since **he is a native of the area**, he introduced a broad familiarity with the traditional culture and customs of the region. I became more interested in the area through his intriguing descriptions.

Posted by Patsy Felix

> 190 ❶ 키워드(Ms. Webb) 확인
> ❷ Webb = our guide, native of the area

STEP 2 두 번째 문서에서 Mr. Webb이 어떤 여행 상품의 가이드였는지를 확인한다.

Dear Ms. Felix,
Thanks for making your trip reservation with **Shawn's Healing Tours**. This is to confirm your booking for one passenger:

Type of Tour: **Hastings and Wanganui**
Departure Date and Time from Wellington: Friday, 10 August, 10:30
Return to Wellington: Sunday, 13 August, 18:30
The total Rate: $175.00 (charged to your credit card)

> ❸ Felix 씨가 선택한 여행 상품 확인

STEP 3 Felix 씨가 관광 유형 중 Hastings와 Wanganui 유형을 선택했음을 알 수 있으므로 Webb 씨는 Hastings 출신임을 알 수 있다. 따라서 정답은 (A)이다.

모의고사 해석
문제 186–190은 다음 광고, 이메일, 웹사이트 반응을 참조하시오.

Shawn's Healing Tours
★ ★ ★ ★ ★
Wellington, New Zealand

Shawn's Healing Tours는 10주년을 기념하기 위해, 모든 여름 패키지들이 작년 투어 가격에서 15퍼센트 할인된 가격으로 제공되고 있습니다. 8월 10일이나 이전에 이뤄진 여행 예약은 이 행사가 적용될 수 있습니다. 저희의 여름 투어는 매주 제공되지만, 예약이 꽉 차기 전에 가능한 한 빨리 당신이 예약을 하시길 바랍니다! 다음은 저희 투어 패키지 목록 일부입니다.

- **Masterton and Palmerston**: 이 2일간의 투어는 New Zealand에서 가장 오래된 항구 중 한 곳을 방문하는 것으로 시작됩니다. 가장 멋진 향토 예술 작품들을 감상하시고, 이 나라의 현대적인 라이브 음악 공연을 들으세요. 투어는 Palmerston으로 향할 것이고, 고대의 성과 유적뿐만 아니라 숲을 탐험할 것입니다.
- **Napier**: Ruapehu 산을 오르고 일부 산맥들을 탐험하세요. 저희의 4일에서 6일간의 투어는 당신을 Tongariro 산과 Ngauruhoe 산에 있는 산맥들로 이끌 것입니다.
- **Hastings and Wanganui**: Hastings 시내는 양식장, 어업, 그리고 다양한 산업들 중에서 조선업을 자랑합니다. 이 2일 간의 투어 동안에, 미술 박물관에 들르시고 Hastings의 뜰을 산책해 보시고 Hastings 대학교 근처의 많은 서점과 카페에 방문해 보세요. 그리고 나서 평화로운 자연 풍경으로 둘러싸인 많은 작은 마을들로 이뤄진 Wanganui로 이동하세요.

투어의 길이와 명소의 유형은 당신의 요청에 따라 이뤄질 수 있습니다.

발신인	horace@reservations.shawnshealingtour.com
수신인	felix@venturetel.net
날짜	8월 2일
주제	예약 확인

Felix 씨께

Shawn's Healing Tours에서 여행을 예약해 주셔서 감사합니다. 이것은 당신의 예약을 재확인하기 위함입니다.

투어의 유형: Hastings와 Wanganui
Wellington에서의 출발 날짜와 시간: 금요일, 8월 10일, 10시 30분
Wellington 도착일: 일요일, 8월 13일, 18시 30분
총 비용: 175.00달러 (당신의 신용카드 청구금액)

저희의 경험 많은 고객 서비스 직원들은 당신이 여행 전에 가질 수 있는 모든 질문들을 항상 기쁘게 다룹니다. 질문이 있으시다면, plans@shawnshealingtour.com으로 이메일을 보내 주시거나 +51(0) 331 654 9266로 전화주세요.

투어 참석 이후의 의견

전문 사진작가로서, 저는 투어의 장소와 풍경이 최고라는 것을 알았습니다. 그리고 또한 직원들이 고객들을 잘 응대하도록 잘 훈련 받았음을 느꼈습니다. 저는 더 많은 모험을 위해 분명히 다시 방문할 것입니다. 저희 가이드였던 Kenny Webb은 경험과 지식이 풍부했습니다. 그는 그 지역 토박이였기 때문에 전통 문화와 지역의 관습에 매우 정통함을 보여 주었습니다. 저는 그의 아주 흥미로운 설명으로 그 지역에 더 관심이 생겼습니다.

Patsy Felix가 보냄

186. Shawn's Healing Tours에 대해 언급된 것은 무엇인가?
(A) 어떤 지역에 새 지점을 막 개장했다.
(B) 새 투어 패키지를 발표할 예정이다.
(C) 한 달에 한 번 이상 투어가 예정되어 있다.
(D) 새로운 시장으로 확장했다.

187. 광고에 따르면, Shawn's Healing Tours가 고객에게 제공할 수 있는 것은 무엇인가?
(A) 전통 행사의 무료 입장
(B) 단골 고객에게 할인된 가격
(C) 유연한 투어 시간
(D) 다양한 운송 선택 권한

188. Felix 씨의 투어에 대해 언급된 것은 무엇인가?
(A) 약 6일이 걸렸다.
(B) 매일 밤 무료 저녁 식사를 제공했다.
(C) 할인된 가격으로 제공받았다.
(D) 오직 전문 사진작가를 위해 만들어졌다.

189. 웹사이트 의견에서, 첫 번째 단락 두 번째 줄의 "serve"와 의미상 가장 가까운 것은?
(A) 주다
(B) 다루다
(C) 제공하다
(D) 교육하다

190. Webb 씨에 대해 언급된 것은 무엇인가?
(A) Hastings 출신이다.
(B) 새로 고용되었다.
(C) 한 가지 언어 이상을 말할 수 있다.
(D) Hastings 대학교를 졸업했다.

191번 문제 풀이 순서

STEP 1   문제에 Lifelong Education Programs가 언급되었기 때문에 답은 첫 번째 문서에서 participants에 대한 내용을 찾아야 하며 Not Question은 보기의 키워드를 본문에서 하나씩 소거해야 한다.

         (A) need / pay / registration fee
         (B) at least 19 years old
         (C) reside / Newcastle Town
         (D) graduates from NIU [졸업에 대한 내용은 언급하지 않았음]

> Newcastle Town
> Lifelong Education Programs - July
>
> All **residents of Newcastle Town** aged **19 and over** are **eligible** for Lifelong Education Programs. Unless otherwise stated, the **programs take place** at the campus of Newcastle International University **(NIU)**. Please refer to page 4 of this booklet for more information about tuition and **registration fees**.

STEP 2   Not Question은 보기의 키워드가 본문에서 검색되지 않는 것이 답이 된다.
         본문에 NIU가 언급된 것은 장소를 언급하는 것이고 졸업에 대하여 언급된 바 없으므로 정답은 (D)이다.

192번 문제 풀이 순서

STEP 1   처음 2줄을 skimming하여 주요 정보와 대략의 상황을 파악한다.
Newcastle Town / 19 and over / eligible / Lifelong Education Programs
take place / Newcastle International University (NIU)

STEP 2   두 번째 문제를 분석한다. [위치 / 키워드 / 유형별 풀이 전략]
192. Who most likely is Bernice Patel?
첫 번째 지문 상단부 / 키워드 Bernice Patel / 유형 - 키워드 옆에 답이 있다.

STEP 3   지문의 상단부에서 키워드를 찾는다. 키워드 근처에 있는 보기가 답이 된다.
Instructor: Bernice Patel, Patel Family Automotive Service

Bernice Patel은 평생 교육 프로그램의 강사이며, Patel Family Automotive Service를 운영하는 사람임을 알 수 있다. 따라서 정답은 (B)이다.

193번 문제 풀이 순서

STEP 1   문제에서 제시되는 사람은 두 번째 문서에 있다.
반면에 첫 번째 문서는 일반적인 내용만을 언급하고 있다. 이 경우에는 특정 사람이 언급된 문서에서 조건을 정리하여 두 번째 문서에서 답을 선택해야 한다.

STEP 2   두 번째 문서에서 Mr. Mullins의 관심에 대하여 먼저 정리한다.
I'm sorry to inform you all that because of another event that she unexpectedly has to take care of, **Ms. Roberts** needs to call off her class.
Robert 씨가 갑자기 맡아야만 하는 행사가 생기는 바람에, 그녀가 그녀의 수업을 취소하게 되었음을 여러분 모두에게 알리게 돼서 정말 죄송합니다.

STEP 3   첫 번째 지문에서
Instructor: **Janet Roberts**, City and State Property Associates

How to Become the Right Person for Real Estate Industry

Ms. Robert가 부동산 업계에 적합한 사람이 되는 방법에 대한 내용을 주제로 강의를 할 것임을 언급했으므로, Mullins 씨가 부동산 업계에 관심을 갖고 있음을 알 수 있다. 따라서 부동산 업계에서 일을 시작하는 것이라는 내용의 (D)가 정답이다.

193. What is Mr. Mullins interested in? 【193 ❶ 문제의 키워드 확인】

TO	Kari **Mullins** (and eleven others)
FROM	Ethel Marshall <emarshall@newcastle.gov>
SUBJECT	Program called off
DATE	July 19

To all,

【❷ Mullins 씨가 듣고 싶은 수업이 최소】

I'm sorry to inform you all that because of another event that she unexpectedly has to take care of, **Ms. Roberts** needs to call off her class. – 중략 –

Sincerely,
Ethel Marshall   【❸ 수업의 강사를 확인】
Program Organizer

Instructor: **Janet Roberts**, City and State Property Associates
How to Become the **Right Person** for **Real Estate Industry**
Tuesdays, 6:00 P.M. - 9:30 P.M.
Bill Community Center, Room 203   【❹ 관심 갖고 있는 수업 확인】

194번 문제 풀이 순서

STEP 1 영어 단어들은 한 단어가 여러 뜻을 가지며 여러 개의 동의어를 갖는다.
따라서 take care of의 동의어는 여러 단어가 있다. '돌보다, 주의하다, 뒷바라지하다' 등의 동의어가 있다.

STEP 2 'take care of'가 해당 위치에서 어떤 의미로 쓰였는지를 먼저 확인한다.
I'm sorry to inform you all that because of another event that she unexpectedly has to **take care of**, Ms. Roberts needs to call off her class.
Robert 씨가 갑자기 맡아야만 하는 행사가 생기는 바람에, 수업을 취소하게 되었음을 언급한다. take care of는 '~을 맡다, 책임지다'의 뜻으로 사용되었다. 따라서 '~에 참여하다'의 뜻인 (A)가 의미상 가장 가까우므로 정답이다.

195번 문제 풀이 순서

STEP 1 프로그램이 원래 열리는 날짜를 확인해야 한다.
두 번째 지문의 Yet, it will be **rescheduled** as soon as possible as the demand for her program is high. 즉, Roberts 씨가 맡은 프로그램에 대한 수요가 높기 때문에, 다시 프로그램 일정을 조정할 것임을 언급하였다.

STEP 2 일정과 관련된 세부 사항을 확인해야 한다.
Once we set the exact date with her, we will let you all know by e-mail and of course, **a new parking ticket** will be sent as well에서 정확한 날짜가 정해지면 이메일로 알려줄 것이며, 새 주차증도 보내줄 것임을 언급하였다.

STEP 3 새로 발급된 주차증인 세 번째 지문의 날짜를 확인한다.
주차증이 사용 가능한 날짜가 7월 23일로 적혀 있으므로 7월 23일에 프로그램이 열렸음을 알 수 있다. 따라서 정답은 (C)이다.

195. On what date was the rescheduled program held?

TO	Kari Mullins (and eleven others)
FROM	Ethel Marshall <emarshall@newcastle.gov>
SUBJECT	Program called off
DATE	July 19

❶ 문제 키워드 확인
일정을 다시 잡는다는 내용

To all,

I'm sorry to inform you all that because of another event that she unexpectedly has to take care of, Ms. Roberts needs to call off her class. Yet, it will be **rescheduled** as soon as possible as the demand for her program is high. Once we **set the exact date** with her, we will let you all know by e-mail, and of course, **a new parking ticket will be sent** as well, since the current one you have received will no longer be valid any longer. Sorry for this last-minute change.

❷ 이메일이나 주차증을 통해 확인 가능

Sincerely,
Ethel Marshall
Program Organizer

Newcastle Town Parking Permit
TEMPORARY-ONLY GOOD FOR A DAY

❸ 주차증으로 일정 확인

Date of Validity: **July 23**
Time stamp: 5:50 P.M.
Section: Lot A2

* This ticket must be visible from outside of your vehicle, so please display it on the dashboard.

모의고사 해석
문제 191-195는 다음 정보, 이메일과 주차증을 참조하시오.

Newcastle 시내
평생 교육 프로그램 - 7월

19세 이상 Newcastle 시내의 모든 주민들은 평생 교육 프로그램에 참가 자격이 있습니다. 달리 언급이 없으면, 프로그램은 NIU 캠퍼스에서 열립니다. 수업료와 등록비에 대해 더 많은 정보를 얻고 싶으시다면, 이 소책자의 4페이지를 참조하세요.

강사: Bernice Patel, Patel Family Automotive Service
자기 소유의 차량을 소유하고 관리하는 것
7월 14일과 18일, 오후 1시부터 오후 4시까지
Newcastle 기술 고등학교, 자동차학과

강사: Johnny Perry, Small Business Development Institution
소규모 기업을 성공적으로 만드는 것: 당신이 해야만 하는 것!
월요일마다 오후 6시~ 오후 8시
Pedro 도서관, 105호

강사: Janet Roberts, City and State Property Associates
부동산 업계에 적합한 사람이 되는 방법
화요일마다 오후 6시~오후 9시 30분
Bill 주민 센터, 203호

강사: Lindsay Scott, 전문 사진작가
사진과 함께 하는 행복하고 즐거운 생활
화요일마다 오후 6시 30분~오후 9시 30분
Bill 주민 센터, 204호

수신인	Kari Mullins(과 다른 11명)
발신인	Ethel Marshall <emarshall@newcastle.gov>
주제	프로그램을 취소한 것
날짜	7월 19일

모두에게

Robert 씨가 갑자기 맡아야만 하는 행사가 생기는 바람에, 그녀가 그녀의 수업을 취소하게 되었음을 여러분 모두에게 알리게 돼서 정말 죄송합니다. 그러나 그녀의 프로그램에 대한 수요가 높아서 가능한 한 빨리 다시 일정을 조정할 것입니다. 저희가 그녀와 정확한 날짜를 정하면, 여러분 모두에게 이메일로 알려드릴 것이고, 물론, 여러분이 받으신 현재 주차증이 더 이상 유효하지 않을 것이기 때문에, 새 주차증도 보내 드릴 것입니다. 마지막에 변경 사항이 생기게 되어 죄송합니다.

Ethel Marshall
프로그램 주최자

Newcastle 시내 주차증

일시적으로 오직 하루만 유효합니다.

유효한 날짜: 7월 23일
타임스탬프: 오후 5시 50분
구역: A2 주차장

* 이 티켓은 당신의 차량 밖에서 보여야 하므로, 계기판 위에 놓아 주세요.

191. 평생 교육 프로그램 참가자들에 대해 언급되지 않은 것은 무엇인가?
(A) 등록비를 내야만 한다.
(B) 최소 나이는 19살이다.
(C) Newcastle 시내에 산다.
(D) NIU를 졸업했다.

192. Bernice Patel은 누구이겠는가?
(A) 고등학교 선생님
(B) 지역 사업가
(C) 시 공무원
(D) 사서

193. Mullins 씨가 관심을 보이는 것은 무엇인가?
(A) 자기 소유 차량을 수리하는 것
(B) 사진을 찍는 것
(C) 자신의 가게를 개업하는 것
(D) 부동산 업계에서 일을 시작하는 것

194. 이메일에서, 첫 번째 문단 두 번째 줄의 "take care of"와 의미가 가장 가까운 것은?
(A) ~에 참석하다
(B) 연기하다
(C) 반납하다
(D) 정리하다

195. 일정이 조정된 프로그램은 언제 열렸는가?
(A) 7월 21일
(B) 7월 22일
(C) 7월 23일
(D) 7월 24일

196번 문제 풀이 순서

STEP 1 기본적인 정보인 문서의 목적을 묻는 문제이다.
목적은 본문에 상단부에서 언급된다. 본문의 첫 문장에서 We are looking for a person who will serve as a liaison coordinator in the Department of Multicultural Education.에서 이 안내의 주제나 목적을 말하고 있음을 알 수 있다.

STEP 2 본문에서 연락 담당자를 채용하고 있음을 언급했으므로 정답은 (A)이다.
(B)는 채용(hire)은 맞지만 교수(professor)에 대한 내용은 언급하지 않으므로 오답이다.
(C)는 신규 학부를 홍보하고 있는 것은 아니므로 오답이다.
(D)는 모집(recruit)은 맞지만 신규 임원(new committee members)을 뽑는 것은 아니므로 오답이다.

Madeline University - Sudbury Town
Seeking a liaison coordinator for students

We are looking for a person who will serve as **a liaison coordinator** in the Department of Multicultural Education. The liaison coordinator will gather together every week with 15-25 students taking undergraduate courses. The students make up the Diversity Committee which offers various supports to different racial, ethnic, and religious groups.

(A) To fill an open position
(B) To hire a ~~new professor~~
(C) To ~~promote a new department~~
(D) To recruit ~~new committee members~~

197번 문제 풀이 순서

STEP 1 구체적인 내용을 묻는 문제이다.
How often, the Diversity committee, meeting, liaison coordinator를 키워드로 잡고 본문에서 스키밍(skimming)과 스캐닝(scanning)을 하여 찾아낸다.

STEP 2 첫 번째 지문의 The liaison coordinator will gather together every week with 15-25 students taking undergraduate courses. The students make up the Diversity Committee를 통해서 Diversity Committee가 학부생이라는 것과 일주일에 한 번 만난다는 것이 언급되어 있으므로 정답은 (B)이다.

Madeline University - Sudbury Town
Seeking a liaison coordinator for students
-중략-

The liaison coordinator will gather together **every week** with 15-25 students taking undergraduate courses. The students make up the Diversity Committee, which offers various supports to diffe...

> **students taking an undergraduate course**
> **= The students**

198번 문제 풀이 순서

STEP 1 문제에서 제시되는 사람은 두 번째 문서에 있다.
반면에 첫 번째 문서는 채용 공고로써 일반적인 내용만을 언급하고 있다. 이 경우에는 먼저 특정 사람이 언급된 문서에서 세부 사항을 정리하여 첫 번째 문서에서 답을 선택해야 한다.

STEP 2 두 번째 문서에서 Mr. Ross의 세부 사항에 대하여 먼저 정리한다.

We are very happy that you have agreed to take **the job as liaison coordinator**.
당신이 연락 담당자로서 일을 맡기로 동의해서 기쁩니다.

Ross 씨가 Madeline 대학교에서 연락 담당자로서 일을 하기로 언급되었다.

STEP 3 첫 번째 지문의 In order to enhance community spirit for the diverse student population, the coordinator is also responsible for organizing events every other month in places throughout the campus.를 통해 다양한 학생들의 공동체 의식을 높일 수 있도록 행사를 기획한다고 언급했으므로 정답은 (C)이다.

199번 문제 풀이 순서

STEP 1 Ross 씨가 받을 물건이 무엇인지 묻는 문제이다. 해당하는 사람이 I / You / 제 3자인지를 확인한다.

STEP 2 이메일에서 Ms. Ross는 편지를 받는 You이고 Miguel Shaw는 편지를 쓰는 I이다.

STEP 3 두 번째 지문의 Within a few days, all of the official papers and tax documents in a welcome packet will be sent to you.를 통해서 공문서와 세금 관련 서류를 받는다고 언급이 되어 있으므로 정답은 (C)이다.

200번 문제 풀이 순서

STEP 1 문제의 키워드인 Harrow Hill 대학교는 세 번째 지문에 있다. 이 경우에는 세 번째 문서를 먼저 확인해야 한다.

200. What is indicated about Harrow Hill College?

Request Form for Transcripts
Harrow Hill College   ❶ 문제의 키워드 확인

Name: (fist) *Jesse*   (last) *Ross*   [Middle Initial: *E*]

❷ Ross 씨가 다닌 대학임을 확인

STEP 2 두 번째 문서에서 성적 증명서를 신청한 이유를 확인해야 한다.

TO	Jesse Ross <jross@juliusmessenger.net>
FROM	Miguel Shaw <mshaw@madelineuni.edu.og>
DATE	October 3
SUBJECT	Give a welcome

Dear Ms. Ross,

– 중략 –

Meanwhile, an official transcript to keep in our files is required because you only sent us a copy, and also <u>an official transcript from the college or university where you last studied needs to be submitted</u>.

❸ 성적 증명서 신청 이유 확인

Sincerely,
Miguel Shaw
Head of Multicultural Events, Madeline University

STEP 3 마지막에 다닌 대학교(Harrow Hill College)의 성적 증명서 제출을 언급했으므로 정답은 (C)이다.

모의고사 해석
문제 196-200은 다음 정보, 이메일, 문서를 참조하시오.

Madeline 대학교 – Sudbury 도시
학생들과의 연락 담당자를 구함

저희는 다문화교육 부서에서 연락 담당자로서 근무하실 분을 찾고 있습니다. 연락 담당자는 매주 학부생 과정을 밟고 있는 15-25명의 학생들과 모일 것입니다. 그 학생들은 다양한 인종, 민족, 종교적 단체를 지지하는 **Diversity** 위원회를 구성하고 있습니다. 다양한 학생 집단의 공동체 의식을 높이기 위해서, 통합 정리자는 캠퍼스내의 몇몇 장소에서 두 달에 한 번 행사를 기획하는 책임을 맡습니다.

게다가 한 달에 한 번 만나기로 한 비슷한 성향의 모임의 학생들과 상담을 합니다. 만약 당신이 이 자리에 지원하고 싶다면, **Madeline** 대학교 인사과 pd@madelineuni.edu.og로 연락주세요.

수신	Jesse Ross <jross@juliusmessenger.net>
발신	Miguel Shaw <mshaw@madelineuni.edu.og>
날짜	10월 3일
제목	환영합니다.

Ross 씨께,

당신이 연락 담당자로서 일을 맡기로 동의해서 기쁩니다. 첫 근무를 시작하기 전에, 몇몇의 서류들이 기입되어야 합니다. 며칠 내로, 공문서와 세금 관련 서류들이 담겨 있는 환영 패키지가 당신에게 배송될 것입니다. 그러니, 근무 첫날에 문서를 기입해서 가져와 주세요. 또한, 새로운 임직원 교육 훈련 프로그램에 관한 정보는 패키지에 포함되어 있습니다.

한편, 당신이 저희에게 복사본만을 보냈기 때문에 저희 파일에 보관할 공식 지원서가 필요하고, 또한 당신이 마지막으로 공부했던 대학교의 공식 성적 증명서도 제출되어야 합니다.

진심을 담아,
Miguel Shaw
다문화 행사 책임자, Madeline 대학교

성적 증명서 신청서
Harrow Hill 대학교

성명: (이름) *Jesse*   (성) *Ross*   [머릿글자: *E*]

취득 학위: 수료증 ☐ / 석사 과정 ■ / 학사 과정 ☐ / 공학 ☐

현재 주소: *231 Wagner Road*
우편번호: *23BX*   도시: *Layton*   주: *Mile End*

성적 증명서가 얼마나 빨리 처리되어야 하는가요?
즉시 ■ / 최종 성적 이후 ☐

※ 주의: 성적 증명서는 발급이 불가능 할 수 있습니다.
1. 학생 기록부 중 일부가 지연된 경우
2. 요금 8파운드가 포함되지 않았을 경우
3. 전액 수업료를 납부하지 않았을 경우

서명: *Jesse Ross*

196. 왜 안내장이 작성되었는가?
(A) 공석에 지원하기 위해
(B) 신임 교수를 채용하기 위해
(C) 신규 학부를 홍보하기 위해
(D) 신규 임원을 모집하기 위해

197. Diversity 위원회와 연락 담당자는 얼마나 자주 만나는가?
(A) 매달
(B) 일주일에 한 번
(C) 일주일 내내
(D) 한 달에 한 번

198. Madeline 대학교에서 Ross 씨는 무엇을 해야 하는가?
(A) 학생들이 적절한 강의를 선택하도록 돕기
(B) 학생 센터에 대한 변화 제시하기
(C) 캠퍼스 내의 다양한 집단 돕기
(D) 다문화교육 부서 관리하기

199. Ross 씨는 며칠 안에 무엇을 받을 것인가?
(A) 성적 증명서
(B) 수락 이메일
(C) 서류 일부
(D) 영수증 복사본

200. Harrow Hill 대학교에 대해 언급된 것은 무엇인가?
(A) Madeline 대학교 근처에 위치해 있다.
(B) 학생 대다수는 해외 출신이다.
(C) Ross 씨가 가장 최근에 다녔던 대학교이다.
(D) 공학과가 존재하지 않는다.